The
Autobiographical
Subject

The
Autobiographical
Subject

Gender and Ideology
in Eighteenth-Century
England

Felicity A. Nussbaum

The Johns Hopkins University Press

BALTIMORE AND LONDON

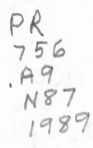

© 1989 The Johns Hopkins University Press
All rights reserved
Printed in the United States of America

The Johns Hopkins University Press
701 West 40th Street
Baltimore, Maryland 21211
The Johns Hopkins Press Ltd., London

The paper used in this publication meets the
minimum requirements of American National Standard
for Information Sciences—Permanence of Paper for
Printed Library Materials, ANSI Z39.48-1984.

LIBRARY OF CONGRESS CATALOGING-IN-PUBLICATION DATA

Nussbaum, Felicity A.
　The autobiographical subject : gender and ideology in
eighteenth-century England / Felicity Nussbaum.
　　p. cm.
　Bibliography: p.
　Includes index.
　ISBN 0-8018-3825-8 (alk. paper)
　　1. English prose literature—18th century—History and
criticism. 2. Autobiography. 3. Authors, English—
18th century—Biography—History and criticism.
4. Autobiography—Women authors—History and
criticism. 5. Women—England—Biography—History and
criticism. 6. Sex role in literature. 7. Self in literature.
I. Title
PR756.A9N87 1989
828'.50809'492—dc20

89-32587
CIP

For Margaret and Luther

Contents

Acknowledgments

My interest in the problem of autobiography was spurred some years ago by Philip Daghlian in his seminar on the Age of Johnson. More recently, I am indebted to several friends who have generously read and commented on various portions of the manuscript, including Shari Benstock, Laura Brown, Gerald MacLean, Mary Poovey, John Richetti, and especially Donna Landry. Mas'ud Zavarzadeh urged me toward a rethinking of this project at an early stage, and I am grateful for that critique. I also want to thank Steve Cohan, Rosemary Hennessy, and the members of the graduate seminar on materialist feminist theory with whom I have ongoing critical discussions. Paul Alkon, Margaret Doody, Christopher Fox, Paul Hunter, Paul Korshin, and John Sitter offered encouragement and help of various kinds during the course of this project, and Isobel Grundy pointed me toward more attention to the Quaker women's narratives at a crucial moment. Jean Howard has been an unparalleled friend and colleague with whom I have shared the evolution of this book, and I am greatly indebted to her in ways both personal and intellectual.

I would also like to thank the National Endowment for the Humanities and the Syracuse University Research Fund for financial assistance. In addition, the Rockefeller Foundation provided the opportunity for concentrated time in a stimulating environment when I was a Fellow of the Institute for Research on Women, Rutgers University. My colleagues there, especially Mae Henderson, Briavel Holcomb, Carol Smith, and Catharine Stimpson, made it possible for me to complete this project. Alexandria Currin has my special thanks for taking on extra responsibilities in order to allow me to accept the fellowship.

I am also happy to acknowledge the generous assistance of the librarians and staff at the Beinecke Rare Books and Manuscript Library and the Boswell Office at Yale University, the British Library, Cornell University Library, Princeton Rare Books Library, and Syracuse University Bird Library in the research toward this book. I have included here, sometimes in substantially altered form, portions of essays that appeared earlier: "'By these words I was sustained': John Bunyan's *Grace Abounding*," *ELH* 49 (1982), 18–34; "Heteroclites: The Gender of Eighteenth-Century Character," in *The New Eighteenth Century: Theory/Politics/English Literature*, co-ed. with Laura Brown (New York: Methuen, 1987), pp. 144–67; "Eighteenth-Century Women's Autobiographical Commonplaces," in *The Private Self: Theory and Practice of Women's Autobiographical Writing*, ed. Shari Benstock (Chapel Hill: Univ. of North Carolina Press, 1988), pp. 147–71; and "Toward Conceptualizing Diary," in *Studies in Autobiography*, ed. James Olney (New York: Oxford Univ. Press, 1988), pp. 128–40. I wish to acknowledge the publishers who granted permission to reprint portions of those essays here. Carolyn Wenger's expert editorial hand greatly improved the final draft of the book.

Most of all, I am very grateful to René Wilett, Marc Wilett, and Nicole Wilett, with whom I share a daily balancing act, for their understanding and support.

Introduction

Eighteenth-century England witnessed a convergence of three phenomena that link together genre, class, and gender: the conceptualization of "autobiography" as a recognizable set of practices, distinct from other kinds of writing; the use of autobiography as a technology of the middle-class self; and the assertion of a female identity in public print. It is the intersection of these practices in the autobiographical subject that is the focus of this book.

In tracing the emergence of the term *autobiography* to dominance in the early nineteenth century, this book examines the ideologies of self-biography across the English Restoration and the eighteenth century. The construction of an eighteenth-century canon of autobiographical writing usually begins with Bunyan's *Grace Abounding* (1666); the canon's secular middle, after a long gap, continues with Boswell and Gibbon in the 1760s; and its fruition comes in the birthing of a continuous organic self in Wordsworth's *Prelude*. My approach here, instead of assuming the authenticity of this narrative, asks what constitutes autobiographical writing in the period and why, when readers consumed multiple editions of *Grace Abounding*, literary historians have found no landmark canonical texts before the time of Rousseau in France, Franklin in America, and Boswell and Gibbon in England. My book questions this interpretive history to ask how the autobiographical subject, both as the genre itself and the "self" at its center, is held in place by class and gender relations. I am using the term *subject* in at least two other ways: to describe the way an individual being is, first, subject to someone else's control and, with limited freedom, positioned within authority relations; and, second, to represent the way this entity becomes subject to its own identity, held within a given self-knowledge—believing that it is free, responsible, and the agent of its own actions. I want to consider then whose interests these narratives of "self" serve, why they proliferate in the late seventeenth and eighteenth centuries, and what forms they take in their private and public manifestations. In addition, pulling marginalized texts, especially women's writing and other unpublished works, from the periphery to the center, I assume that the literary canon needs to be revised to include any representation of reality and identity (including "nonliterary" texts), and consequently I treat memoranda alongside "master" texts.

My methodology here is informed by political criticism, and especially that version of political criticism called materialist feminism, since these theoretical commitments (made explicit in the early chapters of the book) provide the most satisfactorily nuanced approach to the historicity of gender and self-construction currently available. Such an approach makes it possible for a feminist politics to engage the problems of analyzing the representation of the "self" in particular historical moments. Throughout the book I weave back and forth between contemporary texts and those written in the eighteenth century to elaborate how writing the history of any set of literary conventions necessarily engages us in a dialectic between the materials of the present and the past. I am especially interested, then, in locating the traces of the past that allow us to write the history of the "self" and of the genre that is regarded as expressing it, in order to reveal the construction of bourgeois subjectivity in relation to the material conditions of literary production. I pay particular attention to the power relations that situate the gendered autobiographical subject and the sites of resistance to those relations.

Because autobiographical writing purports to tell an individual's story, the critical methodologies most commonly employed to read these texts often wrench the subject from her or his cultural and historical moment under the assumption that language is the expressive creation of the autonomous narrator. My theoretical approach argues instead that the "self" is an ideological construct that is recruited into place within specific historical formations rather than always present as an eternal truth. It is less an essence than an ensemble of social and political relations. Further, the insistence on "I" as a primary mode of perceiving is an assumption that governs the genre in the eighteenth century. "Autobiography" then comes to depict the special position that the "self" exists and that it can be represented in text. This ideology of genre makes it possible to assume a unified and authoritative narrative position of an "I" who holds the discrete particulars together. I am looking, then, at the politics of subjectivity to ask what practices empower the production of this written interiority. Working from the historical signs and the material practices in which they are embedded, I read the autobiographical texts as crucial to the formulation of a gendered bourgeois subjectivity that learns to recognize itself. In short, I regard eighteenth-century self-biography as a matrix of conflicting discourses and practices that produce, reflect, contain, and transform class and gender identities.

The relation of autobiographical discourse to the real is opaque, highly codified, and politically charged; it is entangled in the material reality of lived experience. I also consider the ways that these entanglements are negotiated through the ideologies of genre that make certain kinds of representations of identity and gender legitimate to eighteenth-century readers and writers. I am interested less in the structure of autobiography or its revelation of the events and feelings of an individual's life than in the ways these texts are produced, and the contradictions that an ideological reading of them displays. The nonliterary and non-canonical status of most of the works I discuss (with the notable exceptions of *Grace Abounding* and *The Life of Johnson*) makes them more vulnerable to our unraveling, for the powerful codes of the individuated self surface in these emergent forms. The more fully cultivated ideological fields of the aesthetic are more closed to oppositional readings than those of the "nonliterary" texts. Few of the texts I consider were commercially published in the eighteenth century. They were privately written and privately produced, though many of the authors anticipated that their writings would eventually gain a public audience. In writing outside authorized and institutionalized modes of expression (though always within ideology), Wesley, Boswell, Thrale, and others disrupt old narrative codes or locate new ones as the texts strain to make currently available narrative models, such as spiritual autobiography, stretch to "represent" new kinds of consciousness and experience. In reading these texts, I look then for the ideological crises—crises that are more easily discerned in newly emergent genres because the familiarity of entrenched conventions has not fully glossed over the fissures.

Here I also make use of recent conceptualizations about narrative and ideology that allow us to think of *diary* and *journal* as representations of our imagined relation to reality, mediated by narrator and reader, rather than as failed versions of a life story with a beginning, middle, and end. Certain texts, such as conversion narratives, validate recognized constructs of experience while simultaneously excluding and marginalizing other constructs. This historical period of eighteenth-century England, I further suggest, is a time when identity and character are in particular crisis, and autobiographical writing often sparks nonhegemonic concepts about the self as well as new hegemonies in formation. An analysis of eighteenth-century self-biography, then, provides one pragmatic and local means of addressing these problems of identity.

Narratives of "self" make possible the definition of a gendered middle-class subjectivity that, in producing and reflecting class consciousness, claims territory that was previously unavailable to the lower laboring classes. As class consciousness intensifies, sexual difference of a particular kind also becomes increasingly important in constructing a public identity. I am arguing here that women's autobiographical writing, organized within prevailing discourses, helped to shape and resist the dominant cultural constructions of gender relations and to substitute alternatives. The midcentury memoirists, for example, set out to radicalize ideas of gendered subjectivity, and Hester Thrale's writings, rather than revealing an essential female voice, steadfastly contradict dominant values. In addition, autobiographical texts publicly disseminate that gendered subjectivity as a model for others to follow. In short, autobiographical writing, published and private, serves as a location where residual and emergent notions of gender and class clash to replicate and challenge reigning notions of identity. For the feminist literary historian, understanding the production of the autobiographical subject in such terms will enable movement beyond a critique of the dominant to question its unity and to focus in addition on the resistances of the marginal.

Eighteenth-century autobiographical writing, though spread across class divisions, was largely an activity of the middle class; its proliferation is related to expanding literacy and printing, and to new emphasis on the published self as property in a money economy. It is, in the term Foucault applied to religious confession from its inception as a mandated Catholic ritual in 1215, a "technology of the self," a way of regulating interiority.[1] Through confession, the subject is constructed within power relations as it submits to the authority of priest, God, and church for its validation. Moral technologies of the self such as confession constitute and transform the subject's thoughts, behavior, body, and "self" as individual subjects submit themselves to the divine agency or institution, or its human representative, to make themselves in the prescribed and arbitrary manner. Foucault calls attention, for example, to the early conduct notebooks, the Greek *hypomnemata*, that were written to the self to govern it. The exercise was intended "to collect the already-said, to reassemble that which one could hear or read, and this to an end which is nothing less than the constitution of oneself."[2] Similarly, eighteenth-century autobiography, too, I suggest, may be regarded as a technology of the self which rests on the assumption that its truth can be told.

Making use of Foucault's work for a feminist politics is, however, not without difficulties.[3] Foucault further argues that as sexual activity moved into the private realm in the seventeenth century, its discourses multiplied and the regulation of sexuality increased excessively. These discourses (including medicine, psychiatry, and criminal justice) are secured by power/knowledge relations. In particular, according to Foucault, "peripheral sexualities" attracted regulation. The hystericization of women's bodies and the pedagogization of children's sexuality especially led to increased surveillance. Though Foucault finds that this proliferation of discourses coincides with the "development of capitalism" (HS 5, Vol. 1), he attends very little to the relationship between the economic and the production of sexuality. He seeks instead diverse other centers of power, the locations where intense pleasure and the powers that manage it take precedence. Foucault thus makes possible a conceptualization of sexuality as a historical construct, produced by multiple discourses and inscribed upon the body rather than reflecting a biological imperative. Following this line of thought, we can take account of the way that subjectivity is situated within these power relations. But "sex" in the *History of Sexuality* seems to be limited in its meaning to culturally produced desire and to sexual acts in their many variations and "perversions" rather than to gender or gendered identity. This leads to a virtual exclusion of considering the effect of gender hierarchies in the social formation. For example, a tale of the sexual game of "curdled milk" is told from the point of view of the victimized male villager who was merely dallying in what he assumed to be a socially sanctioned masturbatory act that required a small girl's assistance (HS 31-32). Foucault does not notice the unequal gender relations in the game, for if the male is victimized through prosecution by the village, where is the girl located in the power relations? Nor does he comment on the way the game is regarded as a harmless bucolic pleasure of the peasants, their underclass sexuality portrayed as simpler and more bestial. Further, the children that he finds to be kept under surveillance are schoolboys, and the pervasive myth of "the individual driven, in spite of himself, by the somber madness of sex" (HS 39) is Don Juan, not the newly empowered female.

The question of how gender and class figure in the "political economy of a will to knowledge" (HS 73) is not taken into account. In other words, the privileged male gaze dominates, and unequal gender relations are largely erased as sexuality is restricted to the sexual act. Thus Foucault's *History of Sexuality*, while usefully upsetting the binary of private and public, primarily limits itself to male sexuality in its interest in sexual discourses.

In contrast, feminist critics may begin with the assumption that issues of gender and its hierarchies take precedence. In fact, feminist criticism is *most* able to explain its focus on certain issues rather than others as they pertain to specific historical moments, which enables a questioning of the relations of power so that "the real" is not the sole possession of the ruling gender, race, or class. These issues are addressed throughout the chapters that follow, but they will be taken up in specific historical detail in chapter 6.

What is very much apparent in some new historical and Marxist work is that, as vital and complex as it may be, it still allows for the exclusion of women from its compass. That is, the theoretical grounding does not *require* a consideration of gender. Patriarchal relations, assumed to be natural, are therefore again validated. In sum, even in many theoretically and politically astute texts, the sexual division of labor—intellectual and otherwise—remains fixed: women's writing, reading, and work is rendered invisible.

Feminist political criticism, on the other hand, aligns itself with a rewriting and a rethinking of contemporary historicist theory that requires the inclusion of gender as a category to be considered at every turn, a feminist politics that contests theoretical stances that erase it and foregrounds the differences between a postmodern mode of inquiry that takes account of gender issues and one that does not. Such an approach allows us to think about power/knowledge relations in a way that explains the production and reproduction of exploitation based on gender by linking them to the mode of production and to social relations in an expanding market economy. I take this to be among the goals of a materialist feminist project that moves beyond the new orthodoxies.

My study expands on Foucault's ideas and departs from them to attend more particularly to the ways these technologies of self are bound by class, gender, and nation. In addition, I pursue the political uses of these technologies, widely dispersed throughout the society, as they become the dominant way of regarding the subject. I am arguing in the pages that follow that these first-person texts disseminate a regimen that enables the production of a particular kind of self, assumed to be free and equal, as a class solidifies its alliances. This regimen also calls into place a reader who recognizes herself or himself in text, and subordinates women within its domain. I suggest, then, that by the end of the eighteenth century, a middle class regulates itself through this technology of self, and that the technology is deployed to maintain gender hierarchies.

The book moves from the more specifically theoretical (an explication of the terms by which the reading proceeds and the uses to which it will be put), toward specific instances of ideological crises in first-person texts from late seventeenth- and eighteenth-century England. The point is not to separate theory from history, or methodology from particular-readings, but to indicate the way that theory is always implicated in history, history in theory. The readings, in unmasking what seems to need no explanation, in fact employ feminist political criticism to intervene in the reproduction of naturalized assumptions and to resist their self-evident nature.

I begin by critiquing "new historicism" and redefining its political uses to interpose a feminist agenda. I move on then to discuss the interpretations of eighteenth-century autobiography by nineteenth- and twentieth-century commentators and the implicit suppositions about the genre that operate within their criticism. Redefining autobiography as a code of understanding that shifts its forms as it is produced in particular historical moments, I look at eighteenth-century assumptions surrounding the diary, the journal, and serial autobiography to ask what sort of "I" is called into being in these submerged and discredited texts. I investigate quite specifically the proliferation of private texts and the conditions of their production and distribution to pay special attention to the many revisions of "self" by Fox, Bunyan, Wesley, Boswell, Thrale, and others.

In turning to specific philosophical, religious, and political discourses of the "self" in the eighteenth century in chapter 2, I concentrate on the ways they intersect to evoke certain contradictory self-representations. The questions raised in the debates include whether identity is consciousness, and whether sleep, drink, or injury should change our ideas of sameness through time. In sermons and religious tracts, the demand from the pulpit for self-reflection, bolstered by biblical injunctions, counters the argument that obsessive attention to the self detracts from attention to God. The autobiographical subject is constructed in the conjunctions of the economic and political in which class and the relations of production are crucial, if not always the single most important determinants, in eighteenth-century autobiography. The Lockean political subject possesses himself as a self and yet assents to a contractual relationship with other subjects. Vital to the emergence of capitalism and the consuming subject, the individual subject comes to embody a concept of "self-interest" sanctioned by Mandeville and later Adam Smith, for the state encourages the individual to believe that serving his own interests will benefit the common good.

I focus especially on the competing claims of class and gender on the autobiographical subject, and I lay explicitly theoretical ground to consider the problems of women's autobiography that have impeded its criticism. Turning from a separatist feminism that would claim that women's first-person narrative reveals a true self, I argue instead that the texts may be read within circulating ideologies of gender and genre, and within a politics of difference. As large numbers of women begin to write, a collective sphere of female subjectivity is increasingly recognized. In addition, adopting materialist feminist practice, I pay particular attention to the mode of production in its historical specificity to take account of class relations as well as gender relations. Patriarchy, though pervasive, is unevenly distributed across class lines, and the interconnections of class with patriarchy are particularly instructive and contestatory in eighteenth-century autobiography. It is the resistance to hegemonic ideas of female character in the spiritual autobiographies, scandalous memoirs, and personal narratives of family life written by eighteenth-century women that make possible a reading that exposes the gaps in the ideologies of gender, genre, and class. These contradictions have material effects in woman's legal status and in her construction by a newly powerful male medical profession that manages her body and its relation to "self." These conflicts, then, manifest themselves in constructions of female character and in a private second-sphere subjectivity, an interiority that is defined as subordinate to man in its difference from him.

In the later section of the book devoted to reading particular autobiographies, I have chosen to concentrate on the writing of men and women at three historical moments—roughly the end of the seventeenth century, the mid–eighteenth century, and the late eighteenth century. Bunyan's *Grace Abounding* is made parallel to women's spiritual autobiographies, John Wesley's journals are set in conjunction with the scandalous memoirists, and James Boswell's journals and *Life* are related to Hester Thrale's "Family Book." Rather than attempting a New Critical reading of these texts which would seek the inherent meaning in them or simply accept the political neutrality of the "self" they shape, I read them as locations of uncertainty and of the individual subject's shifting alliances as situated in gender and class relations.

These specific readings include three chapters on men's autobiographical texts and three on women's writing. I segregate the men from the women—not in order to argue for women's inherently different voice but to regard autobiography as one important site where gendered subjectivity is produced. In each chapter I consider strategies of containment and resistance. This involves examining the material conditions in which the text was written and revised, as well as the ways in which it circulated among private and public readers.

Looking first at spiritual autobiography in the period, I find it to be a less stable and coherent corpus than we, from a postromantic perspective, have learned to expect. Though Bunyan's *Grace Abounding* establishes a typical pattern of remorse and resolution, it also displays competing notions of self and soul, as well as ambivalence about the legitimacy of intense self-scrutiny. Bunyan's own revisions of the text reveal multiple attempts to fix a self. Bunyan was a tinker as well as a preacher, and *Grace Abounding* promulgates a technology of the bourgeois self that can possess itself as property, quite literally as an identity to be sold, and more metaphorically as the land, or birthright, unattainable for the working class. At another level, Bunyan seems to be free, yet in fact he wrote *Grace Abounding* while imprisoned for preaching as a Dissenter. Thus *Grace Abounding* strips the Dissenting identity of its radical implications by decontextualizing it and holding it within an ahistorical frame.

Other conversion narratives—Quaker, Baptist, and Methodist—affect and even authorize certain ways in which people perceive and inscribe reality. Women's spiritual autobiographies, while adopting the patterns and language authorized by male Dissenters, carve out occasions for opposition to gender restrictions within their self-reflective texts. Usually not published until after the women's deaths, these diaries and other accounts indicate their thorough indoctrination into the ideology of self-scrutiny, while they attest to the spontaneity and artlessness of their self-revelations. The women frequently disavow sexual difference in order to claim autonomy and equality in spiritual matters. But their resistances to dominance within an androgynous Christ come in their protestations that they dare to preach, albeit as vessels for the Divine

Word. Often persistent in their loyalty to family, women's spiritual autobiographical writings expose the contradictions aroused when their obedience to two patriarchal authorities, God and husband, conflict.

Poised ambiguously between the Church of England and the Dissenters, Methodist identity would seem to lack an essence. John Wesley's
journals propose a pattern for Christian living that he proselytized, and
they help to methodize a public and consistent character for the previously marginal, illiterate, and disenfranchised. The multiple revisions of
Wesley's journals indicate his own lack of resolve about the best way to
represent identity, yet he carefully limited the amount of freedom his
itinerant ministers had in constructing representations of their conversion narratives.

In the section on Boswell's journals, I focus on his gender and class
identity as presented in his private writings. The memoranda declare an
increasingly rigid bifurcation between a public and private identity in
which the *retenu* self cannot tolerate its opposite, the fluctuating *etourdi*.
Fully immersed in self-monitoring that insists on its òwn freedom, the
journals also experiment with class and gender shifts. More than the
other texts I discuss, Boswell's journals construct a quite specifically divided private self that claims resolution within a consistent gentlemanly
character. Boswell seems to seek sufficiently "manly" self-representation
in an attempt to triumph in the newly intensified contest against women
for narrative authority over the minute particulars of private experience.
Similarly, in *The Life of Johnson* gender and class figure prominently, for
Boswell inscribes a "manly" bourgeois Johnson who exhibits a constant
identity. Revised and incorporated into the *Life*, Boswell's autobiographical journals construct a Johnson whose public/private dissonances can be
mediated in his vision of a stable identity that personifies Truth. Wedding the contradictory qualities through the still forceful ideology of
humanism, the *Life* also adheres to the tenets of individual difference
within universal sameness to make (auto)biography and the life it (re)pro-
duces seem to be classless and genderless in its application.

Boswell was among the "gentlemen" who made women of a lesser
status his prey, and the female memoirists at midcentury proclaim their
economic and sexual victimization by aristocratic men as they insist on
their power to determine the "real." These women revised the apologia
form to fit their uniquely female situation—the fall from chastity that
irremediably changed their lives. They are among the first women to

publish autobiography during their lifetime, and thus to shape a public character. Memoirs by Charlotte Charke, Laetitia Pilkington, and others contest the inflexibility of heterosexual binaries as they hold women in a place imagined to be distinctly separate from that for men. The scandal of these texts, as they force the contradictions of the formulations of women's character into print, is that they also make possible revisionary ways of regarding female difference to assert new identities and topple gender hierarchies.

On the other hand, privileged upper-middle-class women such as Hester Thrale would seem to worry little about forging a consistent identity. In her various journals, Thrale finds some limited power in her domestic role as dutiful wife and devoted mother who is positioned within the discourses on child rearing. Thrale's resistance to prescribed identities comes in the formulation of a lifelong habit of recording the "trivial" details of a woman's lived experience and of insisting, however ambivalently, on an inverted hierarchy of values in that private sphere. Women autobiographers in the eighteenth century, then, speak in the language that is available to them in texts that imitate, but also often counter, prevailing notions of female identity and its self-regulation.

In short, I am arguing in the pages that follow that the "self" of autobiography is an effect of ideology and a mediation of its conflicts, and that a politics of writing and reading is implicit within it. I suggest that we may read these autobiographical writings, however diverse in content and form, as confirming the bourgeois self but also making available textual subversions of its new dominance. Diaries and journals, for example, urge readers and writers to recognize themselves in existing social relations, and to believe in a sameness that makes them like all other human beings, as well as in a difference that guarantees their individuation. They also offer a private space for experimentation, revision, and resistance to prevailing notions of identity. In eighteenth-century England, the construction of a female subjectivity or character is given widespread public articulation for the first time, but it is complicated by women's subjugation to the universal "male" in a secondary sphere ascribed to nature and submerged so that it cannot be easily contradicted. In other words, public and private self-writing, for men and for women, is part of the conquest over meaning and the contest over the power to name the real.

I think of this book, then, as a revisioning of a historical episode in the genre of autobiography, and, in its attention to the asymmetries of gender and class, a contribution to the larger collective project of a political criticism. Its hope is that, by rewriting the past in the present, we can begin to imagine the production of new subjectivities in order to refuse what we "are," as Foucault suggests, but also, beyond a politics of negativity, to exceed the current class and gender boundaries that give meanings to "ourselves."

The
Autobiographical
Subject

The Ideology of Genre

There once prevailed, and perhaps, it may not be yet quite abolished, the custom of a man's journalising his own life. Many of these journals yet remain in their MS. state, and some, unfortunately for journal-writing, have been published.
—Isaac D'Israeli, Miscellanies (1796)

He that sits down calmly and voluntarily to review his life for the admonition of posterity, or to amuse himself, and leaves this account unpublished, may be commonly presumed to tell truth, since falshood cannot appease his own mind, and fame will not be heard beneath the tomb.
—Samuel Johnson, Idler 84 (24 November 1759)

I

Autobiography was first conceptualized as a genre toward the end of the eighteenth century, and its definition has been applied retrospectively to the preceding age. Apparently a German, J. G. Herder, first invented the term in 1796 when he entitled a collection "Self-Biographies of Famous Men." The English term is usually first associated with Robert Southey's usage in the *Quarterly Review* of 1809, but in a 1796 essay, Isaac D'Israeli, a statesman and a man of letters, somewhat disdainfully invoked the terms "self-biography" and "self-character." And in a review assumed to have been written by William Taylor, D'Israeli's *Miscellanies* were criticized for making use of the hard word that described a newly recognizable practice: "It is not very usual in English to employ hybrid words partly Saxon and partly Greek: yet *autobiography* would have seemed pedantic."[1] In the early decades of the nineteenth century, then, the various first-person writings of the eighteenth century began to take shape under the classification of a genre.

The first use of the word "autobiography" in an English title may well be in W. P. Scargill's *The Autobiography of A Dissenting Minister* (1834). This work, originally published in one volume, proceeds retrospectively through a linear narrative, yet Scargill recognizes that his work ambles along in a desultory fashion: "Truly I think that I am writing my memoirs in a gossiping kind of way, and that I am discoursing more about others than myself, and I am led off from one topic to another, in a strangely digressive style."[2] In Scargill, the belief is that something called "autobiography" holds these circuitous wanderings together. Unity in "self-biography" was also perceived to derive from a narrator and author who were the same, who existed in history, and who expressed an interior reality. The point of these late eighteenth- and early nineteenth-century texts is that an infinitely varied but unified self exists, and that writing and reading autobiography is morally and aesthetically rewarding.

By the third decade of the nineteenth century, then, the word was so common that it called little attention to itself, and numerous collections of lives appeared. In the introduction to *The Lives of Early Methodist Preachers. Chiefly Written by Themselves* (1838), Thomas Jackson remarks on "these sketches of auto-biography." From 1826 to 1833, thirty-four volumes of earlier titles were published serially as *Autobiography. A Collection of the most Instructive and Amusing Lives Ever Published, Written by the Parties Themselves.*[3] This series of volumes constitutes a kind of eighteenth-century canon, the first of its kind, for the first time, and it affords excellent clues to ascertaining what the editor, who adopts an authoritative and judgmental voice throughout, believes to be included within autobiography. He begins by clarifying the difference between biography and autobiography: "There is such an essential distinction between self-composed and other Biography, that the principal literary object of our undertaking is at once apparent. It is, in fact, to collect into one consecutive publication, genuine materials for a diversified study of the human character, by selecting the most curious and interesting Autobiographical Memoirs now extant." In this collection, then, autobiography seems to be defined exclusively by the fact that it is written by the subject of the narrative, an "I" who holds its threads together. The editor violates his own principles, however, with occasional exceptions such as the *Memoirs of Captain John Creichton*, "arranged and methodized by Swift, yet, having been formed out of his own papers and oral explanations, they retain all the character and spirit, as well as the form of Autobiography" (11, intro.). In general, the editor is more concerned with the instructional or amusement value of the lives in portraying "a wide and diversified view of human character," or its influence on an epoch, than with structural matters (6, intro.). Forty-seven letters written by bookseller James Lackington to a friend are included with an explanation that rambling works may still be of interest: "Although a mere etching, [this life] has something special about it . . . in which originality and variety, rather than high finish and precision, form the leading objects of attraction" (18, p. vi). The editor of the collection, then, makes few claims that the texts can compete with belles lettres.

The editor's definition of autobiography includes material as diverse as David Hume's tiny gem of a life and Phillip Dodington's diary, as well as multivolumed memoirs from Vidocq (the principal agent of the French police until 1827) and James Hardy Vaux ("Swindler and Thief"). Vaux's text, for example, is of interest to "the philosopher [who] may read the workings of an unprincipled conscience, the legislator [who may] be let into the operation of the law upon the criminal's mind, and the citizen [who may] derive a key to the frauds by which he is so easily and constantly beset" (13, intro.). In other words, these early texts are granted their place because the varied lives are curious and original; their scope rather than their tight structure is given primacy. Judged to be worthy specimens of "self-drawing" by authors living and dead, they include diaries, journals, letters, briefest narratives, lengthy memoirs, and even biography.

The reader of these texts, urged to delight in the diversity of his species, is positioned as a student of human nature and as a spectator on it. The justification for including the lives of people such as William Lilly, the astrologer who was Butler's Sidrophel in *Hudibras*, within these volumes is to illustrate "the most eccentric varieties of human character, . . . [in] a collection, the great object of which is to form a comprehensive record of them" (2, intro.). Autobiography, like all literature, the editor argues, is designed "to correct evil propensities by excellent example, to warn by precept, to instruct whilst it delights, and to call into action all those better feelings in the heart of man which tend to individual happiness, and have weight and moral influence on the well-being of a nation" (28, p. 275). The editor repeatedly enlists the principle of "a wide and diversified view of human character" as the rationale for including heterogeneous works. "Truth" seems to matter very little. Apparently embarrassed by the romance element in several of the texts, the editor justifies its inclusion, for *le vrai n'est pas toujours le vraisem-*

blable" (25, p. vi). The effect, in surveying all mankind from statesman to thief, from monarch to bookseller, is to assure the reader that the autobiographical impulse is a universal one, and that the proper study of humans is humans. And this canonization and dissemination of certain eighteenth-century texts also makes the structural and thematic discontinuities of autobiographical work legitimate by placing them within a frame of the humanist self.

More prescriptive definitions of the genre of autobiography did not begin to ossify, however, until the mid–twentieth century under the influence of literary historical, formalist, and, later, structuralist thought. Since then the formal aspects of the genre have been frequently codified as narrative with a beginning, middle, and end which purports to be true, is told retrospectively, and whose author is the same historical being as the first-person narrator and protagonist. These autobiographical theories have derived in large part from the readings of nineteenth- and twentieth-century writing as they are argued in the theoretically sophisticated work of critics such as Philippe Lejeune, Jeffrey Mehlman, Elizabeth Bruss, and Paul Jay.[4] For example, in *Le Pacte autobiographique* Lejeune defines autobiography as "a retrospective prose narrative produced by a real person concerning his own existence, focusing on his individual life, in particular on the development of his personality."[5] Implied within this definition are assumptions of an individuality that is distinct from collective humankind; of the existence of an essence, a personality, which unfolds in the narrative of the past; and of the irrelevance of women's life-writing. All aspects of this definition and others like it present complications when applied to a period before "self-biography" was conceptualized and thus rigidified. When applied to eighteenth-century autobiographical writing, such definitions can only be used to demonstrate the ways in which the texts fail to measure up to generic expectations, the ways in which they are only hesitant thrusts and starts toward autonomous and continuous self-fashionings.

Other contemporary critics who provide readings of the canonical Bunyan, Franklin, Gibbon, or Rousseau, for example, apply these traditional generic limitations of first-person narrative conventions to the earlier texts. Such critics seem to claim that eighteenth-century texts do not imitate the model of spiritual autobiography at one temporal pole or nineteenth-century realist fiction at the other. These constructions of eighteenth-century autobiographical writings often reduce the history of the self to a possible "preromantic" influence on Rousseau and Wordsworth; if the more diffuse forms such as journal, diary, and serial autobiography are included in the canon, it is only as failed versions of the later achievement. Dominated by crisis and closure, both spiritual autobiographies and realist novels present two related hegemonic models of experience that pressure our readings of the inconsistencies of eighteenth-century texts into conformity with dominant notions of a unified self. That is, the effort has largely been one of seeking precursors to the few "classic" later autobiographers such as Mill and Newman and Gosse whose lives are shaped by psychological, intellectual, or spiritual crises that reveal the truth of past experience. But few eighteenth-century autobiographical texts fit the formal critical standard that arises from and replicates these paradigms.

In spite of Donald Stauffer's monumental catalog of life-writing from 1660 to 1800 and William Matthews's extensive bibliographies of autobiographies and diaries that include numerous eighteenth-century entries, the serious critical studies of eighteenth-century autobiography are quite scarce.[6] The more general histories of autobiography usually leap from Bunyan to Rousseau with a quick glance at the intervening period. In order to find detailed criticism of less familiar eighteenth-century works, we must turn back to the historical and descriptive studies of the 1950s and 1960s.

One of the most important works on eighteenth-century self-writing, John Morris's *Versions of the Self*, considers the (male) autobiographers he discusses "as the largely unacknowledged pioneers of the modern sensibility," unwitting agents of the new.[7] Morris seeks continuities between eighteenth-century spiritual autobiographers and the nineteenth-century writers such as Wordsworth and Mill. The kind of self-consciousness that Morris values is the kind that transforms anxiety into strength and sanity, and he reads eighteenth-century works with an eye to finding precursors to the twice-born, those born again to themselves through self-consciousness and psychological regeneration. Morris seeks texts that reveal the power of self-scrutiny to transform a life into a tellable tale. For Morris, good autobiography is "not merely a chronicle of experience but a judgment of it."[8] It presents a powerful and virtuous example for modern man to imitate, a model of the heroic life. Morris pursues themes and patterns, form and closure, in his attempt to identify mental and emotional crises in eighteenth-century texts.

More valuable for our present purposes in thinking about eighteenth-century autobiography is the earlier *English Autobiography: Its Emergence,*

Materials, and Form by Wayne Shumaker, who characterizes the problems inherent in writing a history of autobiography.[9] Shumaker recognizes the dilemma of the eighteenth-century scholar who is caught between the varieties of seventeenth-century autobiography and the restrictiveness of nineteenth-century definitions. He seems, then, to identify the period as a transitional one of conflict. In the section on the eighteenth century, entitled "The Reduction of Heterogeneity," he imagines the eighteenth century as giving birth to the form, meaning, shape, and texture of the great modern autobiographies. "Before 1600, autobiographies of the modern type are nearly impossible to find," Shumaker writes, and "after 1600, they follow one another at decreasing intervals, until at last, about 1800, their authors seem to be writing in a tradition instead of feeling their way into a new literary genre" (5). The eighteenth century is a time, according to Shumaker, of the "emergence" into "the discovery of individuality," of coming to recognition of the "truth" of personhood. Thus, Shumaker is bound by his notion that a pregiven self exists and can be recovered through texts. He values most highly the seeds of modern autobiography in the eighteenth century, the origins of "developmental" autobiography, which emphasize causal progression from one state to another. In short, Shumaker recognizes the diversity of eighteenth-century texts, but his study, too, seeks the precursors to the modern concept of self, particularly "systematic accounts of a whole existence."[10] Shumaker looks for unity. If unity exists, it is autobiography; if it does not, then it is something less. The best autobiography, he argues, displays the characteristics of the nineteenth-century realist novel—form, structure, and dramatic narration. Similarly, Jerome Buckley conflates autobiography and spiritual autobiography to make them share one goal of self-discovery, "the paradoxical dying into life, the finding of the self by losing the self."[11] Both Buckley and Shumaker tame the texts into this familiar order of epiphanic transformation in which identity is lost and recovered. Guided by formalist and traditional historicist methodologies, their critical urge is to stalk the coherent selves hiding beneath the surface of these self-reflexive writings.

Roy Pascal also hunts for a modern self in *Design and Truth in Autobiography*. There he defines the genre as providing "a coherent shaping of the past" and "the reconstruction of the movement of a life, or part of a life, in the actual circumstances in which it was lived."[12] For Pascal, autobiography begins in the late eighteenth century and is inextricably tied to romanticism. The myriad works that do not measure up to postromantic assumptions, including man's centrality and uniqueness, are dismissed from the canon of self-writing. Pascal identifies "the classical age of auto-biography" as extending from Rousseau's *Confessions* (1782) to Goethe's *Poetry and Truth* (1831). Gibbon's and Franklin's works mark the beginning of autobiography because "they recognise in themselves a dynamic inborn quality, their innermost personality, and see their story as its unfolding through encounters with the outer world" (39). Autobiography provides "a coherent shaping of the past" (5) whose "centre of interest is the self, not the outside world" (9); it attempts to relate external reality to that unified and independent self. Centering interest on the self, the "best" apologies and the "best" autobiographies "must evoke the past meaning of an experience" to clarify simultaneously the meaning of past and present (16). In other words, Pascal's desire in reading autobiography is to "savour the quality of the central personality" (20) so that the kinds of autobiographies which he values are unified, evaluative, and developmental. The best autobiographies, then, reveal the truth of the essential self. While I agree with Pascal that autobiography defined strictly according to formalist terms only became common in the latter part of the eighteenth century, he must ignore Gibbon's multiple revisions, Franklin's four fragments, and Rousseau's palimpsest to define this triad as the originary point. Pascal's generic codes have limited applicability for eighteenth-century texts, for they cannot take into account the assumptions in D'Israeli's *Miscellanies,* or the formal variety in the early nineteenth-century multivolumed collection of autobiographies.

Among recent critics of autobiography, only Patricia Meyer Spacks has considered texts marginal to the eighteenth-century canon in any extended way (for example, those by Colley Cibber, Charlotte Charke, Laetitia Pilkington, and Fanny Burney), when she explores the connections between fact and fiction, novel and autobiography.[13] Significantly, Spacks argues that "self" is less a thing than an attitude, a way of reading experience, but she too quickly dismisses the implications of such a radical thought by urging that fictional identity is "more secure than in literal experience" (12). "Selfhood and consistent identity . . . is the underlying obsession and final achievement of the literary imagination in both these related genres" (315), she maintains. Though Spacks implies that eighteenth-century ideas on identity may be disruptive, she confines autobiography and novels to the function of successfully *containing* doubts about substantiality "by [their] firm denial or firm and complex assertion of the reality and importance of consciousness operating on experience." According to this approach, writing the self in a novel or autobiography is a way to get at its essential truth, and thus the notion of self as construct would seem to be abandoned.

Though Spacks indicates that "the eighteenth-century debate on identity became increasingly desperate in tone," the specific content of that debate remains unaddressed. For example, the disquieting implications of Hume's ideas as applied to autobiography are passed over in order to turn immediately to memory as the means to resolve any fear that the self is not progressive, developmental, or empirically grounded. In spite of Hume's wondering about continuous identity, Spacks uses his short autobiographical sketch (which takes "natural equanimity" as its theme) as proof that even the skeptic, when pressed to represent himself textually, finds a coherent self. But perhaps Hume's representation is most telling not in its theme but in its brevity. It suggests that a mid–eighteenth century "self" cannot be sustained in a text longer than eleven pages when it is presented for public consumption.

Spacks's interest is finally in the affirmation of identity: Autobiographies, she maintains, like the novel, "affirm the art of life . . . as stoutly as they affirm human identity" (302). They are optimistic modes that declare a faith "in human stability and growth." She seeks their "underlying principle of coherence" in order to find "their fundamental literary strength" (175). She concludes: "Selfhood and consistent identity, whether by sheer illusion-making or through collaboration with experienced actuality, is the underlying obsession and final achievement of the literary imagination in both of these related genres" (315). Spacks usefully touches on the way nineteenth-century novels shape our expectations about eighteenth-century ones, but she does not apply the same understanding to autobiographical writing. And she has not sufficiently discerned the extent to which our concepts of self and the narratives of identity are historically bound, the extent to which we, as twentieth-century readers, expect the text to imitate our own concept of the self which we think of as natural.

This setting out of spiritual autobiography on the one hand and nineteenth-century romantic self-discovery on the other is implicit in most criticism of autobiography since 1950; but it is perhaps most subtly and convincingly described by William Spengemann in his *Forms of Autobiography*.[14] Like Spacks, Spengemann finds the goal of autobiography, from Augustine on, to be the attainment of true self, which may be present in another or in God. The problem for eighteenth-century autobiographers ("philosophical" autobiography, as Spengemann sets it up), is to mediate between the external "authority" of the universal and the individual's convictions. Franklin resolves the problem by substituting reason for God, and both he and Bunyan are thus seen as transitional figures on the way to Rousseau and Wordsworth. In Rousseau, truth is subjective, based on feeling, and it evolves from the recounting of past events that all have equal significance. But to make Rousseau seem to be an outgrowth of the conflict in Franklin, Spengemann must treat the two autobiographers anachronistically. In sum, the goal of autobiography, according to Spengemann, is what is achieved by the paradigmatic Augustine's *Confessions*, the "reconciliation of protagonist and narrator, of unique experience and comprehensive knowledge, of true being and true consanguinity, of temporal action and eternal form."[15] The search for a center unites the spiritual and the romantic for Spengemann; the romantics sought the center in self, while Augustine sought it in God.

All of these narratives about eighteenth-century autobiographical writing, then, seek a paradigmatic model that will provide a kind of poetics of the genre. They are dominated by the assumption of a self that is both like other human beings and unique, and that can be imitated textually, as well as the belief that the best representations of that self imitate classic realist texts. There is often an assumption that a reality, hidden behind appearances, is independent of its inscription and its reading, and that representation in autobiography corresponds to it. In addition, these narratives presume that autobiographers are the source and center of the meaning of their texts, and that their aim is to write aesthetically satisfying works. If we accept these terms and generic limits, eighteenth-century self-writing can only be an attempt to strive toward nineteenth-century models and notions of self, and our attempts to read it will be constrained by that view.

Though he does not consider eighteenth-century texts, Robert Elbaz's essay on modern autobiography helps move us away from structuralist models toward histories of meanings. Elbaz takes issue with transhistorical definitions that derive from typological views of the genre and from reception theory in his reading of autobiographical texts after Rousseau. Elbaz usefully redefines the category of "genre" to mean "an ideological grid forced upon consciousness."[16] He continues, "Generic classification is a hegemonic phenomenon which restricts literary practice to approved, institutionalized forms of expression."[17] This formulation makes possible the notion that genre, situated in power and knowledge relations, operates under certain constraints. In addition, Elbaz's analysis effectively acknowledges the ways in which autobiographical criticism has constructed a free and autonomous individual who seems independent of social and contractual bonds. Elbaz does not, however, account for generic change—for shifts in the kinds of grids that make meaning in particular sociocultural situations. Nor does he explain the ideologies of hybrid genres—for example, the way that ideologies, themselves always in formation and permeated with oppositions, make resistance to generic codes possible. Most important, Elbaz does not probe the ways that the emergence of the hegemony of a certain genre may serve particular interests. Instead, we may read autobiographical writing, newly imagined as an ideology of genre, in conjunction with economic and political practices, not to fix the meaning of the text or to unfold the essence of a self but to consider the way conflictual discourses are yoked together within ideology to encourage bourgeois subjects to (mis)recognize themselves. Taking up these matters will allow us to move beyond a poetics of autobiography, with its structural models and narratives of the essential self, to a politics of autobiography in the eighteenth century.

❧ II

Rethinking eighteenth-century autobiographical writing along these lines requires a methodology informed by contemporary theories of the human subject, of history, and of culture. New historicism—or cultural materialism, in its more political and principally British version—would seem to enable such an inquiry.[18] Both terms include widely varied methodologies that may be characterized by postmodern reformulations of the relationships between literary and historical texts. These include the problematization of our access to the real, the importance of the critic-scholar as an interested narrator in the construction of history, and the situating of the human subject within power relations within particular historical moments.

Until very recently new historicism has had a rather limited impact on eighteenth-century studies, whose scholars have largely preferred to resist fashionable new theories, including New Criticism, structuralism, and deconstruction. Then too, the topical denseness of its "major authors" (Dryden, Swift, Pope, and Johnson) has led most eighteenth-century critics to assume that, because we have *always* paid attention to historical context and to interdisciplinary approaches, new historicism has little to teach us.[19] Another reason that American new historicism may not have seemed to have great relevance for the eighteenth century is that its focus has been on the peculiarly Renaissance centers of power—the monarchy and the theater—while in the eighteenth century we find a wider diffusion of the power of the state spread among monarch, ministers, and Parliament, as well as into the spheres of education, law, medicine, and the family. But in urging us to reflect on our mode of inquiry, new historicism makes it possible to reimagine the familiar and "natural," and to write genealogies of the institutions of the period (the prison, the madhouse, the hospitals) as well as of the underclass, the enslaved, and women of every class. These genealogies attend especially to the "accidents" of history to question history's continuities; they turn to the instability and confusions of historical events to show the conflictual aspects of what previously seemed to be fully uniform. As Foucault writes, genealogy "disturbs what was previously considered immobile; it fragments what was thought unified; it shows the heterogeneity of what was imagined consistent with itself."[20] Such an approach reconstitutes the conceptual object from a point of view located in the present so that the narrative produced has the power of intervention in present knowledge, and it argues for strategies of action. In other words, new historicism offers a conceptual base, however problematic, to critique more traditional methodologies.

New historicists argue that rather than knowing history directly, as objective intractable fact, we can know it only in textual artifacts about which a (literary) historian situated in the present composes a narrative. In other words, our perceptions of the historical past depend profoundly on what we bring to the foreground of our perception. The historian or narrator always speaks and writes from interested positions (whether or not those interests are acknowledged) and reflections on those positions become an inherent part of the narrative she or he fashions. As Fredric Jameson has written, "That history . . . is *not* a text, for it is fundamentally non-narrative and nonrepresentational; what can be added, however, is the proviso that history is inaccessible to us except in textual form, or in other words, that it can be approached only by way of prior (re)textualization."[21] While a category of the "real" exists, our access to it is constrained and held within certain textual and ideological bounds. Jameson, however, apparently regards the aesthetic as *the* single category mediating the contradictions of text and culture, but the texts that readers and writers determine to be aesthetically satisfying in a given age comprise a historically determined category, the terms of which shift and change according to time, class, and gender. In other words, "literature" and the canon are not sacrosanct, but are themselves the products of history and culture, and the autobiographical canon is among those that is most in need of reformulation.

In addition to redefining the relationship of the historian to "fact," the new historicism also calls special attention to the ruptures and discontinuities of history. Most studies of autobiography rely on a history of ideas which is thematic and continuous. The methodology of the history of ideas, when employed by literary historians, gives historical "context" the power to *explain* the literary text. In such studies, the progress of a particular object such as "identity" or "self" is traced through history to its culmination in the present. Such an approach demonstrates the way that events and ideas of the past lead inevitably to the concepts of self prevalent today. In contrast, writing the new history of any set of conventions is an activity in which past and present are intermingled as we attend to the ways that we have access to the past only through the present. In fact, the history of the ideology of the self, and of its texts, can only be written now that the autonomous and rational "self" expressive of a secret inner core is becoming an artifact of a moribund and newly historicized humanism.

One of the radical breaks of new historicism with the past, then, is in the constructedness of history and in the ways in which our access to a material reality is always mediated by language and ideology. What is at stake is, in part, the claim of objectivity in traditional historiography or whether "real" or "true" history can be known. New historicism helps us avoid the naive assumption, for example, that even the most detailed autobiography transparently describes an objective reality, or that it is the principal task of the literary critic to determine the "accuracy" of that self-representation. The struggle instead is over the consensual code by which we will make intelligible meaning of events. Hayden White, for example, is among those who, in reconceptualizing traditional historiography, conceive it "to be a 'message' about a 'referent' (the past, historical events, and so on) the content of which is both 'information' (the facts') and an 'explanation' (the 'narrative' account)."[22] The facts must meet both coherence and correspondence tests to claim certain value as truth.

Intellectual history after the linguistic turn—as John Toews indicates—cannot remain the same as it has been; that is, the history of *ideas* has become instead a history of *meaning* with its concomitant questioning of the status and validity of reason as the "universal, species-defining, and thus 'highest' form of human activity . . . [so that] language can no longer be construed as simply a medium, relatively or potentially transparent, for the representation or expression of a reality outside itself."[23] This places empirical history in question, for "language not only shapes experienced reality but constitutes it."[24] It is not that nothing exists beyond meanings, but that the conditions for the production of that meaning are in doubt. Within these new understandings it becomes important to determine why particular semantic codes gain precedence or relinquish ground in the social formation. Consequently, the "meanings" of history are constructed and made rather than discovered. History is not background or context in which we place the superior aesthetic object that is somehow truer or more real than the text that is traditionally defined as literary. Instead, literature and history work reciprocally to expose the limitations and misrecognitions of each, and the sanctity of the canon is violated.

New historicism, then, has brought with it a welcome attention to the multiple crossing discursive domains in any given text. It has blurred boundaries between fictional and nonfictional genres such as Swift's *Journal to Stella* or Fielding's *Voyage to Lisbon*, sometimes taken as historical truth, to regard discourse instead as an organizing principle. Such work in the eighteenth century may, for example, set the discourses of sexual impotence and castration in conjunction with Fielding's plays, or relate the production of "woman" to consumerism, the emergence of tourism to landscape painting, the reformist tracts on prisons to Goldsmith's *Vicar of Wakefield*, or the female body in medical tracts to women's images of themselves.[25] Broadly put, new historicism may be deployed to question the reciprocal relations of representation and reality, the production of subjectivity and human agency, and the contradictions of ideology.

The critics of new historicism range from those who want to reclaim "real history" to those who find it lacks the status of theory or science. In other words, the issues focus on "history" (especially of empirical fact) and on "theory" (or the desirability of claiming that historical conjunctural analysis can have larger explanatory power). Certainly new historicism in its many versions often displays an ambivalence toward how systematic it is to be, as well as toward the empirical status of its inquiry, and I take this to be a reason to put pressure on its theoretical aspects and especially its feminist and other political alignments. Some versions of new historicism allow power to produce its opposite or its own subversion only in order to disenable it. Thus successful change, even through collective opposition such as the women's movement, cannot be satisfactorily explained. Another very important pressure on new historicism comes from the cultural materialist strain that is more interested in theorizing resistance than containment, in finding ways for the poor and the otherwise oppressed to effect change.[26] New historicism, in its alignment with some versions of feminism and Marxism, needs to take more account of the dissonances that emerge from the juxtaposition of strongly held contestatory subject positions through history to consider the mode of production, as well as class, gender, and race relations. The relationships among them cannot be adequately conceptualized if discourse is imagined to float free of lived experience. More exactly, without a notion of the materiality of ideology, new historicism fails to establish a hierarchy of causes and effects and thus displays a relative indifference to these social relations and hierarchies.

Foucault himself refuses the appellation of science or theory for his work, regarding it instead as a critique of what counts as knowledge in power relations. That is, Foucault argues against the possibility of a scientifically valid theory with "truth-value" that would have sufficient explanatory power as a theory of history. Because power for Foucault is spread throughout the social formation, rather than lodged in the dominant class, he avoids Marxist interpretations of history that insist on the primacy of the economy in maintaining and reproducing dominant social relations. Alternatively, power is a diffuse force that simultaneously authorizes certain knowledges and excludes alien modes of discourse. According to some interpretations of Foucault, power extends beyond the dominant ideology of the state or the mode of production, and it is so diffuse in the social formation that it always reproduces itself, making it difficult to theorize the possibility of change for the human subject. Thus, the disruption of dominant "meanings" cannot be explained.

The subject of power and knowledge, as defined in Foucault's works, nevertheless attempts to recover a continuous history. In the very close interactive relationship he posits between history and the human subject, the subject attempts to restore that which is lost or unrecoverable: "Continuous history is the indispensable correlative of the founding function of the subject: the guarantee that everything that has eluded him may be restored to him; the certainty that time will disperse nothing without restoring it in a reconstituted unity; the promise that one day the subject—in the form of historical consciousness—will once again be able to appropriate, to bring back under his sway, all those things that are kept at a distance by difference, and find in them what might be called his abode."[27] The autobiographical act would seem to be, then, on the surface at least, an attempt at making this abode of reconstituted unity into a textual form. To read it from a new historical perspective, however, contests these continuities: "Genealogy does not pretend to go back in time to restore an unbroken continuity that operates beyond the dispersion of forgotten things: its duty is not to demonstrate that the past actively exists in the present."[28] I am suggesting, then, that eighteenth-century self-writing sets out the subject's fragmentations and discontinuities, its repetitions and revisions, though its readers may be compelled to make all the pieces of self and experience fit an identifiable mold as conflicting concepts of identity interplay within them. It is the ideologies of these molds that pertain here, for the "knowledge" that the human subject possesses about itself figures within discursive systems of power that are available at a given historical moment. There are, then, aspects of new historical work that make a revisionary reading of autobiographical practices possible. But a study of discursive practices, such as the writing of conversion narrative or the keeping of a journal, must also be a critique of the ideological frames that produce and limit such accounts of subjectivity. To erect a politically viable genealogy of the self and its textual traces requires a methodology that, unlike the Foucauldian project, turns its technology on itself to disclose its ends, and examines its own interest in adopting certain positions, its own stake in the power/knowledge relationships it seeks to unveil.

❧ III

We can, then, attempt to discern the ideologies of narrative operating in autobiographical texts, and the economic and political interests that they sustain. Such an approach also begins to make possible the destabilizing of our notions of the genre of autobiography. In first-person narrative, the "I" arbitrates reality through cultural codes to make "experience" intelligible and to place it in a familiar framework. The very articulation of events determines the evaluation of them. "Meaning" is encoded in the selection of words, the sequence of phrases, the assignment of dialogue to self or to another as we answer the ultimate narrative question, "So what?"[29] Thus, as much as authors of diaries, journals, and other serial accounts assume that they are themselves the origin of meaning, autobiographical writing, even in its most private renditions, makes use of what has been thought and said more publicly.

Diaries and journals, like other historical forms such as chronicles and annals that present themselves in less continuous forms, have commonly been judged to be inferior to more "finished" forms of narrative. Autobiographical writing parallels historical writing in its claims to represent what *is*, and recent revisions of traditional historiography and narrativizing history bear importantly on the question of the nature of reality that operates in those texts to produce the effect of truth.[30] The value attached to narrativity in the representation of real events arises from the desire to make sense of real events. Narrative, as Hayden White defines it, requires a meaning and a moral. But in his analysis historical annals and chronicles generally refuse to take shape as recognizable stories, and diaries, too, resist the imposition of plot. History proper, as White has pointed out, is usually assumed to be a text in which "the events must be not only registered within the chronological framework of their original occurrence but narrated as well, that is to say, revealed as possessing a structure, an order of meaning that they do not possess as mere sequence" (5). The historical chronicle lacks closure, while the annal simply lists events. Many eighteenth-century autobiographical texts avoid plot lines and avoid drawing moral consequences from the discrete particulars that are included within them.

Eighteenth-century autobiographical writers, for example, often violated the familiar generic codes of biblical paradigms or Theophrastan character. The representation of reality that they found most "natural" was something different from historical narrative, but something that recounted public and private events in their incoherence, lack of integrity, scantiness, and inconclusiveness. While it may have been Pepys's or Swift's or Wesley's desire to replicate the plenitude that they expect to find in experience, it may also have been their recognition that such an order can only find its contours through careful construction. As White argues, we expect narrative to "display the coherence, integrity, fullness, and closure of an image of life that is and can only be imaginary" (27). Many eighteenth-century autobiographical writings resemble the discontinuous historical forms he discusses, for they may not be "the imperfect [representations of self and experience] that they are conventionally conceived to be but rather . . . particular products of possible conceptions of historical reality, conceptions that are alternatives to, rather than failed anticipations of, the fully realized historical discourse that the modern history form is supposed to embody" (6). The list of dates in annals, for example, may frustrate a sense of continuity as much as provide one. The diarist or journalist, like the annals writer, may well attempt to imitate human chronology without overt rearrangement of events or evaluation of their significance. The diary or journal, then, may be considered to be the fragmented resolution of the contest over the authority for constituting a written representation of identity and lived experience in the midst of competing versions of the narrative representation of reality.

White seems bound to an idea of narrative as transhistorical and transcultural; that is, his argument suggests that there are certain features of narrative which must be universal, and he looks sympathetically on the definition of narrative as a metacode, "a human universal on the basis of which transcultural messages about the nature of a shared reality can be transmitted" (1). The multiplicity of eighteenth-century autobiographical texts, however, testifies that we cannot assume that the world presents itself to us in any fixed or transhistorical form, for our perception of it is always influenced by the ways we make it intelligible; using language, we mediate the world to our limited discursive frames. A historian must speak to a generation in narratives that encode the conventions of intelligibility at a particular time, for history is always a construct situated in the historian's moment. Narrative, situated within ideologies, functions to efface contradiction and make us believe that it imitates universal human codes; but, in fact, it is possible to imagine a world without narrative as we currently know it. No one narrative form is essential to being human, and culturally sanctioned narrative models are early implanted in our consciousness. In short, while it is crucial to acknowledge the way history is always someone's story, it is equally important to historicize narrative, to recognize its embedment in its particular moment and sociocultural situation, and to note the ways in which its various readers over time assign its varying meanings.

Our perceptions of eighteenth-century ideologies of autobiographical narrative, then, may be revised to incorporate texts that have ill-defined beginnings, middles, or ends, and that do not explicitly assign moral significance to the events they record. These conflicting notions of narrative and identity may have been tolerated, even encouraged, in the emergent genres of the period, including meditations, descriptive poems, the early novel, and memoirs in which the principle of organization may simply have been an associative train of ideas. Journals and diaries, for example, like chronicles and annals, would seem to question what tenet, other than human time, is powerful enough to connect events. In short, eighteenth-century works of self-biography are less quests toward self-discovery in which the narrator reveals herself or himself than repetitive serial representations of particular moments held together by the narrative "I."

It seems important, then, to consider how diaries, journals, and autobiographies were produced in the eighteenth century, what categories of authors wrote them, and how they were circulated in order to trace the autobiographical subject. We tend to think of a *printed* text as a fixed entity rather than a textual space that is always undergoing revision, in part because an author's name encourages a reader to regard a text as all of a piece, the "expression" of a subjectivity coherently held. But eighteenth-century narratives, private and public, underwent numerous metamorphoses, including total transformation before publication, and abridgment and expurgation both before and after publication. Even standard eighteenth-century novels, such as *Moll Flanders* and *Jonathan Wild*, were issued throughout the century in competing versions so that the "authentic" version cannot be firmly verified. Pat Rogers, in a study of chapbooks in the period, notes that "the radical adaptations of *Roxana* date from the last quarter of the eighteenth century and totally supplant the original in general consciousness."[31] As a consequence of this kind of textual history, a book bearing a certain signature or one that is recognizable because of a certain character cannot be discussed in terms of its "original" version since multiple versions of the text coexist. The idea of a standardized edition, itself in formation, was in conflict with making texts cheaply and readily available as the printing of varieties of literary products increased. In the first half of the eighteenth century, it was particularly common to sell books in installments at a price many could afford with the idea that the numbered portions would eventually be bound up and placed alongside each other on the owner's shelf. Readers in the lower and middle classes became accustomed to the serial mode of consumption as well as production.[32] A given autobiographical text, then, is also a series of accumulating acts of writing, revision, and reception.

What was true of the published fictional texts was equally true of the purportedly nonfictional in the eighteenth century, though the multiple versions of autobiographical texts less frequently reached the public domain: often the texts remained unpublished, or were only published post-

schedules for studying, memoranda, accounts of personal finances, records of his reading, and notes and quotations that might become sermons.

Wesley's conversion, unlike Bunyan's or Augustine's, comes at the very beginning of his published diaries in May 1738, and yet he continues for seven volumes to describe the activities of the converted self. His textual "self," then, or autobiography, was *meant* for scrutiny and revision. He wrote and rewrote his journals, including the Georgia journal that apparently existed in at least five unpublished versions, sometimes in cipher or untidy shorthand, sometimes with rules and resolutions in the imperative like Boswell's memos to himself, later to be revised and inserted into the journals. Wesley, like Fox before him, edited and censored autobiographical texts that members of his flock submitted to him before approving them for publication. Thus many Methodists wrote *and* lived under the strictures Wesley had designed. The crisis of conversion narrative involves the anxiety of not being able to tell a providential story; the daily event and the story of human agency take its place.

Similarly, the crisis of the eighteenth-century self reflects, in large part, the attempt to render secular experience in the terms of paradigmatic biblical models. Secular autobiographical narratives display multiple and serial subject positions that may not add up to a coherent self. Pepys's apparently extemporaneous diary was written in five carefully crafted stages: (1) notes, (2) accounts and expanded notes, (3) revision of general entries, (4) diary entry, and (5) reading and revision.[37] Pepys's revisions occasionally appear in the manuscript, but more often they predate the diary entry, for he worked from notes and memoranda, much as Boswell did. His written diary registers an orderly self-examination—on a daily, weekly, monthly, and annual basis, Pepys subjected his written self to review and revision. Another text written from multiple narrative stances is Swift's *Journal to Stella,* a series of sixty-five letters from Swift to Esther Johnson (Stella) and Rebecca Dingley, written for the most part in continuous journal form. In the journal, the personal and the political intermingle. Swift purposefully attempts to position himself in journal and letter simultaneously as the elusive, playful "PDFR" who loves Stella and the serious clergyman on a political mission to gain the First Fruits and Twentieth Parts. The journal-letters end without resolution, the political never fully reconciled with the private. Boswell, Thrale, and Burney also kept voluminous journals that measure

their identity in its daily repetition but remark on the contradictory positionings of the self from moment to moment, day to day, year to
year. Each collected notes or memoranda that, in time, were revised to
produce new versions of selves.

Hester Lynch Thrale Piozzi compiled numerous diaries and journals,
including the "Family Book," volumes of Johnson's sayings, journals
of the remarks of famous contemporaries, and books of her daughter
Queeney's achievements; from 1776 to 1809 she regularly made entries
in *Thraliana,* her diary of anecdotes and personal history, among the first
English ana. In addition, she kept a "New Common-Place Book," various small diaries, and, as Mrs. Piozzi, she prepared a five-volume literary
autobiography for her adopted son. Mrs. Thrale wrote and rewrote herself and her experience, which she apparently considered too copious to
confine to one version. Similarly, Boswell kept memoranda, condensed
notes, journals, and revised journals, and then transcribed revised journals into *The Life of Johnson*—all varied discourses of a self perpetually in
formation that adopts contradictory subject positions.

Even with regard to the more canonical autobiographies such as those
of Gibbon, Rousseau, or Franklin, the fragmentary nature of the texts is
often ignored by modern critics in the interests of defining a cohesive
genre. Benjamin Franklin's autobiography, far from being a continuous
narrative, consists of four distinct sections written at four distinct times
over twenty years, sections that lack connective tissue or summary;
though he lived until 1790, the narrative stops at 1758. The portions we
remember best (the arrival in Philadelphia as a penniless waif, the acknowledgment of his life's errata, the scheme for moral perfection) occur
in the first two sections—but Franklin did not prepare a definitive version that neatly fits the parts together, and what we know as the *Autobiography* was not published while he was alive.

Similarly, Gibbon wrote six autobiographical fragments, never bringing the narrative to completion in his lifetime. His telling and retelling
of himself suggests his crisis in believing that he was, indeed, the source
and center of his own life, and brings to the foreground the arbitrary nature of the individual subject's construction of the real. Franklin's and
Gibbon's autobiographical writings are multilayered revisions of themselves, their public coherence only arrived at through assiduous editing
by later generations. The texts never settle on a finished self. Repetition
helps the "I" constitute itself through reiteration of an identity, and this
constant revision is an attempt to create a perfect past, something that

may well have been possible in constructing some versions of spiritual autobiography but something quite impossible if the unpredictable present intrudes on the idealization of a whole and finished "self."

While these journals, diaries, and fragments of autobiographies may well be devices to construct, imagine, and declare an identity, they are also demonstrations of the difficulty in finding new paradigms for quotidian experience, and they are testimonies to the uncertainties and incoherences of eighteenth-century "selves" as experienced through time. The texts of "self" and experience, then, in turn produce and reproduce, confirm and undermine, these ideologies of perceiving and representing reality. Particularly in their private forms, these texts may often reinscribe the pervasive public ideologies of identity which they seek to resist and subvert, yet these texts may also display the incompatibility of the various notions of identity, class, and gender in circulation.

❧ I V

A more specific discussion of one type of private serial autobiographical narrative, the diary, will tease out some of the ideologies of genre governing it during the eighteenth century. The diary and journal have only recently become the subject of theoretical discussion.[38] Some of the reasons for the neglect of serial narrative forms are practical ones, while others relate to critical assumptions: diaries often remain unpublished manuscripts; their length may make reading tedious and difficult; they lack the formal cohesiveness that lends itself to New Critical readings; and, in spite of their articulation of human chronology, diaries are not classic realist texts. Donald Stauffer is typical of formalist critics in his argument that we should ignore the diary when he writes, "The diary makes no attempt to see life steadily and see it whole. It is focussed on the immediate present, and finds that the happenings of twenty-four hours are sufficient unto the day. It becomes, therefore, not the record of a life but the journal of an existence, made up of a monotonous series of short and similar entries. Furthermore . . . the diary has scant claim to consideration, for it makes no pretence to artistic structure."[39] The diary, then, is dismissed from consideration because it does not fit into existing aesthetic categories.

If published eighteenth-century autobiography defies nineteenth- and twentieth-century paradigms of the genre, then unpublished diaries and journals conform even less to demands for theme, pattern, structure, and certain meaning. Because it was so seldom published, the diary in the eighteenth century had little burden of the past to contend with. As William Matthews has written, "Except for religious diaries and certain [others] . . . diaries are mostly written without reference to other diaries and without influence from them, and so the form has no history except in the most general sense."[40] Because diarists often believe that they write in a vacuum without reference to other similar texts, they are especially susceptible to claims of originality and spontaneity.

Though diaries and journals certainly existed earlier than the seventeenth century, that historical period marks the moment of *proliferation* of the serial autobiographical text.[41] Modern usages of the words *diary* and *journal* began to appear in the sixteenth century. When the word *diary* is used in the title of seventeenth- and eighteenth-century texts, it often refers to medical, astronomical, or meteorologic accounts, or, as in the case of the popular *Ladies Diary* (1752), it means a kind of almanac or even a housekeeper's pocketbook. Such diaries, seldom designed for publication, were kept rather as private record books. Most of the diaries included in Matthews's bibliography of British diaries were not *published* in the eighteenth century, and so did not reach the public domain until the nineteenth or twentieth century. For example, Samuel Pepys's diaries were first published in 1825 and Evelyn's in 1818. Though Matthews's list is not exhaustive, it is indicative of general trends. Among those he lists, I can find only one that was both written and published in the sixteenth century, and approximately twenty-five similarly treated in the seventeenth century. Fewer than twenty were both written and published between 1700 and 1750, and there are twenty-three in this category between 1750 and 1800. Though the diary form was integrated into the novel as early as *Robinson Crusoe* (1719) and *Pamela* (1740), the first complete novel-diary was not published until 1777.[42] The diaries that *were* published in the eighteenth century are not introspective or personal but are most often travel- or military-oriented sea diaries or daily accounts of battles. By the nineteenth century, diaries were often published relatively soon after they had been written and without waiting for the death of the author. The diary, in other words, was largely a private document in the seventeenth and early eighteenth centuries, but by the nineteenth century it was both a private and a public document, no longer confined to secrecy.

We can find traces of new ideological assumptions regarding identity in the spate of diaries produced and published in seventeenth- and eighteenth-century England. These include the belief that the private inner "self," somehow more authentic than the public one, will be marked by more fluctuations and vacillations than the public; and, by the end of the century, that a private "self" exists which conceals dangerous and even criminal thoughts that ought not be made public. Thus there is an assumption of a real and pregiven person behind the text and, correlatively, the feeling that private subjectivity should remain private, its only legitimate reader the diarist or journalist.

One way to mark out some of the presuppositions about serial narrative in the period is to analyze retrospective comments written late in the eighteenth century, in particular those concerning the most marginalized self-biographies, for, as in the case of autobiography, only near the end of the century did diary and journal begin to be conceptualized. One exception is Thomas Warton's parody of the diary's minute attention to details and the importance it assigns to the trivial when he mocks an academic journal written by a senior fellow at Cambridge. The parody in the *Idler* ridicules the repetitive nature of diary with its hourly entries, as well as the idleness of academic life that breeds diary keeping:

> *Monday, Nine o'clock.* Turned off my bed-maker for waking me at eight. Weather rainy. Consulted my weather-glass. No hopes of a ride before dinner. . . .
>
> *Ditto, Twelve.* Drest. Found a letter on my table to be in London the 19th inst. Bespoke a new wig.
>
> *Ditto, One.* At dinner in the hall. Too much water in the soup. Dr. Dry always orders the beef to be salted too much for me. [43]

Warton's mockery oddly reverses itself with an incongruous nationalist argument for the superiority of English universities over foreign institutions, in spite of the laziness and luxury evidenced in the diary as characteristic of Cambridge and Oxford. Diary writing, though humorously treated, is interpreted here as a threat to stalwart masculinity and Church of England virtue.

Increasingly it was the act of *publishing* a diary rather than writing it that stigmatized it. In *Idler* 84 Samuel Johnson wrote favorably of diaries when he suggested that we can only guard against self-love and ulterior motive in writing our lives if they remain private accounts. And even later in early nineteenth-century reviews of recent self-biographies, publishing autobiography is compared with a violent and insane malady that strikes writers who are hungry after fame, for "if the populace of writers become thus querulous after fame, (to which they have no pretensions), we shall expect to see an epidemical rage for auto-biography break out, more wide in its influence and more pernicious in its tendency than the strange madness of the Abderites, so accurately described by Lucian." There is fear of an autobiographical plague: "Symptoms of this dreadful malady (though somewhat less violent) have appeared amongst us before. London, like Abdera, will be peopled solely by 'men of genius.'"[44] Similarly, an anonymous reviewer of the *Life of Peter Daniel Huet*, referring to Samuel Johnson's *Idler* 84, lamented that "self-biography" seldom provided a frank picture of one's motives or interests, and merely satisfied vanity: "It may perhaps be said, notwithstanding all professions to the contrary, that no one ever published memoirs of himself, entirely for the benefit of others."[45] In this sentiment toward prohibiting the publication of diaries, we see the paradoxical demand for revelation of those details that are most difficult to tell and the demand for published diaries to transgress existing boundaries between private and public.

In Isaac D'Israeli's "Some Observations on Diaries, Self-Biography, and Self-Characters" (1796), one of the first full conceptualizations of the diary that has not been previously remarked upon, journal writing seems to be a practice in recession, in spite of biography's recent popularity.[46] D'Israeli, writing in a slightly sardonic vein, argues that the interest in the diary arises simply because it recounts the experience of a fellow being: "Our souls, like our faces, bear the general resemblance of the species, but retain the particular form which is peculiar to the individual. He who studies his own mind, and has the industry to note down the fluctuations of his opinions, the fallacies of his passions, and the vacillations of his resolutions, will form a journal to himself peculiarly interesting, and probably, not undeserving the meditations of others. Nothing which presents a faithful relation of humanity, is inconsiderable to a human being" (97–98). D'Israeli assumes that a journal will isolate variations and changes of thoughts, feelings, and decisions; that it will be perused at a later date by its maker; and that its truthfulness will be useful to others. D'Israeli recognizes that there may be some pleasure in using diary as a mnemonic device to spur memories of a dinner fifty years earlier, but he takes instead as his object of satire diary's giving priority to recording details of personal hygiene: "Dates of birth, and settlements of marriage, may be pardoned to the individual; but to give the importance of history to the progress of a purge, and to return divine thanks for the cutting of a corn, . . . is giving importance to objects which should only be observable in the history of any other animal, but man" (99). Thus such a hierarchy of values is necessary in order to distinguish a category of being called "man." In sum, the journal produces a sincere yet change-able "self" that asks its readers to make something smooth and finished of the text, to reproduce a recognizable and full human being.

In fact, D'Israeli considers the subgenre of the diary to be private, true, and even a little dangerous. Throughout his essay there is a some-what coy contradiction between the requirement to keep one's "self" pri-vate yet make it readable enough to tantalize a public readership. This coyness also appears in the anonymous prefatory material to George Whitefield's *Journal of a Voyage from London to Savannah*. The journal proper is described by the editor as displaying "a wide and diversified view of human character," but he excuses its publication on the grounds that a surreptitious copy was previously published without the author's consent: "He knows himself too well to obtrude his little private con-cerns upon the world, especially when intermixed with such passages re-lating to others, as none but an unthinking person could judge proper to divulge."[47] The journal is paradoxically judged worthy of a large public audience if the author is excused from responsibility for its escape from his hands.

The diary affords a place where one can converse with "that other Self, which Shaftesbury has described every thinking being to possess; and which, to converse with, he justly accounts the highest wisdom" (101), D'Israeli writes. Dividing the self from the self, the diary sets out an alternative self to ponder. And by declaring that divided self tex-tually, autobiography renders self-division increasingly commonplace and natural. Thus, D'Israeli thinks of the function of the diary as display-ing the most intimate and incriminating of details; it requires delicate strokes and regular diligence. To write a diary reassures others of one's honesty, D'Israeli assumes, and it is an occasion to address the reader without reserve; if deceit is detected, the entire project will surely be jeopardized. The diary provides a "faithful relation of humanity" that in-terests other human beings, a text that serves comparative purposes and helps to create a recognizable category of human qualities. D'Israeli's commentary, then, like Whitefield's journal, may well be read as reiter-ating the commonplaces in circulation about self-biography, and particu-larly the diary, near the end of the eighteenth century. That is, popular ideas about this form can be more readily articulated at the moment when it begins to shift to a more public and standardized mode than had previously been known.

The diary and journal, then, are representations of reality rather than failed versions of something more coherent and unified. In spite of the fact that the diary and other serial narratives imitate traditional and emergent generic codes (romance, epic, drama, comedy, tragedy), by being written in "private" they affect to escape preexisting categories, to tell the "truth" of experience. By eschewing known narrative codes and opting for discontinuity and repetition, diaries and journals often attempt to seem spontaneous, and thus avoid assigning meaning or a hierarchy of values. The diarist pretends simply to transcribe the details of experience, but clearly some events are more important to the narrative "I" than others, and the minute particulars of an interiority increasingly become the diarist's focus. In addition, the diary usually claims that it is secret, in spite of its apparent invitation to the "self"—and perhaps others—to read it at a later date or after the diarist's death. Finally, the diary produces a sincere yet changeable narrator and reader, whether self or other, who delights in smoothing over the contradictory strands in the text. In sum, the eighteenth-century diary produces and reflects an individual who believes she or he is the source and center of meaning; it inscribes the dominant ideologies of empiricism and humanism while it also, through its discontinuous and fragmentary form, may disrupt the ideologies it seems to espouse.

These prenarrative and antinarrative forms serve certain ideological functions in culture and history. Autobiographical texts in the period issue from the culture as much as the individual author, and as marginalized versions of identity and experience, they contest the culture's more public and institutionalized constructs of reality. Remarkably unfixed texts that were only infrequently published during the eighteenth century, they invalidate our expectations of narrative. Far from being incidental to eighteenth-century identity, revisions and changes were crucial to its reproduction. But the emergence and proliferation of these various forms raise further questions about notions of reality in the eighteenth century, as well as questions about whose interests the production of a private much-revised subjectivity reinforces.

In short, a rethinking of the ideologies of genre in the eighteenth century must include the recognition that eighteenth-century English diaries and self-biographies existed in multiple versions, seldom reached the public eye during the life of the author, and often remained unpublished until later centuries. The mid–eighteenth century, then, cleared a *public* space for writers and readers of documents about the private "self." What had seemed private to the early eighteenth century had become a desirable commodity by the end of the century, but the practice of diary writing was believed to wane as its publication became a conventional, if sometimes disreputable, practice.

If private autobiographical writing constituted a place for experimentation and sabotage of prevailing class and gender categories, as well as political and religious doctrines, it does not however escape the familiar ways of making meaning in a given historical moment. That is, diaries can only be relatively autonomous from the culture they inhabit, for there is no truly private language or practice. The subject of serial autobiography is a subject positioned within struggles to claim individual difference, autonomy, freedom, and privacy. Writing oneself in autobiographical text, even in asserting the existence of a private self, is complicit in the political and economic production of that subject. Private autobiographical writing in the eighteenth century serves the purposes of various institutions in anchoring a self-regulating body of individuals who perceive themselves to be autonomous and free. But it also functions to articulate modes of discourse that may disrupt and endanger authorized representations of reality in their alternative discourses of self and subject. As such, it poses tentative textual solutions to unresolvable contradictions, largely within the private sphere. An eighteenth-century serial autobiography, read through the ideology of genre, is the thing itself rather than a failed conversion narrative or an incipient realist novel.

CHAPTER TWO

The Politics of Subjectivity

[Self] by its Nature, is purely and simply One.
—Zachary Mayne, An Essay on Consciousness (1728)

But self or person is not any one impression, but that to which our several impressions and ideas are supposed to have a reference.
—David Hume, A Treatise of Human Nature (1748)

In what personal identity consists, is an important question, which has been frequently agitated and variously discussed; and on this account it may appear presumptuous rather than prudent in me, to attempt an investigation of a subject on which the learned world has been so much and so long divided.
—Samuel Drew, An Essay on the Identity and General Resurrection of the Human Body (1809)

I

The prevailing views of the eighteenth-century subject, those views that we have long associated with common sense, assume that knowledge is the product of experience and that a universal human nature exists outside the confines of history. In other words, each individual participates in a transhistorical human nature that is distinguished from the nature of other species by its ability to make ethical decisions and its reverence for the past; most important, human consciousness is assumed to be uniformly capable of making symbols. In spite of its universality, humanism, as it was understood in its various manifestations in eighteenth-century England, tolerates contradictions within its ideological frame, for it relies on a dualist concept of a split human nature that is paradoxical and even inconsistent. In fact, humanism assumes that moral duplicity is fundamental to the uniform nature of man. As Paul Fussell puts it, "To the humanist, inconsistency is necessarily Man's lot:

to expect consistency from him is to deny by implication the paradoxical dualism that makes him man."[1]

This humanist model further encompasses the notion that the pursuit of happiness is man's goal, and his failure to achieve it can only be a failure of will. Man's will is free, so liberated that Samuel Johnson argues strongly against the ruling passion or other inherently determinative forces on character. We are capable of controlling our own desires. He writes in the *Rambler*, "Nature will indeed always operate, human desires will be always ranging; but these motions, though very powerful, are not resistless; nature may be regulated, and desires governed; and to contend with the predominance of successive passions, to be endangered first by one affection, and then by another, is the condition upon which we are to pass our time, the time of our preparation for that state which shall put an end to experiment, to disappointment, and to change."[2] In Johnson's interpretation, what is changeless in our nature is the insatiability of human desire, for men resemble each other more than they differ. But that capacity for change is always circumscribed by the universal equalizer, death, and by the changelessness of eternity. In short, eighteenth-century humanism allows for inconsistencies within individual consciousness and between man and society. But the divisions are sufficiently knotted together so that any individual identity may finally become explicable and comprehensible, its essence pregiven and known and its plenitude displayed.

In analyzing these familiar eighteenth-century assumptions of the "self" through postmodern theory, we can rethink the autobiographical subject to interrupt our notions of a coherent, stable human self who originates and sustains the meaning of his experience. I want to first define more fully the autobiographical subject that is at issue here, and then turn to consider the conflictual discourses in circulation in particular eighteenth-century texts. Of particular relevance for redefining the concept of narrative consciousness in autobiographical texts is Émile Benveniste's distinction between the "I" who speaks and the "I" who is spoken. For Benveniste, language constructs subjectivity, and in turn subjectivity writes language: "*I* refers to the act of individual discourse in which it is pronounced, and by this it designates the speaker."[3] Benveniste proposes a split subject: "It is in and through language that an individual constitutes himself as a *subject*, the I who is uttering the present instance of the discourse"[4] between the agent of speech and the subject engendered in discourse, speaking and spoken. The "I" is a shifter, always changing its referent in time and space. The split subject, then, allows for the recognition that the "I" who is writing is distinct from the "I" who is written about. This disparity between parts of the "self" has also been taken up in contemporary psychoanalytic theory by Jacques Lacan, who, in his rereading of Freud, has decentered the self as we have known it since Descartes.[5]

Bridging the social and the psychic to theorize the way the fragmented subject is articulated within discourse, Lacan argues that the subject is constructed in language. No longer the origin of meaning, knowledge, and action, the individual consciousness in its infancy is both as diffuse and as unified as a broken egg—the "*hommelette*" of Lacan's formulation. For Lacan, universal symbolic categories describe and define the human subject through its developmental stages when it loses its androgynous unity and shifts from the diffuse infant to a subject who differentiates herself or himself from the (mother) parent. The human subject, moving through the imaginary stage of identification and duality, sees an ideal image reflected in the mirror and simultaneously recognizes and misrecognizes that image. That mirror stage or movement into the symbolic realm is the beginning of the "self" dividing from itself. According to Lacan's system, the mirror stage also marks the moment of the production of the unconscious—of the unspoken and unsaid—as well as the foundation of desire. In a reinterpretation of Freud's *fort-da* story, the child's entrance into power relations comes at the moment of attempting to gain control over an object that has disappeared from view. And finally there is Lacan's stage of signification, in which the subject emerges into language. In order to enter into society, the child must begin to learn and manipulate language. The entrance into the symbolic is also the moment of recognition of the sexual split, of the split into a gendered subjectivity.

While Lacan's premise that there is no unmediated experience or access to reality without the use of a sign system is useful, his theory of language is inadequate to a politically viable critique of autobiographical writing because it isolates the subject from the real, confining it forever to the realm of signification. Lacan's theories conceptualize a contradictory subject who nevertheless seems freed from history and culture, one who is entrapped and incapable of change. Lacan pays little attention to the ways in which the symbols that describe the individual's emergence into language and identity are themselves produced within ideology. That is, the Lacanian subject, without being sufficiently embedded in

the economic and the political, erases the variations of particular sociocultural formations. This lacuna can be circumvented in part by attending more specifically to the particular historical situations of the specific
discourses that produce the subject, and to the production of "individual" desire at the conjunction of these discourses. For the politically situated subject, human consciousness is less the origin and center of meaning than the reproduction of social and historical relations. Discourses
too, then, participate in these relations rather than remaining only expressive products of an individual self, and a single consciousness is no
longer perceived to be the originating impulse. Thus, I find an emphasis
on a discursive subject placed in its historical specificity more productive
than a universal symbolic system that explains all subjects through time.
In addition, Lacan's discourse of universal difference, of binary opposition that replicates a transhistorical heterosexual sex/gender system with
its fixed hierarchies, poses serious difficulties for feminist criticism because it cannot address the material conditions of oppression based on
gender.

In other words, we feel compelled as writers of ourselves and readers of
autobiographies to construct a "self," but that interest in a closed, fixed,
rational, and volitional self is fostered within a historically bound ideology. One consequence of the subject's entering into the culture's language and symbol system is a subjectivity placed in contradiction among
dominant ideologies while those ideologies simultaneously work to produce and hold in place a unified subject. In order to preserve the existing
subject positions, individual subjects are discouraged from attending to
the ways in which the discourses are incongruent. We *believe* that the
different positions make an autonomous whole, but the *feeling* that we
are constant and consistent occurs because of ideological pressures for
subjects to make order and coherence. Though we have confidence that
the conflicting positions will add up to a whole, it is partially that we
attend to the particular memories that match the available codes and
make us believe in a fundamental unity. If human subjects give heed instead to inconsistencies, the reformulated "self," an intersection of competing discourses, may seem less obviously continuous and explicable. As
Mieke Bal has described subjectivity, "The discourses [that language]
produces are (located in) common places, be it institutions, groups or,
sometimes, and by accident, individuals. Those common places are the
places where meanings meet."[6] All the moments may not fit, and the
subject positions may strain against each other. In short, the emergence

of language takes place within a system of semiotic power relations to displace the universality of human nature and to substitute a historically located subject. Autobiographical texts, then, may specifically resist a self made whole by humanist ideology, Cartesian philosophy, or Christian theology. Thus, a model of multiple discursive formations which calls a historically located individual subject into being proves more flexible for producing new ways of regarding gender, identity, and narrative.

In order to locate this subject of power, we may then ask whose interests the production of this autobiographical subject serves. Marx's notion of ideology as "false consciousness" would emphasize the way in which ideology is opposed to what is true, and it would seem to be the possession of a ruling class that is then imposed on the underclasses. That is, the ideology is in the hands of the dominant class, and power moves from that class downward.[7] There are, however, important alternative ways of viewing ideology. In his landmark essay, "Ideology and Ideological State Apparatuses" (1971), Althusser attempts to account for the position of the subject of power in relation to material practices.[8] In that essay, Althusser defines interpellation as a process by which the subject comes to recognize itself as it is hailed in language. For Althusser, ideology functions to disguise the real conditions of the production of the subject: "Ideology represents the imaginary relationship of individuals to their real conditions of existence."[9] The subject produced in capitalist societies is one ready to claim that it is the free author of its own "expression," but because ideology obscures the conditions of its production, the subject cannot recognize the real conditions of its subjection. If we follow these assumptions, the autobiographical subject would believe in its agency to express and know and regulate itself without discerning the economic and political powers that limit its expression.

In any sociocultural situation, Althusser further argues, multiple contradictory forces are at play in the formation of material and discursive practices. Rather than the individual's being the source of her or his own language and ideas, ideological state apparatuses (ISAs) such as the church, the family, and the educational system produce that consciousness and assign systems of meaning which individuals absorb and adopt. The individual also unwittingly reproduces the conditions that allow the institutional state apparatuses to persist in their assignments of meaning. Ideological practices, he argues, are inscribed in the rituals and other material practices of everyday existence. The agency for these practices is widely scattered because the ISAs are not the product of any one class or monolithic power group. While literature, for example, may be the attempt of one class to control another, it may also subtly voice several contradictory codes at one time. Ideology then interpellates or constitutes individuals as subjects, defining and confining them in part, so that they achieve "free" recognition of their subject positions.

For Althusser, the social formation is not simply a reflection of the economic, but is produced by multiple conflictual levels that are themselves "relatively autonomous." While the economic level is determinative in the last instance for Althusser, as it was for Marx, other elements of the social formation (the family, state, religion) may dominate at a given moment. Though Althusser does not take up the issue of gender, his formulation enables the possibility of other revolutionary forces, such as feminism, gaining hegemony and transforming ideology.

It is the materiality of ideology which I want to stress here, as well as the way in which ideology is not monolithic or exclusively aligned with a particular class as the only hegemonic force. Everything need not have a direct economic cause or reflect the economic interests of a class, as in reductionist versions of Marxism. Antonio Gramsci, for example, usefully argues for a more interactive notion of class hegemony as an ensemble of social relations articulated together, "a *process* of class relations in which concrete and determinate struggles for cultural, economic and political power or jurisdiction represent the decisive terrain of specific historical analysis."[10] That is, though the economic has powerful effects, the ideological, economic, and political are mutually determining forces within which subjects are produced. In this way, the economic is productive of the real rather than merely reflective of a reality that is already given. These social relations work to reproduce existing relations, but oppositional force is situated in the subjugated which may find avenues to make itself known. Nonhegemonic ideologies may contest dominant ideologies and make the contradictions felt. For Gramsci, domination or power may come through ideological struggle rather than being exerted exclusively by one class upon another. Recent theories of ideology, then, may regard ideology as a "material matrix of affirmations and sanctions," as a system of assent to regulation, produced within ideological struggle.[11] We cannot say with conviction that a particular ideology is the uncomplicated possession or product of a particular class, such as the aristocracy or the working class; nor can we say that a particular ideology belongs exclusively to one gender. In the definition I am using here, ideology is itself a set of conflictual practices and class antagonisms that legitimate exploitation and its favored modes of production. In other words, though class may be more intensely constitutive for men, or gender more crucial for women, at particular historical moments, these are applied asymmetrically. In perpetual struggle and subject to co-optation by particular political programs, ideologies may elide contradictions in the interests of declaring a "self" that matches hegemonic ideologies about the individual in culture. The interstices between them may encourage imagined alternatives to the status quo as ideologies vie for dominance in the determinative order of intelligibility within textual practices. It is here, in the contradictions within the materials of culture, that we may locate the oppositional subject necessary for a materialist feminist politics. Such a project, then, requires a model of ideology which acknowledges contradiction within it in order to allow subjects to misrecognize themselves in prevailing ideologies and to intervene in producing new knowledge.

Particularly important for regarding this reformulated subject of ideology is the way in which "meaning" is produced at the conjunctions of conflicting discourses. Michel Pêcheux's theories of transformation of the subject place particular emphasis on theorizing the way that human subjects take up language within power relations. He argues that once we abandon the notion that words have transhistorical meanings, we begin to see how their meanings shift and slip in the crevices between discourses as they are deployed at particular times. Pêcheux writes that "*words, expressions, propositions, etc. change their meaning according to the positions held by those who use them,* which signifies that they find their meaning by reference to those positions." [12] In a given social formation, then, at a particular historical moment, the power of certain discourses to determine knowledge may be uneven, and an ensuing struggle occurs in human subjects, in texts, and in the management of those texts. Pêcheux has argued that individuals may readily accept the ways they are interpellated in society, and are then defined as "good." Or they may counteridentify, refusing and acting against the available subject positions. A third alternative is that they may disidentify, in which case a "transformation-displacement *of the subject form* may take place." [13] Such disidentification may occur because such subjects are held in subject positions that are incompatible, and the ideologies are brought into contestation. "Disidentification" in text or in the world may make visible the previously invisible aspects of ideology that produce subjects, and new positions may be made available through which change may be effected.

It is not only relevant that language *means* in relation to itself and its linguistic system, but that language practices, and thus meanings may vary radically according to the subject position of its users and the extent to which they are enabled to contest dominant ideologies. In an example of disidentification, though the underclass and the female gender may use the same words as the dominant class and possessors of male privilege, they may be dismissed from the category "knowledge." In addition, especially pertinent to materialist feminism is Diane Macdonell's insight that different domains of language use exist and are taken up in relation to each other—they are interactive and even transgressive.[14] The human subject, she suggests, is one location of the *interdiscourse*, or the place where these conflictual discourses meet. Those who control meanings of words and concepts are empowered, though resistance to that power may occur at the intersections of conflicting discourses. For example, women's scandalous memoirs in eighteenth-century England are a collectivity of discourses aimed at mocking masculine privilege and at libeling the dominant classes; but at the same time, the female memoirists usurp the language of the oppressors to redefine dominant notions of their disreputable characters and of their inferior status.

I am suggesting, then, that these theoretical notions of the subject make it possible to read eighteenth-century autobiographical writing as one textual location where women and men, privately and publicly, experiment with interdiscourses and the corresponding subject positions to broach the uncertainties of identity. Autobiographical writing allows the previously illiterate and disenfranchised to adopt a language sufficiently acceptable to be published, and, at the same time, it enables them to envisage new possibilities in the interstices between discourses or to weave them together in new hybrid forms. In its public and private manifestations, autobiographical writing is a discursive and material practice in which gendered subjectivity is constructed, confirmed, and sabotaged. Such texts may work simultaneously for and against the ideologies of identity which prevail. They may sometimes seem to resolve certain manifest contradictions in order to affirm the humanist self, but just as often the texts may be read as subverting hegemonic formulations of identity, thus arrogating the power to change dominant knowledges regarding the human subject.

By stepping outside narrative conversion models and privately experimenting with other forms, the autobiographical writers at once form the private self necessary for an emergent market economy and produce a space for interrogating received assumptions about identity. The period from 1660 to 1800 might be read then not as the movement toward the formation of a human subject who is the source of his own meanings but, rather, as one crucial period for representing and revisioning the experience of human subjects in formation, subjects constructed in multiple conflicting domains, through which the ideologies of the "self" are made known.

II

In eighteenth-century England, "identity," "self," "soul," and "person" were dangerous and disputed formations, subject to appropriation by various interests. Heated rhetorical battles were waged throughout the century after Locke's An Essay Concerning Human Understanding (2nd. ed. 1694), in which the issues at stake were the meaning that each word would be granted and the implications of those words for the individual's legal, moral, and spiritual responsibility in relation to church and state. The controversy concerning identity set out these imperatives in order to fix identity and to recoil from the heretical notions of skepticism. Here I will argue that these competing discourses of identity are redundantly in evidence from the end of the seventeenth century until they wear themselves out with repetition by the 1790s. The intensity, diversity and duration of the controversy indicate that the issues they touched were vitally linked to the social formation. Autobiographical writing, though seeming to be a benign search for an essential "self," affords first a private occasion and later a public forum for attempting to resolve these problems.

Throughout the century, questions surface about the mystery of human identity and the ways language can be enlisted to probe that mystery. The concept of identity seems a particularly important focus in seeking consensual agreement about human nature, in part by differentiating men from brutes and seeking their universal qualities. In deciding what elements constitute the difference between humans and animals, philosophers centered especially on the degrees and duration of consciousness. For example, if consciousness chiefly determines humanity, then a concomitant concern arises about the nature of the connective fabric that holds the disparate moments of consciousness together to make a self. In these philosophical texts, memory, the imagination, sensibility, and fiction making are each in turn forwarded as an explanation of the continuing principle of consciousness, the linkages that make up human identity. In tracing the trajectory of these arguments here, I am attempting to gauge the ideological impact of such arguments, and to reconsider the way that the "individual" is implicated within power relations. By looking at these written exchanges, we can discover that the contemplation of identity was posited as an act that took place outside ideology, but within the search for truth. This allowed the philosophical and religious debates to withdraw often from issues of class and gender and assume quietly that conceptualizing identity is unrelated to political or economic matters.

The cause for alarm in these treatises is in part the threat of releasing the unified and rational Cartesian self from responsibility for its actions through time, as well as the threat of subverting the Christian self whose immortal body, consciousness, and soul must be sent to another world intact. For example, Dissenter Joseph Priestley, discussing the subject of identity in his "Observations," carefully establishes himself as a believer in "the proper *unity of God* the maker and governor of the world," and he assures his readers that his views are not irrational and "certainly not *dangerous.*"[15] In what is perhaps the first "Essay on Consciousness," which Zachary Mayne calls "a rude and imperfect Beginning," he seeks to refute "a very dangerous and pernicious Opinion, which prevails almost every where, viz. 'That Brutes have the same Powers or Capacities of Understanding with Mankind.'"[16]

Another very strong impulse in these discourses is to identify the *Principium Individuationis* that makes each human different from others and to locate that difference within sameness. One of the concerns is simply over the terms of the struggle. The problem is partially conceptualized as a linguistic one, a problem of naming rather than of the thing itself. For example, Catherine Cockburn Trotter, writing with impressive philosophical power and extraordinary vigor, points out that Thomas Burnet has misconstrued the meaning of the terms of the argument: "But perhaps he takes the *soul, man,* and *person,* to signify the same thing, and so they may to him . . . [for Locke] does not use those three terms in one and the same signification."[17] Most of her treatise clarifies the distinctions among these and other contested terms. Similarly, Joseph Butler writes, "Nor will language permit these words ["identity" and "same person"] to be laid aside; since if they were, there must be I know now what ridiculous periphrasis substituted in the room of them."[18] Vincent Perronet, too, thinks the problem rests in words. He remarks that once we decide what a "person" is, then it is easy to determine if an individual is the same or a different person.[19] A man in a frenzy, for example, is a man or a living agent but not a person.

All of these debates on identity in the decades between Locke's *Essay Concerning Human Understanding* (2d ed., 1694) and Hume's *Treatise of Human Nature* (1748) are reflected in the autobiographical writing, published and private, in the eighteenth century. First-person narrative, then, makes the self subject to the competing claims of philosophy and religion, and visible as property. For Locke, this "knowing" subject divides itself from itself, and takes itself seriously as an object of understanding. Among the other concerns that repeatedly arise in the debates are the questions of whether the self is consciousness or material substance; whether consciousness and substance are dependent on each other for existence; whether consciousness is continuous and if it persists through time; whether consciousness can be transferred to another body; and whether identity persists after death and is connected to a body. All of these questions center on the definition of human nature. Are we "ourselves" when we are unconscious or in altered states of sleep, insanity, or brain injury? If these states are altered, is there responsibility under the law or to God for human activity? Are personality and identity permanent and essential, and if they vary through time, are we the "same" person? These questions debate the possibility of a continuous consciousness and make possible its translation into autobiographical texts.

Critics have inaccurately placed the beginning of these debates about identity in Hume's *Treatise of Human Nature,* but philosophers and divines take up positions regarding the term from the last decade of the seventeenth century when Locke's *Essay* appeared. In the much repeated phrase that became so familiar to eighteenth-century readers, Locke defined personal identity as consciousness rather than substance, as "a thinking intelligent Being, that has reason and reflection, and can consider it self as it self, the same thinking thing in different times and places."[20] Locke, rather than Hume, was the first to pose the problem of identity (especially the *duration* of identity) in a way that troubled his readers.

What was particularly unsettling to Joseph Butler, Anthony Collins, and other interpreters of the *Essay* in the early decades of the eighteenth century was Locke's assumption that the "same Man" can, quite literally, be so altered as to seem to be another person, as in instances of amnesia, senility, madness, or loss of consciousness (2.27.19–20) or in Locke's example of a friend who believed his soul was Socrates'. According to Locke, man is responsible even for that which occurs when he does not have consciousness. This is because when a person loses his memory, or is *"beside himself"* or *"is not himself,"* he is nevertheless the same self. Locke appeals to empirical "proof": "Experience then convinces us, that *we have an intuitive Knowledge of our own Existence,* and an internal infallible Perception that we are. In every Act of Sensation, Reasoning, or Thinking, we are conscious to our selves of our own Being; and in this Matter, come not short of the highest degree of *Certainty*" (2.27.6). What was disturbing to readers of Locke was the possibility that the self may be *only* consciousness, discontinuous in time and identity. The permanence of the personality, then, is paradoxically fixed in an immaterial substance that does not change through time. Locke defines an individual life as "the same continued Life, by constantly fleeting Particles of Matter, in succession vitally united to the same organized Body" (2.27.6). For Locke, the consciousness may be connected to one individual immaterial substance.

Again and again, the controversy that Locke instigated requires definition and redefinition of the words related to "identity." For example, Locke asks whether the same soul or consciousness can enter several different bodies over a period of centuries. This may be, he suggests, but the person who has much in common with Nestor is not Nestor, not the same man (2.27.14–15). The concept of "Man" implied a continued life, but the concept of "identity" requires only consciousness. Similarly the pervasive fear that Anthony Collins voices is echoed by many others, for he thought that Locke's theory implied the impermanence of personality, "that it lives and dies, begins and ends continually: that no one can remain one and the same person two moments together, that two successive moments can be one and the same moment: that our substance is indeed continually changing; but whether this be so or not, is, it seems, nothing to the purpose; since it is not substance, but consciousness alone, which constitutes personality; which consciousness, being successive, cannot be the same in any two moments, nor consequently the personality constituted by it."[21] But what if, as Anthony Collins wrote, "no Man has the same . . . Consciousness to Day that he had Yesterday," then how is a person to know himself or another?[22] Can identity be fixed in time and space?

These arguments about the nature of identity, like others in the early eighteenth century, bear significantly on the forms that first-person writing takes in the period. Locke seems to enjoin individuals to assure themselves that they are the same through time by writing to recollect their past and present actions, and thus he offers a secular motive for keeping accounts of oneself. Locke claims that identity reaches forward and backward through time in a continued life: "And as far as this consciousness can be extended backwards to any past Action or Thought, so far reaches the Identity of that *Person;* it is the same *self* now it was then; and 'tis by the same *self* with this present one that now reflects on it, that that Action was done." For Locke, then, consciousness comprises the self, and it persists through time in spite of variations in the material substance of a being (as through the progress from child to adolescent to adult) in which identity is preserved. For Locke, the self *is* a thing, a "conscious thinking thing," and he emphasizes the importance of remembering what one has done as marking identity.

David Hume's *A Treatise of Human Nature* encapsulated ideas current in a cultural climate troubled by Locke's notion that consciousness, not substance, constituted the self. Hume's works, deeply preoccupied by the problematic of "self," voice the skeptical challenge to British empiricism, questioning whether knowledge can come only from sense experience. Both in the body of his treatise and in the appendix, Hume puzzles over his difficulty in making his ideas consistent on the subject. He assumes there is a uniting principle of identity, but he finds himself unable to name it: "'Tis certain there is no question in philosophy more abstruse than that concerning identity, and the nature of the uniting principle, which constitutes a person." [23] In the appendix he writes, "But upon a more strict review of the section concerning *personal identity,* I find myself involv'd in such a labyrinth that, I must confess, I neither know how to correct my former opinions, nor how to render them consistent" (633). Yet if there is no certainty to human identity for Hume, he remains convinced that the identification of a universal human nature is the function of history: "Mankind are so much the same, in all times and places, that history informs us of nothing new or strange in this particular. Its chief use is only to discover the constant and universal principles of human nature by showing men in all varieties of circumstances and situations." [24] In other words, Hume's uncertainties about identity are nevertheless recuperated to make them serve a humanist self.

While Hume connects the various perceptions that seem to constitute identity, his treatise also draws on the common understanding of the

connection between disparate perceptions as consciousness (defined as
"reflected thought" or "perception"). But he is stymied by the question
of what unites "our successive perceptions in our thought or consciousness. I cannot discover any theory which gives me satisfaction on this
head" (*Treatise* 636). There is, he determines, an irreconcilable inconsistency in these two propositions "*that all our distinct perceptions are distinct
existences*" and "*that the mind never perceives any real connection among distinct existences*" (*Treatise* 636). In partial resolution, Hume posits the idea
of a continued existence, distinct from other existence, which may come
through the imagination rather than through reason or senses so that the
"self" is a fiction. He adds, "Identity is nothing really belonging to these
different perceptions, and uniting them together, but is merely a quality
which we attribute to them, because of the union of their idea in the
imagination when we reflect upon them" (*Treatise* I.4.6). We assume
that objects have duration, constancy, and coherence, as we connect our
perceptions in the past and present. Though our tendency is to seek uniformity from incoherence, it is only by the fiction of imagination that we
are able to have an idea of identity. We *imagine* that there is no interruption or variation; these gaps can only be resolved through the imaginative creation of "the fiction of continued existence" (I.4.6).

Similarly, in perhaps his best-known formulation, Hume writes that
the mind "is a kind of theatre, where several perceptions successively
make their appearance; pass, repass, glide away, and mingle in an infinite
variety of postures and situations" (I.4.6). Why, Hume asks, do we insist
on giving an identity and sameness to fleeting and successive perceptions
"which succeed each other with an inconceivable rapidity, and are in a
perpetual flux and movement?" It is the contradiction between the apparent identity or sameness of an object or self, and the diversity among
its forms, that he attempts to reconcile with a concept of self. Hume also
places that union of various and successive ideas in memory, for "the
memory not only discovers the identity, but also contributes to its production, by producing the relation of resemblance among the perceptions" (I.4.6). Our identity exceeds our memory, however, just as character, he writes, can be varied without losing identity because it is
separate from identity.

Identity for Hume, then, depends on resemblance, contiguity, and
causation. Memory discovers identity in finding connections among the
various perceptions. But throughout Hume's discussion, as he reiterates

in the appendix, the question of personal identity continues to perplex him, and "all the nice and subtile questions concerning personal identity can never possibly be decided." In fact, his pondering the radically disturbing problem of identity pushes him toward indulging melancholy: "I cannot forbear feeding my despair with all those desponding reflections which the present subject furnishes me with in such abundance" (623).

Attempting to defuse the substantial questions of identity at stake, other thinkers simply take refuge in the perplexing and incommunicable nature of identity. As one anonymous essayist put it, "A continuation of thought, then, is absolutely incommunicable, and distinguishing, and thereby certainly fixes particular Personal Identity."[25] The essayist continues, "Thus we easily know ourselves the same, but *why* we are so, being an enquiry of less moment, is attended with much greater difficulty" (88). Such an identity, he claims, is essential, in spite of its multiplicity or diversity or incommunicability: "The objects & c. of our thoughts are most diverse and innumerable, but what we conceive as essential to their nature, is simple and immutable." In other words, identity is *assumed* to exist in spite of the inability of philosophical discourse to provide a powerful explanation. It must be taken on faith as the natural state of things.

The natural "self" in these philosophical debates is also under considerable pressure to remain sane and consistent. For Vincent Perronet (as for Locke), lucid remembrance—that is, present consciousness of past actions—is necessary for moral and legal responsibility: "And indeed in his [Locke's] Opinion, that God Almighty will punish no Man here after for any Crime, but what is first brought home to his Mind and Conscience."[26] From others there is also similarly a great outcry affirming the unity of every man and mocking the irrationality of presuming that several different people could become the same person. Philip Doddridge writes, "If by *knowing* it [that he thinks], be meant remembering it, (which it must mean if it be at all to the purpose) they cannot be different persons, according to Mr. *Locke's* principles of identity, unless every instance of forgetfulness makes a man a new and different person: and then how many thousands and millions is every man."[27] Speculations on the ways one man can be a hundred different persons, or on the complication of losing one's identity through sleep or loss of memory, lead to sarcasm and hilarity throughout the century.

Joseph Butler, like other commentators who participate in the debate, appeals to "our natural sense of things"—that is, to the status quo and to the generally acknowledged—to refute what he perceives to be the absurdities of the identity debate. Butler also argues against those such as Anthony Collins who carry Locke's ideas to the extreme by claiming that "any number of persons whatever may be the same person." [28] Such arguments err, he thinks, in paying attention to the *substance* of identity for, as we have seen, Collins believes that personality perpetually changes. As Butler conceptualizes the problem, consciousness, however, does *not* constitute personal identity, and individual agents are not necessarily conscious of it. Our actions in the past may be forgotten, yet we are the same agent who performed them. Following this line of reasoning, autobiographical writing then would tend to confirm identity, to reassure writers and readers uncertain of the sameness of "self" that it could be defined and set in place: "By reflecting upon that, which is my self now, and that, which was my self twenty years ago, I discern they are not two, but one and the same self" (388). Writing a first-person narrative, then, ratifies one's natural, sane, and continuous existence and acts as a spur to forgotten moments of consciousness.

But for Butler, whether we remember or forget past activities and happiness does not determine or negate identity. Because we are sure identity exists, it *must* exist. In the end Butler begs the question about those mad, frenzied, or stupified persons whose consciousness fails them. There is considerable skepticism in his conclusion when he writes that we cannot know what identity consists of because we can only use those same contested faculties to determine it: "For it is ridiculous to attempt to prove the truth of those perceptions whose truth we can no otherwise prove, than by other perceptions of exactly the same kind with them, and which there is just the same ground to suspect; or to attempt to prove the truth of our faculties, which can no otherwise be proved, than by the use or means of those very suspected faculties themselves" (396).

These early debates about Locke's categories of identity continue long after Hume's treatise, into the later eighteenth century and early nineteenth century. The issues of self, consciousness, and substance, as fixed or fleeting, fiction or fact, persist until familiar assumptions about identity become accepted as the prevailing mode of thought or, as frequently, the writers take refuge in the mystery of it all. Self-reflective writing, then, displays and sometimes mediates the contradictions between the idea that identity exists through time, and the idea that its existence is uncertain. The (male) philosophical texts authorize the construction of a technology of the self in a particular historical formation and make available interdiscourses where conflictual meanings meet.

ᴄᴧ III

Among the important philosophical texts on the discourses of identity that continue to bear on these issues throughout the century are Kames's *Essays on the Principles of Morality and Natural Religion* (1751); Edmund Law's *A Defence of Mr. Locke's Opinion concerning Personal Identity* (1769, reprinted in the 1812 edition of Locke's *Works*); the anonymous *Essay on Personal Identity* (1770); and Priestley's *Disquisition relating to Matter and Spirit* (1771). To a large extent, the debate turns toward materialism and the emphasis on the body (the "germ" that constitutes the self), but at least one essay on identity, long, cogent, and anonymous, stalwartly defends its antimaterialist stance. The *Essay on Personal Identity* is worth considering in more detail because it is not widely known, and because it serves as a textual summary of the continuing concerns after Hume. The anonymous author is interested in matters of consciousness and substance, of memory and being, as she or he attempts to refute Locke and to resituate the individual in the larger social formation. In this essay, the author makes reference to the intricate controversy, beginning with Locke and the Bishop of Worcester, and most recently having been taken up by Isaac Watts. Remarking on the late passion for classification, Watts notes it is odd that "on the subject of PERSONAL IDENTITY, as to what distinguishes one intelligent, rational Being from another, we are readily contented with any hypothesis" (7), and he wishes to fix the truth of it once and for all. Arguing against Locke, the author bases his urgent refutation on the necessity for gaining a life after death. Quite specifically he fears the implications of Locke's ideas will bring an end to moral obligation, to debts and gratitude, to rewards and punishment. Thus, according to this author, both personal salvation and the social contract that binds individuals requires them to possess firm notions of identity and obligation.

First, he enquires whether consciousness constitutes personal identity (Watts had this Lockean premise) and whether the body is a necessary part of personhood. Consciousness, he counters, does not constitute personal identity, for consciousness is "that, whereby we are sensible to ourselves of this personal identity" (20). He then redefines person as a "thinking being, one intelligent substance, which is always the same, whether it be, or be not mindful of its own actions in different times and places" (11). Unlike Locke, the author thinks that identity exists even if we are not conscious of our actions, and he questions whether we are responsible for past forgotten actions. According to Locke, forgetfulness of the event clears the person of the deed. But, counters the anonymous author of this piece, is it "reasonable to suppose, that God would unite to the same body many different persons, or to the same person several different bodies?" (15) Would personal identity be ended if memory were lost? Locke, by arguing in the affirmative, had provided decades of sanction for the production of a written memory that creates an identity and makes one accountable. According to the author of the essay, however, identity is always present whether one is conscious of it or of past action: "It is impossible, also, for the mind of man to be conscious even once, much less continually, of all the actions, & c. of its past existence" (23). No person, he says, ever maintained the same consciousness or perpetual present consciousness of past action. In refutation of Locke, therefore, "it is . . . not only improbable, but impossible, that the same consciousness should constitute the IDENTITY of a person" (40), for identity does not consist of consciousness, personality, or matter. To think unceasingly is to exist, but one need not be perpetually conscious in the present of past action: "Spiritual or Personal Identity, therefore, wholly depends upon an uninterrupted continuation of thought, which, consequently, is its real and proper constitutent" (67). We are responsible for our crimes, he maintains, at the Judgment Day, whether we have done penance for them or reflected on them. The author's definition further becomes bound up with religious conversion narrative when he cites the example of Paul, whom Locke claims is different "persons" before and after conversion; the anonymous author appeals to common sense to refute this radical change, and he counters that Paul became a different *man*, not a different person. To claim he was two different persons, he suggests, would also absolve the "person" of moral responsibility for crimes of the past. The same man can be two or more different persons, the essayist argues, as long as there is "an uninterrupted continuation of thought." Any kind of thought is sufficient to constitute identity, but when it terminates, identity does. In short, according to this author, the function of reflecting on one's own identity, of producing a subjectivity and an interiority, is to make oneself conscious of past action; but the responsibility for one's actions exists whether or not it is acknowledged. This would seem to suggest that keeping journals may heighten one's consciousness, but one is responsible even for the omissions.

The lengthy second part of An Essay on Personal Identity, "An Attempt to discover the real Constituent of Personal Identity," elaborately addresses the problem of the essential self. There personal identity depends "upon something, in its own nature, absolutely incommunicable" (5). We know we are the same, but why we are so seems impossible to ascertain. It is essential and cannot be taken away or transferred. Equally important is the attempt to distinguish one individual from another. But no "universal principle of individuation" can be discovered; the question of identity then remains mysterious and unresolved: "But concerning this let every one determine as to himself seemeth best: it is certain, however, that no universal principle of individuation has ever yet been discovered" (92). In short, identity for him is continuous thought, not consciousness. It is not material or communicable, but essential, immutable, and simple, though not yet discoverable.

The author of this essay makes clear that the questions of consciousness that Locke had raised a century earlier were still current. If Locke was interpreted, at least by some, as seeming to claim that anyone who is not conscious of what she or he did an hour before is a different person from the one who performed that action, then the role of serial autobiographical writing in reassuring the individual of personhood takes on new significance. The author appeals to reason, common sense, and experience to persuade readers of the absurdity in Locke's claim that consciousness constitutes identity, as he postulates a constant succession of persons changing as rapidly as one's thoughts. Confident of his ability to find the "truth," the real constituent of personal identity, the essayist fixes on the continuation of thought as the continuing principle: one must think, but not necessarily about oneself, and when thought (broadly defined) terminates, identity ends also. At a time when diary writing apparently began to lose its grip as a fashionable private activity, the author seems to argue against keeping written records of one's subjectivity as reassurance of an identity. In other words, the reasons for producing a technology of self-regulation in these and other philosophical texts are in as much dispute as the nature of the "self" in question, but preoccupation with matters of identity continues to make self-interest seem perfectly natural.

IV

Eighteenth-century autobiography often affects to be a reflection of a true identity that is largely class-free yet dependent for definition on social station. Samuel Johnson gives authority to the view of self-writing as the great leveler in the *Idler* when he writes, "The prince feels the same pain when an invader seizes a province, as the farmer when a thief drives away his cow. Men thus equal in themselves will appear equal in honest and impartial biography; and those whom fortune or nature place at the greatest distance may afford instruction to each other."[29] We can, however, begin to discern that conceiving of individual differences among human beings has economic uses and consequences in eighteenth-century England. In the *Wealth of Nations* Adam Smith claims that human beings belonging to various economic classes do not display as much difference as exists between breeds of dogs: "By nature a philosopher is not in genius and disposition half so different from a street porter, as a mastiff is from a greyhound, or a greyhound from a spaniel."[30] These differences, he argues, have no uses among animals, but the differences in men, subtle as they are, not only distinguish them from animals but are the condition on which production, distribution, and exchange depend. Smith writes, "Among men, on the contrary, the most dissimilar geniuses are of use to one another; the different produces of their respective talents, by the general disposition to truck, barter, and exchange, being brought, as it were, into a common stock, where every man may purchase whatever part of the produce of other men's talents he has occasion for."[31] Overriding all the differences between men and dogs, between humans and beasts, there is in Smith's opinion, a governing benevolence that gives moral order and validity to the economic relations among individuals. The economic well-being of the nation requires uniqueness.

Similarly, Bernard de Mandeville in his *Fable of the Bees: or Private Vices Publick Benefits* had earlier made familiar the notion that man had a bestial nature. For Mandeville, the gratification of appetites should not be called vice but rather is "the great support of a flourishing Society."[32] Virtue, he argues, is the deception that skillful politicians manage to urge on humanity in order to encourage self-denial, and, by analogy, it is not unlike the flattery a mother employs in teaching her children manners. In Mandeville's formulation, flattery erases class and gender distinctions to make the lowest wretch believe he is king. Thus Mandeville gives legitimacy to the lowest "natural" passions and encourages luxurious indulgence of them as a means of ensuring the wealth of the nation. Though man in his natural state is ruled by various passions in turn—including lust, pride, and selfishness—he need not conquer these passions but must instead relegate them to the private arena where they may be kept secret: "But a Man need not conquer his Passions, it is sufficient that he conceals them."[33] The self, then, consists of both public virtue and private vice, the one concealed from the other. Mandeville, in encouraging individual desire, legitimates the accrual of capital as one distinguishing element. For both Mandeville and Locke, the self possesses itself, but the "self" is imagined as capital, as property that it willingly surrenders to a social contract among equal beings. In large part, however, the economic and political implications of constructing a universal yet individually differentiated self seem largely invisible to eighteenth-century autobiographical subjects.

Autobiographical writing in the period extended most widely among the newly literate body of writers that emerged between the working class and the aristocracy, though they were not exclusively from "the middling sort." Though the concept of class is a vexed one, the historian of the working class, E. P. Thompson, has constructed a useful model of "class" in eighteenth-century England as resting in the individual consciousness—"Class is defined by men as they live their own history, and, in the end, this is its only definition—though he qualifies this statement by indicating that class is a historical designation that shifts over time and "eventuates as men and women *live* their productive relations, and as they *experience* their determinate situations, within 'the *ensemble* of the social relations,' with their inherited culture and expectations."[34] Thompson believes in the real *experiential* historical process of class formation. He would seem to want to find the *truth* of history, albeit through intricate and detailed study of particulars, by means of the clear vision that he apparently believes exists outside of ideology. Confined within what seems to be a humanist and empiricist model, Thompson forwards a powerfully persuasive argument for historicizing the notion of class, in which class is a cognitive category. In other words, for Thompson, class does not seem to exist until it is recognized by an individual as his place in the social and political system.

Thompson is right, I think, in finding that the middle class became more and more aware of itself as such throughout the eighteenth century in England, but the categories of class may exceed an individual's own

understanding of that position. Consciousness does not simply emerge
nor does it simply take shape when individuals recognize it. Produced
and reproduced through complex formations that serve larger political
interests, the belief that consciousness develops and evolves is *itself* an
ideological production that may be used to reproduce the relations of
production. Class is a cognitive category constituted within the material,
and individuals may be situated within contradictory class positionings.

If class designations increasingly cohere in the eighteenth century,
the ways in which subjects recognize themselves within those designations is not always clear. The middle class, for one commentator in 1756,
is recognizable as the central and largest one among the five classes, for it
consists of "the Men of Trade and Commerce, in which I comprize the
Merchants, and all those that are usually distinguished by the Epithets of
genteel Trades and good Businesses: such as require Figure, Credit, Capital, and many other Circumstances to conduct and support them." In
many nations, he continues, this middle class is so distinct as to seem a
country in itself, but the situation in England confounds simple classification: "*England*, a trading Nation, connects more closely the whole
Body of People. . . . The Man of Trade marries the Daughter of the
Gentleman; the Gentleman the Tradesman's Daughter; and again, the
Gentleman makes his Son (younger at least) a Man of Trade. Hence
arises the Difficulty of separating them; nor can it indeed be altogether
done."[35] Class restrictions, like individuation, exist only to be erased and
realigned. The restrictive divisions unite the populace, defined in economic terms, so that it is imagined as a whole seamless unit where confusions are sorted out and settled. The autobiographical subject, I have argued, consists of a network of positions situated among many discursive
and material practices. To recognize her or his own class position, to
have a cognitive understanding of it, may give such a subject an illusion
of control over her or his own identity as it comes into possession of her
or himself. It may also, however, obscure the way and the extent to
which class positionings as determined by the relations of production
affect consciousness and its subjection to political and economic interests. Eighteenth-century autobiographical writing is a location that tolerates inconsistencies, and it both constructs and propagates this new class
consciousness to become a moral technology of that class formation.

We might instead consider class without assuming that individual
agents are free to recognize their class alliances. Subjects may not be
aware of the ways they are implicated in class struggle, yet may find

themselves engaged in such conflicts when ideological gaps emerge. The class slippage among women is of course especially pronounced. Women, for example, serve as agents of class linkage through their conversation and manners. Eighteenth-century women, in particular, are privileged or deprived according to their husband's or father's status, but without their taking on the economic benefits that come from earning the income. In other words, subjects may be positioned in highly mediated and ambiguous ways in relation to economic and political power, or they may be situated across classes so that other factors such as gender figure more crucially in their lived experience. No matter what the class designation of women, various kinds of social and educational regulations reinforce their secondary status to supersede class. The same treatise that identifies the large, distinctly middle class advises men that, although "a Father should be very careful to fix in his Son a tender Regard to the opposite Sex," the laws will always grant men superiority regardless of their class. A woman of the middle class should be taught "that a Degree of Subjection is allotted her; but that it must never be base, nor ever need be mean."[36] Oppression based on gender, mediated by testimonies of benevolent domination, cuts across class lines.

To be "out of oneself" or "beside oneself" not only threatens one's individual salvation and sanity but also has consequences for the social order. In the eighteenth century insanity was, at least on some occasions, defined as an attempt to participate in the supposedly essential characteristics of another class, and sketches of the Bedlam inmates are filled with examples of upstarts who are deluded into believing they are members of the nobility or gentry.[37] Madness, according to one essay, is "the Deprivation of Common Sense." Deficiency in common sense, the author R. Freeman argues, "is not a Want of sufficient Capacity to act agreeably to the Station of Life they are in, and to make a proper Use of the Reason and Talents Nature has given them; but some strange mistaken Principle about themselves; some desire to appear what they are not, or more than they are."[38] The author continues to assert that a clear and consistent concept of identity is the appropriate mechanism for maintaining distinctions in rank between cobbler and prince. He seems to echo the more specifically philosophical arguments encountered in Locke and others: "For should the Soul of a Prince, carrying with it the consciousness of the Prince's past Life, every one sees, he would be the same Person with the Prince, accountable only for the Prince's Actions; But who would say it was the same Man?" (355). "Knowing oneself" is a principle useful in maintaining class boundaries and in teaching a population to believe that subjectivities possess certain natural characteristics.

"Body," "soul," and "man" are different categories, according to this account, and they can only be held together through the concept of "character." Public character, Freeman argues further, requires a transparent correspondence between conduct and the requirements of the world, and anything less deserves scorn: "If a *Magistrate* should take it into his Head to *drive* his own *Coach,* or to appear in the *Execution* of his *Office* with a Whip in his Hand, and a *leather Belt* about him, would he not be *ridiculous?* . . . If a *clergyman* should all of a sudden turn *Bricklayer,* whip on a leather *Apron,* stick his *Rule* on *one Side* and his *Trowel* on the *other,* would he not make a *whimsical Figure?* But why so? Why certainly, because he suffered his *Whim* to get the better of his *Reason,* so far as to betray him into an *Action* injurious to his *Reputation,* as being inconsistent with his *Character*" (354). Real character exists, Freeman maintains, and people ought to stay fixed in it. But paradoxically, it seems that developing a consistent character that is known to the world may require a divided self that separates the public part one plays from the private true self, especially if one's rank is mistakenly judged.

The question then becomes, whose purposes are buttressed by the production of a sane middle class that privately and publicly believes itself to possess an interiority as figured in these philosophical tracts, and attempts to give it stability? This question will be addressed throughout the chapters that follow, and here I suggest a few general directions that discussion will take. In particular, these narratives allowed a literate class to define its supposed superiority to an illiterate one. By producing a particular category of experience of self-scrutiny and self-knowledge, writers of journals or memoirs could maintain and actively create a sense of distinction from and superiority to those who were unable to write reflexively and to make that technology into a property that gathered political and economic power to it. "Knowing oneself" allowed an individual subject to exercise privilege, as well as discipline and regulate, the behavior of those who did not "know" themselves. Also, autobiographical writing encouraged a consciousness of a more particular sense of uniqueness from others in the species, and allowed the definition of that uniqueness as requiring realization through self-interested pursuit. Thinking of oneself as bourgeois justified pursuing one's own individual self-interest, while believing that self-interest to be virtually synonymous with communal interest. Unlike the working class, whose identity was determined in large part by region of birth or by communal rituals that fostered a group sense of identity, the emergent bourgeois formed a class that would begin to keep an unprecedented record of its individual selves.[39] If the concept of self in the lower classes, reconstructed from its traces, was one of alliance with others, including collective and organized action, to be middle class requires thinking of "self" differently—individually, rather than as serving class or communal interests. Elizabeth Eisenstein has remarked on the growing atomization of the reading public: communal solidarity was displaced by the assumption of society as "a bundle of discrete units." Printing, she suggests, increased the bifurcation between public and private, society and self, between that which is subject to public scrutiny and that which receives special protection from it.[40] As writing materials became widely available and printing expanded, ordinary people could advertise their written lives and make them into intellectual *property*. The pattern of collective lands with relatively equal access to means of subsistence gave way to new emphases on attending to self-interest *through* rather than *in* collective activity. The collective rights of the working class, long served by the communal grounds, roads, flora and fauna, were increasingly designated as private. Small farms were combined, and the principles of a mercantile capitalist economy came to dominate throughout the country. The state encouraged game laws and high duties on foreign goods, as well as turnpike tolls and conscription, all of which emphasized the location of power in the ruling class and its usurpation of the laboring people's traditional rights. In short, class designation and identity, as displayed in material practices, were in considerable disarray.[41]

There was, then, a presumption that social inequality—that is, hierarchy and domination—was required in order to maintain a stable state. Earning a better wage than another (rather than working toward a subsistence wage supplemented by communal rights) became more important in a newly regulated money economy, and consciousness of class increases the separation between individuals and bolsters the idea of the uniqueness of each individual. It concomitantly signals that the human species has commonalities. Similarly, writing about an "I" reproduces a subjectivity essential to a market economy, a partriarchal symbolic and social order founded on separate hierarchical spheres for each sex, and a self-conscious class that regulates itself in part through its own private autobiographical writing. The problematic of "self" is, in no small part, a class predicament in eighteenth-century England, and it is especially problematic for a middle class that looks toward its own recognition and regulation.

If eighteenth-century autobiographical writing, as a nexus of subjectivities, helps to construct the necessary monolithic and unitary subject of the political and economic, it also questions and revises that concept of "self." In the multiple versions of eighteenth-century self-writing, including private writings in diaries and journals, these suppressed and oppositional voices may be heard. By reading those voices *within* culture, we can begin to determine the ways in which they violate and comply with dominant ideologies of the self. Such writing brings diverse discourses into mutual articulation as it both reflects and produces a subject positioned in ideologies. Writing in contradiction, the subject of autobiography recognizes and misrecognizes itself as a free, whole, and rational individual who can translate consciousness into written and sometimes published representations to confirm its existence. Reading eighteenth-century autobiographical writing anew means questioning the ways in which these texts, in spite of their exclusions based on gender and class, have been seen as transparent versions of reality and as emanations of an individual self, always already "he," operating in a "free" space outside ideology.

Women are not given special status in these philosophical and religious discourses on identity, for they are largely subsumed within the male, and, by that omission, are subject to erasure as an identity or subjectivity. Though women themselves rarely participate in the debates, in part because so few have access to philosophy's "regime of truth," Catherine Cockburn Trotter (whose defense of Locke's essay was mentioned earlier) is an exception who takes on a male persona throughout her anonymous defense of Locke. She writes metaphorically as a male defender of a lady's honor. In her letters she commissions Locke's opponent, Thomas Burnet, to be fair to women in believing that a woman's intellectual work is her own, and she insists that she stands competent to write philosophical prose without a man's assistance: "It is not to be doubted, that women are as capable of penetrating into the grounds of things, and reasoning justly, as men are, who certainly have no advantage of us, but in their opportunities of knowledge."[42]

At the end of the century another woman, Hester Thrale, resorts to mocking the controversy that, by then, seemed to her hackneyed and stale. The issues are trivial, she writes in *British Synonymy*, and there is nothing new to be said:

Identity and Sameness would be nearly synonymous in conversation language, I believe, only that as the first is a word pregnant with metaphysical controversy, we avoid it in common daily use, or at best take it up merely as a stronger expression of unchangeable SAMENESS. Mowbray and Tourville with their everlasting IDENTITY are complained of by Lovelace in his anxious agony of mind, as companions he could not endure—while Hume would have told him, that although their manners resembled one day what they had been the last, such resemblance was not proof of IDENTITY, however it might give a SAMENESS to their character. Those indeed who resolve to doubt all they cannot prove, give themselves much unnecessary fatigue concerning the consciousness of their own existence—doubting, in good time whether they are themselves the same persons, who, before they became philosophers, readily believed that if they set an acorn an oak would come up—and that a chicken would surely be hatched from an egg, if warmth sufficient were adduced to cause the necessary change of appearance in what was before a chicken in potentia? But such doubts and such doubters are best despised, as some of them may possibly have a real interest in considering their existence to be dubious, that escape may be effected from accounting for its errors and crimes. We should therefore be aware of these scepticks, and as little as possible I think dip into their books; from whence little amusement or instruction can be derived, but much SAMENESS, particularly in their discourse upon IDENTITY.[43]

Thrale finds little that is relevant in the controversy, perhaps in part because she too is a woman excluded from the intricacies of scholastic learning and philosophical language. For Hester Thrale in 1794 the issue is simply too dull to pursue; when pressed, she resorts to common sense to dismiss the abstract reasonings of Hume and others.

In sum, in eighteenth-century England the public struggles over the construction of a coherent, rational, and self-authorizing identity are located in philosophical and religious language to make the individual seem distinct from society and outside of history, blind to class and gender. Eighteenth-century readers and contemporary readers alike efface these contradictions to produce the coherent subject of the emergent capitalist society. Its necessary claim to an unalterable human nature disguises daily change. The "subject" of autobiographical writing, positioned in these discourses as resting outside politics and the social formation, often retreats into private writing. This ideology of the individual as an instance of a universal human nature distracts attention from the plurality and tensions of identity. In addition, it discourages collective enterprise and accedes to the intervention of church, state, and political authority in maintaining the status quo. The baffling quality of personal identity—whether it is continuous or not, whether it has substance or immortality—is repeatedly described as defying human understanding. These ideas, then, are constantly defended as the truly human ones, to the exclusion of all others: each individual is an instance of the universal, and each self, a free and indivisible unity.

Autobiographical texts, public and private, negotiate the contradictions of these philosophical and religious discourses of the self, to produce, revise, and subvert an individuated self that partakes of the universal essence and transcends the distinctions based on class and gender. Diaries, journals, and autobiographical writing of all sorts effect uneasy resolutions to the ideological contradictions of the bourgeois gendered self that believes, however uncertainly, in its own existence and authority, and in the necessity for its self-regulation within the fluctuating boundaries of self-interest.

CHAPTER THREE

Dissenting Subjects

Bunyan's *Grace Abounding*

But in the great Day, wherein the Secrets of all Hearts shall be laid open, it may be reasonable to think, no one shall be made to answer for what he knows nothing of; but shall receive his Doom, his Conscience accusing or excusing him.
— John Locke, *An Essay Concerning Human Understanding* (1694)

Yea, look diligently, and leave no corner therein unsearched, for there is treasure hid. . . . Have you forgot the Close, the Milk-house, the Stable, the Barn, and the like, where God did visit your Soul? Remember also the Word, the Word, I say, upon which the Lord hath caused you to hope.
— John Bunyan, *Grace Abounding* (1667)

I

I want to turn now to specific autobiographical texts written by Bunyan, Wesley, and Boswell, as well as by Quaker and Methodist women, scandalous memoirists, and Thrale, to consider them as instances of the conflicting discourses of genre, gender, and identity that prevailed in the late seventeenth and eighteenth centuries. These narratives—in Puritan Richard Baxter's term, "Book[s] of *Heart accounts*"—have in common the attitude toward subjectivity that is conceptualized later as "self-biography." Within each of these sets of texts, I want to investigate the conditions of circulation and distribution, as well as the subjectivities produced within them, to consider which categories of texts remained private documents, which were published, and what uses their readers made of them. From the carefully structured *Grace Abounding* to the serial volumes of the scandalous memoirs or the unpublished lifelong journals of James Boswell, these autobiographical writings in the eighteenth century represent coherent textual identity for an emergent middle class, but these texts may also be read as locations where autobiographical subjects disrupt certain notions of the bourgeois self. Though these subjects are positioned within seemingly consistent ideologies, the contradictions in and among them make resistance and change possible.

Spiritual autobiography in its most prescriptive forms fastens on a compelling model of experience and encourages the production of a textual identity that is consensually agreed upon.[1] In particular, spiritual autobiography takes for granted that human beings participate in the divine Subject to share the same characteristic traits, so that the story of one individual conversion is the story of all. The spiritual autobiographical subject accepts the terms of submission to the Absolute (male) Subject, yet believes in the free initiation of his or her subjection. The expected pattern, firmly located in the orthodoxies of God, church, and state, was promoted orally as well as in privately circulated and publicly distributed documents that testify to the converted self. The wide dissemination of these autobiographical writings encouraged imitation of the technology of public confession, thus ensuring its perpetuation and solidification as a mode of making experience intelligible.

Speaking within transhistorical discourses that avoid history and politics, spiritual autobiographies often call into place a reader who can avoid close and uncomfortable attention to the material conditions of their production. We may also discover instances in which the conversion narratives invert or even sabotage the categories available for constructing an authorized identity in texts. In spiritual autobiography, uncertainties, both formal and experiential, emerge in the gaps between subject positions to challenge the very identity that autobiography seeks to establish—a converted "self" that interpellates itself in harmony with the patriarchal divine. Thus autobiographical writing in this period may be understood as the textual struggle of subjects positioned among competing claims of authority for definition. To begin to address some of the terms of the conflicts, I will look first at religious discourses on identity that parallel to some extent the philosophical discourses we have already examined, and then focus more particularly on the autobiographical subject called into being in Bunyan's *Grace Abounding*.

At least two contradictory religious discourses compete to define the spiritual "self," a word often used interchangeably with "soul" in sermons of the period. On the one hand, they call for intimate self-knowledge, while on the other they warn about the dangers of self-absorption. From both perspectives, the self is described as a continuing consciousness, variously related to a material being that seeks existence through eternity; but whether self-contemplation is to be desired or eschewed, questioning its efficacy makes a public space available in which to cultivate a private subjectivity that "expresses" that self.

These religious debates about identity rage throughout the Restoration and eighteenth century and are complicated by crossing with the philosophical. When preachers and philosophers quarrel about the materiality of identity in this world and the next, for example, the controversy centers on whether an essential material core exists that will survive in the afterlife. Early in the eighteenth century, Nonconformist Isaac Watts accused John Locke of denying the resurrection of the same body. Wishing to fix "identity" for this world and the next, Watts finds the clue to identity in its union with the body, *"the same soul united to the same body."* He scoffs at Locke's definition of "person" which allows a man to change: *"Personality* and *Sameness of Persons* either in this World or the other must not stand upon such a shifting and changeable Principle, as may allow either one Man to be two Persons, or two Men to be one Person, or any one Man or Person to become another, or to be really any thing but himself."[2] The controversy over these theories centers on Locke's questioning whether the body remains the same before and after resurrection. Even if the resurrected body includes new material particles, it is, according to Locke, an identical body to the one that lived on earth; but the Bishop of Worcester argues the opposite point of view. Distinguishing her arguments from Dr. Holdworth's "vulgar sameness" and "vulgar consideration of identity," Catherine Cockburn Trotter wrote in defense of the Bishop: "In a Word, it is impossible for a human body to be restored at the resurrection, to any one particular of that, in which its supposed sameness consisted in its vital union with the soul here."[3] It is the immaterial *soul* rather than the material body that is resurrected, according to Worcester. If "soul" is equated with "self" rather than with the body, and if "self" is consciousness, then human beings have hope of an individuated existence not only in this life but in perpetuity.

Extending the definition of "identity" beyond human beings, Joseph Priestley in "Observations on Personal Identity" maintains that even though all of nature is constantly changing (including rivers and forests), it remains the same object.[4] Priestley takes refuge in the Christian tradition to declare that "it is my own opinion that we shall be *identically the same beings* after the resurrection that we are at present." (156). Even, he argues, if every thought that "in the course of nutrition, digestion, and egestion, every particle of the body, and even of the brain . . . was entirely changed . . . we should, I doubt not, still retain the idea of a real *identity.*" (158). Priestley here uses "identity" to mean sameness, but it is that very sameness that is in dispute. He further distinguishes, like many divines before him, between the identity of "man" and the identity of "person." For Priestley, whatever the change in the "man" (by which he seems to mean the material substance), there would be no change in the "person" (by which he means the immaterial soul, self, or identity). Here "person" comes to mean identity, and thus identity is not material or substantial.

Similarly, Priestley gives attention to the idea of a consistent "germ" (sometimes material, more often immaterial) that constitutes the principle of individuation. Because the *germ* of the body remains the same after the resurrection, we will be able to recognize each other by our essential core of identity after death. Thomas Morell, annotating Locke in 1794, insists on the materiality of this "germ": "*Thinking substance and person should be one and the same thing.*" Mere *existence* is not the *Principium Individuationis:* "viz. since our own bodies must rise at the last day, &c. there may be perhaps some *original fibres* of each human body, some stamina vitae or primeval seeds of life, which may have remained unchanged through all the stages of life, death, and the grave."[5] According to these thinkers, the materiality of the germ remains uncertain because the final appeal concerning the nature of identity—an essential nature— rests with God who alone can know the extent to which personhood (also called "self" or "soul") changes in various states.

The issue seemed settled to Samuel Drew, however, who in 1809 argued that we can have identity without consciousness. The search is for the "immutable, intransferable," and unchanging identity: "Nothing can be a greater mark of folly, than to conceive that our personal identity can consist in that which is fleeting, transitory, and unstable."[6] Like Priestley he seeks sameness, the sameness that rests in the human body and more specifically in a "germ" or "stamen" that is immutable in spite of the shift of various particles of the material body. This sameness through time enables individuation and self-regulation, but its placement in the body makes it especially susceptible to sexual difference, whereas the soul is generally assumed to be without gender.

Beyond the question of the corporality of personhood or the possibil-

ity of recognizing individuals after death is the question of how to prepare
that self for judgment, whether through strict scrutiny or studied indifference to it. Religious discussions position subjects between the conflicting ideologies of self-denial and self-knowledge (including the revelation
of the secrets of the heart at the Judgment Day). They enjoin the reader
to "know thyself" while, in contradiction, other Christian doctrines cau-
tion against the perils of self-indulgence and argue for the urgent necessity to ensure immortality through self-denial. According to these treatises, self-knowledge allows us to identify a "self" or "character" that can
be recognized and described; but, at the same time, only the Absolute
Subject can know the "self." Thus, it is an impossible and even heretical
task to compete with God's understanding of one's "interior."

Self-denial is crucial in producing a state of holiness, and sermons on
the subject abound. Methodists in particular were charged with preaching "self" instead of Christ, a practice that was frequently condemned
because it leads away from contemplating the divine. Similarly, for
Quaker William Penn, "self" was almost synonymous with indulgence.
The "Self" that he urges his followers to deny is one of "conveniency,
ease, enjoyment and plenty. This Doctrine of *self-denial* 'tis the Condition to Eternal Happiness."[7] Oddly, the discourses surrounding self-
denial argue against telling one's own story or preaching a narrative
about that conversion.

In contrast, in *Self Examination Explained and Recommended*, Samuel
Clark urgently exhorts his followers to examine themselves: "Though
formed capable of reflection and foresight, they live in this respect like
the brutes, who are void of understanding; scarce ever considering the
end."[8] Methodically outlined, Clark's six-step process for determining
character requires divorcing oneself from public life, and "conversing"
daily with oneself. Self-examination is dangerous, but not to examine
oneself seems equally dangerous: "Such are the fatal consequences of In-
consideration, that so to honour and usefulness, parent of vice and misery, source of all that self-deceit, which blinds men's eyes, and leads
them on to their own destruction" (2). The purpose of all this self-study,
Clark maintains, is a recognition of our real character—"to enquire seriously and impartially into the state of religion in our minds; that we may
form a true judgement of our real character in the sight of God, and may
be the better able to regulate our future conduct." (34) In other words,
these sermons produce a subject that is inscrutable to others, something
"interior" and secret, an inner private order. Part of the purpose of self-

examination is also to reveal one's ruling passion: "It is evident therefore, that in order to know our true character, it is necessary to be acquainted with that part of our constitution, and seriously to examine what share it has had in determining our conduct" (14). Self-examination, listening "to the secret springs of our conduct," then, prescribes its own rigorous methodology and its goal of recognizing one's "true character" by seeking out the most hidden and dangerous inner recesses.

In midcentury Laurence Sterne voices the same contradictions in his sermon on self-knowledge: "To know one's self, one would think could be no very difficult lesson. . . . If a man thinks at all, he cannot be a stranger to what passes there—he must be conscious of his own thoughts and desires, he must remember his past pursuits, and the true springs and motives which in general have directed the actions of his life: he may hang out false colours and deceive the world, but how can a man deceive himself?"[9] But he then acknowledges that men daily enact self-deceit: "Scripture tells us, and gives us many historical proofs of it, besides this to which the text refers—that the heart of man is treacherous to itself and *deceitful above all things.*" Self-reflection, Sterne maintains, counters the tendency toward disguising one's motivations. It is a way of distinguishing men from beasts, "yet in fact, in generally so inattentive, but always so partial an observer of what passes, . . . he is as much, nay often, a much greater stranger to his own disposition and true character than all the world besides" (81). Man therefore cannot know himself impartially, only God can, yet man is distinguished from the brutes only by his capacity to be self-conscious. But, in fact, self-scrutiny will "make him rather sorry, and ashamed of himself, than proud" (102). Sterne laments that self-examination may be doomed to failure, simply because human beings are blind to God's omniscience: "These are some of the unhappy mistakes in the many methods this work is set about, wiser for all the pains we have taken."[10] Knowing oneself may paradoxically breed the desperate irrational thoughts that threaten the very identity the practice would hope to secure.

Religious advice throughout the century, whether from Anglicans or Dissenters, was deeply divided in its demand to reflect on oneself yet avoid excessive self-love in the pursuit of an elusive spiritual identity. These religious debates set out oppositions for the subject who painstakingly examines himself in an attempt to fix an individual spiritual character, alienated from itself yet seeking self-consciousness. In the reassuring ideology that takes shape, even eternity will be populated with individuated selves who, fully in possession of a stable personhood that withstands divine judgment, can recognize themselves and others. These discourses provide, then, the religious and philosophical rationale implicit in conversion narratives such as John Bunyan's Grace Abounding in their straining toward defining a sanctified "self" that urges readers to forget the conditions of its production.

☙ II

The most popular and most unified of seventeenth- and eighteenth-century spiritual autobiographies, Bunyan's Grace Abounding (1666), created a prototype for generations of readers and writers in its shaping of an ideal Dissenting self within the context of religious injunctions for self-examination. The primary generic paradigm that figures regularly in historical accounts of spiritual autobiography is the human's journey to his heavenly home and to his new identity as a child of God through self-scrutiny, and in many ways, Grace Abounding exemplifies this classic Puritan conversion.[11] That such a formulation spoke poignantly to its contemporary readers is evidenced by the six editions of Grace Abounding published in Bunyan's lifetime; by 1804 fifty English editions, as well as French, Dutch, and Welsh translations, had appeared. In addition, the book was bowdlerized, excerpted, and printed in chapbooks throughout the period. As Frank Mott Harrison puts it, "The text of the book became grossly mutilated as the editions proceeded," and Joan Webber has noted that it was "used up like a commodity . . . it was literally read to pieces."[12] Bunyan's version of his life, along with Pilgrim's Progress, caught the imagination of writers as diverse as Addison, Swift, Pope, Wesley, Hume, and Boswell, and as early as 1708 a catalog of Bunyan's works had appeared. Anne Williams Dutton's A Brief Account of the Gracious Dealings of God was among the many imitations of Bunyan's autobiography.[13]

Admission to one of the Dissenting sects usually came through providing a public declaration of spiritual change, and many such narratives arose precisely because they were required to be spoken or read before a member was accepted into a congregation. Only certain patterns could be accepted as authentic in these public acknowledgments of conversion. As various commentators have pointed out, early in the seventeenth century Puritan ministers adopted the practice of telling the story of their conversion to certify their converted identity and to qualify them to minister to others.[14] The "self" conveyed the sense of an individual who claims to be unlike all others, "the chief of sinners," in Bunyan's own definition. Such a practice prevailed to grant an identity legitimacy, and gave the illusion that such a person was "known" to the congregation. It also made possible the formation of a tenuous collective identity as each jockeyed for position as the sect's worst of sinners.

The attention that we give to any such individual or collective pattern, however, veils the many divergencies from it. It is not so much a question for these spiritual autobiographers of recording exactly what happened, but of attempting to fit lived experience and subjectivity within the parameters of credible frameworks. Such patterns may be thought of less as the natural expression of reality than as recognized codes pressed upon the real. These generic conventions hold identity and experience to certain recognizable categories as they construct the subjectivity they reflect. In other words, especially in autobiographical texts, identities interact with generic conventions; identities are produced through genres, and autobiographical genres, through conceptions of identity.

Although the programmatic narrative of some spiritual autobiographies fostered a kind of generic pattern, I want to sound a cautionary note about making generalizations from that pattern. Neither the Dissenters nor the Church of England was a monolith; rather, different factions with varying political and religious projects jostled for power over time, and the issues at stake and the textual shapes they take varied accordingly, as the very different forms of Fox's journal or Bunyan's *Grace Abounding* make clear. For example, the tripartite division focusing around the conversion moment is the most familiar in spiritual autobiography, but other formulas also appear in the period. For all the many conversion narratives that follow a three-part structure, an equal number, including some of the best-known, do not. Baxter's *Reliquiae Baxterianae* describes a gradual change rather than a sudden conversion, and it alternates between setting a model for others on the one hand, and humbly refusing paradigmatic status on the other.[15] Jane Turner, for example, in her *Choice Experiences of the Kind Dealings of God before, in, and after Conversion* (1653), divides the conversion experience into six sections, while *The Life of Adam Martindale* (1624–1686) separates life into seven parts; James Fraser (1670) employs eight, and Elizabeth Cairns uses nine.[16] In many journals and autobiographies, including Bunyan's *Grace Abounding*, the numbered paragraphs hint that the work originated as a journal and, in any case, mark the constant vigilance required in monitoring one's soul through time. The numbering demonstrates Bunyan's strong sense of daily, even hourly, torment over his uncertain salvation, as well as a sense of repetition and redundancy that imitates the lack of constancy in the battle: "By these words I was sustained, yet not without exceeding conflicts, for the space of seven or eight weeks: for my peace would be in and out sometimes twenty times a day."[17] But, finally, the number of prescribed divisions becomes less significant than the narrator's assumption that her or his written life advances toward radical change, and that each section affords an occasion to assess one's movement toward achieving a converted self and a godly life.

In short, eighteenth-century readers took Bunyan's account to be a model three-part pattern of conviction, conversion through God's revelation and grace, and postconversion trials and resolution. From the beginning until the point of the first and most important conversion, as he constructs it, Bunyan stresses that there was a providential explanation for both his tribulations and his pleasures. God allows him to attend school, to learn to read and write, although interpreting divine benevolence is complicated by Bunyan's nearly drowning. Bunyan records his assaults on God's authority, and he is punished with terrible dreams and visions. According to the narrative, God chastizes him for blaspheming and for playing games, especially tipcat. But Providence also grants him the blessing of a devout wife who guides him toward God; and through God's mercy he escapes death from an adder's sting, and from a musket bullet. Thus, Bunyan would seem to affirm that the traditional paradigm with its explanation of a single originary conversion is sufficient to assign meaning to his life within a recognizable pattern. Through religious discourse, Bunyan is recruited and recruits into being the sovereign Subject of ideology, the Subject in whom all subjects partake. The words of Scripture serve as a corollary text while the autobiographical narrator seems to proclaim the authority of God's word, and the force of his autobiographical "self" competes as a substitute textual authority, a devotional guide that replaces the Scriptures and the Absolute Subject.

This apparent order, however, obscures the ways in which the text is itself a much-revised and careful manipulation of lived experience rather than the spontaneous effusion inspired by God's grace it appears to be. Bunyan, among the first professional evangelists to use print, apparently substantially revised Grace Abounding between the first and third editions, adding fifty-seven paragraphs to the third edition and another ten to the fifth edition.[18] The revisions, including the famed bell-ringing epi-

sode and the description of his acquaintance with Antinomians, emphasize the extremes of his emotional states. They underscore his hypocrisy
and his sin, his depths of despair and heights of joy; they register his alliances with the pleasures of the laboring classes, and his relegation of
such pleasures to the category of sin.[19] They pointedly suggest that the
converted self aspires to the middle class. In short, the revisions intensify
the separation between the preconversion and postconversion selves to
emphasize Bunyan's isolation, daily devotion to self, and the disruption
of class boundaries that the process of conversion may entail.

The many revisions also indicate that, as the original title page made
clear, the formal question of unity is more problematic than the brevity
of the book might suggest. The first and longest part includes the conversion, temptations, and a tentative resolution of the struggle. The crucial
moment comes when God sends him to Bedford. The section including
his first conversion (introduced by the briefest of prefaces and concluded
with a catalog of his current abominations) is complicated, however, by
Bunyan's moving swiftly to apparent conversion in thirty-seven paragraphs, only to recount more temptations for another two hundred paragraphs.[20] This protracted attention to the postconversion period is
unusual, and it reflects the persistence—in spite of conversion—of Bunyan's fear that he was excluded from the elect. Each section of *Grace
Abounding* culminates in a tentative resolution, but the various addenda—the two accounts and the catalog of abominations—disclose
that any resolution describes a fragile construct rather than a stable or
unified converted identity. The converted "self" threatens to break apart
at every turn.

The two postscripts to the body of *Grace Abounding*, then, offer new
risks that the conversion will be undone. "A Brief Account of the Author's Call to the Work of the Ministry" and "A Brief Account of the
Author's Imprisonment," solipsistic centers of "I" and "me," reiterate
the contradiction between Bunyan's daring to recognize his blessed state
and remaining humble, between self-absorption and self-denial. The first
of these postscripts, the account of the work of the ministry, is a treatise
on the vicissitudes awaiting one who is "addicted to the ministry of the
saints." At times Bunyan seems perilously close to suggesting that *he* personifies God's word, but the confidence that he is God's instrument, the
cymbal on which God plays, alternates with his "still counting my self
unworthy" (87). Uncertain of God's grace when it preaches, the narrative "I" positions itself as a converted subject that cannot reconcile an

"inner" and an "outer" self: "I can truly say, and that without dissembling, that when I have been to preach, I have gone full of guilt and terrour even to the Pulpit-Door, and there it hath been taken off, and I have been at liberty in my mind until I have done my work, and then immediately, even before I could get down the Pulpit-Stairs, have been as bad as I was before" (88). In addition to these instances of revision, new paragraphs, added to the fifth edition, reiterate Bunyan's humility, yet he argues that his slanderers and imprisoners can only heighten his martyrdom.

Bunyan's revisions also betray certain assumptions about the gender of converted souls. As earthly patriarch to his group of children, Bunyan "fathers" his flock, while his wife "mothers" his soul by bringing him pious books. Women may instigate and verify conversion. Just as his conversion narrative begins with his wife's leading him to holiness, it concludes with telling her that he is convinced of his salvation. In another dramatic conversion moment he attributes to female agency, he hears "three or four poor women sitting at a door in the Sun" talk of God. He "was greatly affected with their words, both because by them I was convinced that I wanted the true tokens of a truly godly man, and also because by them I was convinced of the happy and blessed condition of him that was such a one" (16–17). Bunyan does not gender his self as "manly," as Boswell will do in his journals, but he divides female souls into the conventional categories of pious and wicked. Bunyan, empowering women in his text to enact spiritual change, also limits their authority to that which is granted to them by men. Women are positioned in the text both as potential agents of salvation, as in the case of his wife and the poor women of Bedford, and, on the other hand, as the source of carnal desire.

Bunyan pays a surprising amount of attention to sexual desire in *Grace Abounding*, probably because he wanted to divorce himself from the eroticism of the Ranters. Accused of having Antinomian or Ranter leanings on numerous occasions, his revisions painstakingly dissociate him from their libidinous tendencies, "abominating those cursed principles" (19).[21] He thanks God for keeping him from such fleshly temptations, "I being but a young man and my nature in its prime." He knows there are accusations against him, especially from among other Dissenting sects, concerning sexual philanderings with a fellow Dissenter, Agnes Beaumont, and he counters these charges with an image of himself as father and family man: "But that which was reported with the boldest confidence, was, that I had my *Misses*, my *Whores*, my *Bastards*, yea, *two wives at once*, and the like" (95). Especially in the revisions, he defends himself against rumors of adultery and fornication by insisting that his soul is innocent, that his "self" is without sexual desire.

In large part, however, the labyrinths of self and soul, often interchangeable terms, claim to be indifferent to gender: "What! will you preach this? this condemns your self; of this your own Soul is guilty; wherefore preach not of it at all, or if you do, yet so mince it as to make way for your own escape" (92). Clearly, Bunyan's search is for salvation as much as for an identity. "Soul" and "self" at other times interact, as when, subject to torments of the flesh, his "Soul" makes his "self" vulnerable to the vindictive force of eternal justice. At times it seems that his "soul" belongs to God, but his "self" is his own: "I was loath to conclude I had no Faith in my soul: for if I do so thought I, then I shall count my self a very Cast-away indeed" (21). Elsewhere his "self" takes solace in "all manner of vice" on the Sabbath (12), his "Soul" becoming an inner man who is subject to despair (13, 23, 82). The problems surrounding the self's fragility are partially resolved through Bunyan's revisions that equate personal salvation with firm notions of identity.

In fact, the very idea of salvation seems to hold within it both the promise and the threat of the loss of identity.[22] Bunyan wants to step outside his identity in order to escape the pain and guilt, once he has recognized his sin: "Oh, how gladly now would I have been anybody but myself! Any thing but a man! and in any condition but mine own!" (47) But finding God is also finding a consistent individuality in *Grace Abounding*, however much it may need to be persistently recaptured: "Thus, I say, I could recal myself sometimes, and give myself a help." (64). Before conversion, Bunyan's "self" is a mere cipher for the devil, while the converted self in contrast imitates "Jesus Christ himself, *the same yesterday, and today, and for ever*. Heb. 13.8" (74). In other words, a truly Christian self is one fixed in perpetuity. But the narrative conversion in its various layers indicates the necessity to reexperience conversion; that is, in spite of the protestations, the saved self is not permanent: "Well, I would I had a pen and ink here, I would write this down before I go any further, for surely I will not forget *this* forty years hence; but alas! within less than forty days I began to question all again" (32). These conflicts among the multiple positionings of the self urge the self toward regular revision in spite of its claims of stability.

Grace Abounding, then, establishes a satisfying pattern of conversion within the religious discourses that command the regulation and denial of self and soul. It also, subversively, posits an alternative "self," divided and distanced from God and from itself, requiring constant revision, to suggest the vexing way in which even a converted self may vanish. It imitates the expected pattern and yet violates it. In spite of its status as an exemplary spiritual autobiography, *Grace Abounding* pushes against the traditional conversion experience to render conversion and tempta- tion as a torturous, unending process. In its revisions, as well as its link- age of biblical and personal texts, the problematics of loving attention to the spiritual self surface: *Grace Abounding* produces an identity that threatens to fracture and to subvert its own confident assertion.

⚙ III

The critics of spiritual autobiographies such as *Grace Abounding* often assume them to be the unguarded revelation of an interior truth at the core of an individuated self, a confession that makes the uniqueness of the individual paramount. Such readings apply psychoanalytic categories to textual identities through history to stress the personal in the text. In Bunyan's case, his struggle is represented as that of an individual diseased psyche that reliably expresses itself through the written word.[23] Recent psychoanalytic approaches seem to remove Bunyan's text from history to make it the common tale of every individual's anxious struggle over ex- cessive guilt.[24] Roger Sharrock, for example, speaks of Bunyan's "nagging anxiety and uneasy conscience," and he seeks to find the "secret of the book" that will explain its continuing appeal.[25] Such readings insist on positioning the autobiographical religious subject as the subject of desire, rather than the subject of history, culture, and ideology. They erase the material conditions of the production and circulation of these texts to claim that an individual's psychology represents Everyman's desires.

Spiritual autobiography in seventeenth-century England was in large part literature written in antipathy to the Church of England, the official church of the state, and Dissenting preachers such as George Fox, Richard Baxter, and John Bunyan were harassed and imprisoned for their activi- ties in defiance of the legal restrictions against them. Puritan autobiogra- phy's construction of an individual subjectivity, then, also made possible rebellion against the sovereign and the law. The Dissenters were sub- jected to considerable—if somewhat erratic—persecution in the mid and late seventeenth century. They were fined, tortured, and sometimes killed. Such persecution led many to attempt to practice their faith within the fluctuating limits of the law, and to accept Charles II's friendly edict to permit their activities so long as the peace was not disturbed. The state and church in the late seventeenth century tolerated dissent in some measure by teasing it with the threat of imprisonment, albeit a state of incarceration with occasional, if temporary, reprieves. Bunyan, for example, was imprisoned in Bedford for twelve years, from 1660 to 1672, but as Michael R. Watts has pointed out, "he was allowed out of prison to attend church meetings in 1661, 1668, 1669, and 1670, and was elected to the pastorate of the Bedford Congregational church in January 1672 while still a prisoner."[26] And in that year the king issued a Declaration of Indulgence suspending penal laws in ecclesiastical matters. Similarly, Richard Baxter was imprisoned and freed several times beween 1670 and 1686. But even after the deaths of their leaders, Bunyan (1688), Fox (1691), and Baxter (1691), the Dissenters did not yet possess full equality under the law.[27] It was during one of Bunyan's respites from prison that *Grace Abounding*, written between 1660 and 1666, was published. Of course the very act of writing *Grace Abounding*, a prison document and a sermon in defiance of church and civil authority, challenged the very authorities who denied him a preaching voice; and yet he would have been freed if he had been willing to say that he would forego preaching.

In short, there was apparently increasing collusion between the persecutors and the persecuted, an alliance that took the form of tacit cooperation with Anglicans. The dominant powers of church and state engaged in close interaction with the Dissenting forces, in a series of inconsistent strategies ranging from containment to torture, and *Grace Abounding*, as well as other spiritual autobiographies, adjudicates the contradictions in a variety of ways.

As a Puritan, Bunyan's relationship to parental, civil, and divine authority was certainly complex and troubled. We might make something of the fact that his mother died in June 1644, his father remarried in September, and Bunyan entered the army (*not* on the side of his father's Royalist loyalties) in November.[28] But beyond disturbances deriving from the family, most Puritans were victims of an oppressive state power. Roger Sharrock, Bunyan's biographer and editor, describes the Puritan's enigmatic connection to authority in this way: "The Puritans, whose ideal aim was to make use of the state so as to confirm their own authority over men's souls and conduct, found themselves driven by the logic of events to fight for freedom from state interference and to attempt to wrest concessions from the civil power."[29] *Grace Abounding* was produced, then, in a climate of resistance and persecution, but the conditions of its production have been virtually obliterated from the minds of its readers, both by Bunyan's subtle evasions in his text and by critics' failure to question the apparent artlessness of that tactic. Bunyan's concentrating on producing an inner life, what he calls the "unfolding of my secret things" (57), makes references to the historically specific seem insignificant or even irrelevant. Though his contemporary readers knew of Bunyan's imprisonment and certainly read with that in mind, the effect of the text as it was reproduced throughout most of the eighteenth century allowed readers to ignore Bunyan's historical circumstances and make *Grace Abounding* into a personal yet universally applicable spiritual exemplum. Bunyan's apparent isolation and self-absorption both intersect and collide with a collective identity for the "poor people of Bedford." But positioned this way within an ideology of universalization, Bunyan's "I" also seeks the commonalities, across class and sect boundaries. The collective subjectivity constructed and conveyed in spiritual autobiography of the period helps produce a self-regarding middle class who, in large part, serve the interests of early capitalism by fostering the private individualism that comes from religiously authorized self-scrutiny. In *Grace Abounding* John Bunyan also sets out a prescription for the laboring and increasingly literate classes to become a "middling sort"—for them to *regard themselves*—and in so doing, to believe they possess an autonomous and unified self.

Bunyan draws on the affinities between his "experience" and that of the reader he recruits. Christopher Hill finds this realism and folksiness (the "flat, matter-of-fact, real-life narrative") subversive, since "its hero is a lower-class itinerant whose major temptations occur when playing tipcat."[30] But this subversive realism also allows readers to transcend the specific historical circumstances of the production of the text, and to make the unpremeditated discourse of realism and plain style seem to be Bunyan's natural choice, even a divinely ordained one. Bunyan writes, "God did not play in convincing me; . . . wherefore I may not play in my relating of them, but be plain and simple, and lay down the thing as it was" (5–6). *Grace Abounding* is complicit in these readings by its scant attention to the historical particulars and material conditions of Bunyan's political circumstances. Such omissions undoubtedly permitted its publication; Roger Sharrock argues that it would have been "difficult to

obtain a licence for a work of this character between 1660 and 1666." [31]
The emphasis on generic characteristics of *Grace Abounding* and other
similar spiritual autobiographies by critics and scholars has surely been
prompted by an attempt to explain its enduring appeal and to equate aesthetic value with historicopolitical transcendence.

One effect of Bunyan's claiming that his predicament transcends history is to command a larger body of sympathetic readers and to make his
text serve as a spiritual guide. Though Bunyan notes that he is taken
from his followers and bound up, he makes other specific references to his
imprisonment more general by appealing to scriptural metaphor: he is between the "Teeth of the Lions in the Wilderness" (3). But it is only in
another text he wrote in prison, unpublished until long after Bunyan's
death in 1765, *A Relation of the Imprisonment of Mr. John Bunyan*, that
the details of the accusations against him can be recaptured. Sharrock
points out that such accounts were usually included in such autobiographies during this period: "We should expect an account of trial and imprisonment to appear in the full autobiography, and not elsewhere. Such
accounts begin to be included in the autobiographies from the time of
the first application of the Conventicle Acts after the Restoration. . . .
They form a regular feature of this class of writings and the pattern they
follow is often that of a verbatim account with the speeches assigned to
the several participants." [32] Thus, it seems all the more remarkable that
Bunyan's was omitted, and that the most popular spiritual autobiography
of the eighteenth century did not include this convention.

In the *Imprisonment* the narrator Bunyan presents the importance of
his trade as coequal with that of his preaching, one a part of the other:
"And again, I did look upon it as my duty to do as much good as I could,
not only in my trade, but also in communicating to all people where-
soever I came, the best knowledge I had in the word" (114). Yet the
justice, as reported in his dialogue with Bunyan, tries to interrupt Bunyan's interpretation of the Scriptures, and, quite specifically, to fix him as
a known: Bunyan is acceptable as a tinker, not a preacher—as a poor
man, not economically independent. When Bunyan cites scriptural authority that "every man has received a gift," the justice counters, "Let
me a little open that Scripture to you. *As every man hath received the gift;*
that is, said he, as every man hath received a trade, so let him follow it.
If any man have received a gift of tinkering, as thou hast done, let him
follow his tinkering. As so other men their trades" (121–122). Thus, the
justice brushes away Bunyan's ability and authority to interpret Scrip-

ture, and he urges him to return to his recognizable subject position as a member of the working class who only performs his craft.

In addition, the poignant portrayal of Bunyan's wife's testimony on his behalf makes the domestic and economic consequences of his imprisonment strong and urgent: "She told him [the justice] again, that he desired to live peaceably, and to follow his calling, that his family might be maintained; and moreover said, my Lord, I have four small children, that cannot help themselves, of which one is blind, and have nothing to live upon but the charity of good people" (131–32). Pregnant when her husband was first jailed, she reports that she lost the child she was carrying. In response, one of the judges chides her for claiming her poverty and argues that Bunyan's preaching, not his tinkering, gave the family its income. Again, the question of whether Bunyan is to be defined as tinker or preacher arises:

> *Hales.* What is his calling? said Judge *Hales.*
> *Answer.* Then some of the company that stood by, said, A Tinker, my Lord.
> *Wom.* Yes, said she, and because he is a Tinker, and a poor man; therefore he is despised and cannot have justice."
>
> (132)

In short, Bunyan's crime, as it appears in the *Imprisonment,* is that he is a tinker, that he is poor, and that he is contesting the authority of church and state. In contrast, in the brief account of imprisonment that concludes *Grace Abounding,* Bunyan's narrative "I" insists that his crime is his preaching of God's word and that his achievement is the conversion and salvation of his individual soul. The *Imprisonment* makes his incarceration a class issue as much as a religious one, and the religious purposes of the autobiographical text, *Grace Abounding,* would have been muddied by its inclusion.

Class references are explicit when, by the early nineteenth century, *Grace Abounding* was frequently republished in abbreviated form, usually with some allusions to "the unlearned tinker of Bedford," the "tinker-teacher," or the ordinary preacher "without a mitre." [33] *Grace Abounding* also signals to the alert reader a strategy of survival, or rebellion within persecution, for the landless working class for whom finding an identity within Christ takes on economic connotations. For Bunyan, his conflict settles within the person of Esau and his loss of birthright. Bunyan tortures himself with the idea of committing the one unpardonable sin, and for a hundred paragraphs he searches Scripture for a sin equally as horrid as his imagined error. He draws an analogy between himself and Judas's urge "to sell and part with this most blessed Christ" (43). Using a conventional Puritan metaphor, Bunyan thinks of the possession of Christ's spirit as property, and he uses the biblical narrative in Leviticus to compare Christ to land. He becomes obsessed with the phrase, "*sell him, sell him.*"

It is Esau's story that Bunyan finds most riveting as a metaphor for his greatest fears, in spite of his attraction to various literary models in Peter, Judas, Christ, Saul, David, Solomon, and his living friend and mentor, Mr. Gifford: "*Or prophane person, as Esau, who for one morsel of meat sold his Birth-right; for you know how that afterwards when he would have inherited the blessing, he was rejected, for he found no place of repentance, though he sought it carefully with tears,* Heb. 12.16,17" (45). Like Esau, he is tempted to sell his birthright, which he defines as Christ, or property; like Esau, he fears that he will find "*no place of repentance*" though he seeks it. In his struggle he is obsessed with the phrase "no place of repentance." He stresses his desire to assume another identity: "And *now* was I both a burthen and a terror to myself. . . . Oh, how gladly now would I have been anybody but myself!" (47).

After finding a more exact double in Nathaniel Bacon's *A Relation of the Fearful Estate of Francis Spira in the year 1548* (1649), Spira's anguish becomes Bunyan's own for a time. Finally drawing parallels between Spira, Esau, and himself, he reinterprets Esau in the light of the New Testament and determines that Esau's being denied a place of repentance ("though he sought it carefully with tears") was less the denial of a birthright denied twenty years earlier than the search for a blessing from his father. Birthright, then, is reinterpreted to mean the right to regeneration and blessing, to eternal inheritance, a lesson of reassurance to the laboring classes.

That "birthright" Esau sought, that "place of repentance," comes to have a very tangible meaning for Bunyan, who speaks in terms of a place, a room, a home. Of course, Dissenting preachers such as Bunyan frequently were itinerants, and literally had no fixed place for gathering. In longing for a birthright as a believer, Bunyan and his followers, unlike the Anglicans, possessed no church building. Yet somehow one subject position Bunyan adopts is to turn that fictional ideal into the particular, a place from which to participate as a Dissenting subject. It is the *space* of conversion that Bunyan wants to enter. After a year's search through the

Bible, the narrator describes Bunyan's finding the words that he reads as having specific personal application: "*Compell them to come in, that my house may be filled, and yet there is roome,* Luke 14. 22, 23. These words, but especially them, *And yet there is roome,* were sweet words to me; for, truly, I thought that by them I saw there was place enough in Heaven for me, and . . . when the Lord Jesus did speak these words, he then did think of me" (72). Finally the words "*I must go to Jesus*" reverberate and speak to him. The words that call him to Zion, "to the City of the living God"—within the fiction of *Grace Abounding*—create a place for him in his imagination.

Apparently the common food for the poor, "pottage," referred to in Esau's story, was common parlance for the *Book of Common Prayer* to the seventeenth-century reader, and Jack Lindsay makes a convincing case that "birthright" also held revolutionary significance when it was used by radical religious groups.[34] Certainly possessing a place, or a piece of land, must have held class connotations for a man such as Bunyan. E. P. Thompson points toward the way in which social mobility in the seventeenth and eighteenth centuries required the acquisition of land,[35] and *Grace Abounding* exemplifies that desire. Similarly, calling attention to Bunyan's radical religious and political connections, Christopher Hill specifically notes Bunyan's class consciousness in *Pilgrim's Progress*, his allegorical denunciation of hypocrisy and the Antichrist personified as gentlemen.[36] But while Hill finally reads *Grace Abounding* as a radical political and religious tract calling for the economic and legal freeing of the poor, the homeless, and those without land, I have been less concerned to recover "Bunyan's" beliefs than to define a series of conflicting and revised subject positions that Bunyan's narrative "I" occupies, and to identify ways in which readers can appropriate his "life" to find a whole and unified consciousness, authorized by the divine. In spite of obvious textual contradictions and gaps, *Grace Abounding* depicts a subject bound to the control of state and church, while it promotes individual salvation, freedom of choice, and hope for the future.

In the early eighteenth century, Daniel Defoe provides a kind of secular progression to economic well-being. In his *Review* for 25 June 1709 Defoe categorizes the population of early eighteenth-century England as "the great, who live profusely," "the rich, who live very plentifully," "the middle sort, who live well," "the working trades, who labour hard but feel no want," and the country people, the poor, and the miserable.[37] It is those who wish to be the "middling sort" that Bunyan addresses in claiming a free and consistent self for those who believe in God. And it is this "middling sort," and those who wish to be, who in large part produce textual representations of self and experience in the period, and who turn to public published declarations of a fractured identity seeking to claim a coherent one. The place of property, or of identity, becomes increasingly the public declaration of self.

Bunyan's "I" presents itself as one of those who became literate in spite of his parents' low condition—"notwithstanding the meanness and inconsiderableness of my Parents" (7). As Margaret Spufford has pointed out, Bunyan "was fully conscious of having had educational advantages which exceeded his parents' social position" (what she elsewhere calls "slithering down the social ladder"), which explains the apparent anomaly of a tinker's literacy. Spufford provides convincing statistics for her point: from "1580–1700, 11 per cent of women, 15 per cent of labourers and 21 percent of husbandmen could sign their names, against 56 per cent of tradesmen and craftsmen and 65 per cent of yeomen."[38] But other literate laborers, artisans, and tradesmen such as tailor Arise Evans and shoemaker Nicholas Smith wrote spiritual autobiographies. What is probably unusual is that Bunyan *published* his text, a violation of the prevailing notion of what a tradesman ought to do. Once a text becomes public (in an apparently radical act of publishing what had previously been considered a private document), it paradoxically loses the subversive quality of a text prepared for private circulation, and, at least in Bunyan's case, *Grace Abounding* was quickly absorbed into the customary and the expected in its repeated imitations and adaptations in the eighteenth century. Bunyan's text, then, became the exemplary spiritual autobiography for the middle class, in spite of being authored by a Dissenting tradesman. In its private journal form, Bunyan's autobiography may have been a site of resistance, but in its public form it urged readers to think of themselves as subjects of self-regulation under the legitimating banner of religion. As the magistrate insists, the private has become publicly legislated so that "it is your private meetings that the law is against" (123). Bunyan's *Grace Abounding*, then, raises questions about the politics of privacy, a question of who controls and commands what is constructed as the secrets of the heart.

As I have remarked earlier, the autobiographical subject may describe subjection to an authority's control, while being bound to a belief that one is a free agent with an independent conscience and self-understanding. In fact, it would also seem that the production of a "practice of the self," the subject positioned in self-scrutiny, is ultimately a conservative act, an attempt to *conserve* private identity, a practice of the self that is useful to an emergent consumer economy that requires the formation of a publicly coherent bourgeois subject. Thus, spiritual autobiographies such as Bunyan's function as a potential location for abrupt and pronounced shifts in class status, as well as threats against church and state; but the potential power that *Grace Abounding* musters toward acknowledging the dissonances among subject positions has been largely obscured by the preaching tinker who, from within the prisons of church and state, offers an exemplary model for a bourgeois identity. Specifically, the formal conventions and inattention to the material circumstances of the production of *Grace Abounding* allow it to be received as a text that contests the dominant religious powers but within the prescribed, if ambiguous and unarticulated, limits.

The Bunyan of *Grace Abounding* is permitted, within the ideology of a converted self, to argue against the very church and state that incarcerate him, and to forge, ironically, its most dominant pattern for perceiving a spiritual "self" throughout the eighteenth century. *Grace Abounding*, then, stops short of constructing a subject sufficiently qualified to enact major changes in the controlled subjection of that subject. Bunyan's example would seem to validate the claim that ideological conflict occurs in part because "subjects" are qualified within that ideology to contest it, or to take up transformative positions within it, but are not qualified *enough* to escape their subjection.[39] In this case, free autonomous rational subjects are called into being as readers and writers of autobiographical texts in the eighteenth century even as they are writing from prison or in danger of persecution. Bunyan's text effaces his physical imprisonment, postulates a freedom in eternity, and Baptists, while eventually achieving state toleration, accept the status quo and are not empowered to control the state. Thus *Grace Abounding* participates in the effective strategy of producing a new "practice of the self," one of self-scrutiny which extends to self-regulation of conduct. The religious subject hailed in spiritual autobiography worships a (male) God who, though seemingly classless, possesses sufficient land and capital to dispense the inheritance the subject seeks. In short, *Grace Abounding* provides a persuasive model for the quiescent and orderly transformation from a working-class itinerant to a bourgeois self who possesses his own "unfettered" domain of self. This practice of self-regulation, rather than relying on a more direct state control of behavior, reproduces a dissenting subject that welcomes its construction as a "self" under God and finds a satisfying explanation for its economic and ideological imprisonment and co-optation while offering within the material conditions of its production, the unsaid of a revolutionary reading.

CHAPTER FOUR

Methodized Subjects

John Wesley's Journals

How unspeakable is the advantage, in point of common sense, which middling people have over the rich! There is so much paint and affectation, so many unmeaning words and senseless customs among people of rank, as fully justify the remark made seventeen hundred years ago: Rarus enim ferme sensus communis in illa Fortuna. *[For in such an elevated condition of life, common sense is generally very rare].*
—John Wesley, *Journals* (29 June 1758)

[Wesley's journals are] no life at all in the ordinary sense of the word, but only a mere string of preachings. His journals are like the notebooks of a physician—a curious monstrous, wonderful narrative.
—Margaret Wilson Oliphant, *Blackwood's Magazine* (1869)

I

By the early eighteenth century those who spoke from outside the boundaries of the Church of England were tolerated without the daily danger of harassment and imprisonment, though they still had not achieved civil equality. It was certainly possible to be both an aristocrat and a Dissenter, but for such a person, barred from full participation in the state, the consequences were forbidding. Unable to attend university, and unable to serve the king, aristocrats or those otherwise eligible for high place in large part avoided professing religious beliefs that would destroy their chances for advancement. In fact, shortly after the death of Queen Anne in 1714, most of the 6 percent of the population who considered themselves to be Dissenters were concentrated in the poor and working classes. Though the paucity of evidence prevents sweeping generalizations about the economic conditions of Dissenters, Michael R.

Watts does indicate his conviction that "a much higher proportion of Dissenters than of the population at large were engaged in commerce or manufactures as merchants, tradesmen, or self-employed artisans, and the social and legal pressure of the eighteenth century helped to confine Dissenters to such occupations."[1] In addition, Dissenters were increasingly successful in recruiting members from the urban centers where they were less subject to retribution from landed Anglican gentry, who still exerted considerable control over the more rural areas. The Dissenting subjects, then, formed a relatively homogeneous body—still more rural than urban, made up of more working and middle-class people than gentry, and containing few landowners.

Though in the late seventeenth century they were the object of persecution, the Dissenters of the early and mid eighteenth century sought state sanction and authorization. In other words, Dissenters began to vacate the space of contestation and instead actively sought validation within existing structures. At this same historical moment when Dissent was becoming institutionalized and its total numbers were waning, John Wesley's group at Oxford began to gather regularly for devotion. Though not distinct from or in opposition to the Church of England until later, they were called Methodists "from their custom of regulating their time and planning the business of the day every morning."[2] Certainly Dissenters were still excluded from Oxford and Cambridge, but by 1732 they were an organized band of dissension that possessed a certain stature, no longer simply a subversive lot. Laymen sat on their Board of Dissenting Deputies, and two members were chosen annually from the Congregationalists, Presbyterians, and Baptists. This board initiated efforts to gain greater religious freedom and civil equality, including the repeal of the Test Act.[3] Yet state sanction brought with it an inevitable second-class status. For example, Dissenting ministers' pay equaled that of the lesser Anglican clergy, and unlike the Anglicans, the Dissenters were granted no housing or tenure.[4] In fact, by 1730, the Dissenting population had declined sufficiently to prompt Strickland Gough to question the reasons for its losses in "An Enquiry into the Causes of the Decay of the Dissenting Interest." The Methodist Church was not institutionalized until after Wesley's death in 1791. Thus, the Church of England increasingly contained and defused the power of the radical opposition even as it legitimated its presence.

For newly literate eighteenth-century readers, no matter what their sect, the spiritual accounts of seventeenth-century Baptists and Quakers continued to hold the power to shape experience and to transform lives. I have already noted the immense popularity of Bunyan's *Grace Abounding* throughout the eighteenth century. In fact, John Bunyan helped legitimate Dissent for an audience drawn from the Church of England and other sects. John Haime, for example, in a life published in *Arminian Magazine* (beginning in April 1780) takes Bunyan's account to be exemplary, in spite of his own Methodist leanings: "Among many old books which were here, I found 'Grace Abounding to the chief of sinners.' I read it with the utmost attention, and found his case nearly resembled my own."[5] Equally popular were the numerous Quaker journals and testimonies. Many Quaker "autobiographies" were published before 1725, the most widely read of which, George Fox's *Journal* in its revised and abbreviated form edited in 1694 by Thomas Ellwood, apparently sold between 2.5 and 4 million copies in the period.[6] George Fox had prescribed and controlled the kind of Quaker autobiographies written and published, and John Wesley similarly exerted strong influence on the texts submitted to him by his followers. In spite of their spanning the latter half of the eighteenth century, John Wesley's journals are now little read and seldom cited in studies of autobiography. John Morris, for example, chose not to include them in his study, saying the journals had little influence on the genre of spiritual autobiography: "The Wesleys produced no great seminal model that could serve the faithful as Fox's *Journal* served the Quakers."[7] This seems to me to be somewhat inaccurate, both because Wesley's and Fox's journals were equally rambling and digressive and because Wesley's published journals chided others into producing conversion stories. Wesley's methodized day and self were publicly circulated and much imitated, and his urging of his ministers to write their lives in a similar manner founded an entire community of discourse. Taken together, Wesley's journals and his ministers' published lives demonstrate the power of text to shape both "experience" and the printed representation of that experience. These contemporary texts, like those written by the Dissenters, taught readers how to narrate and order their lives as they displaced more remote biblical models and substituted more immediate "realistic" ones. Conversion narratives in the eighteenth century, especially those written within the Methodist camp, thus take on an ideological framework that acquires paradigmatic force to affect and even determine the way people perceive and inscribe reality.

If Bunyan stresses the singularity of his experience and its applicability to all sinners, Wesley prefers the redundancy of multiple forms and repetitive conversions. Wesley's autobiographical writings, and those he encouraged his ministers to write, interweave the provisional and the structured to monitor conflicting representations of reality for a growing body of Methodists. These hybrid texts offer alternatives for the written representation of the consciousness of an individual subject. These writings in their varied forms allow for the representation of the uncertain status of a sect that repeatedly insists on its unity with the Church of England while questioning the church's doctrine.

Methodism emphasizes an individualism that freely consents to participate in a larger religious movement and, in addition, a collectivity of individual members.[8] Methodism encouraged the emergence of a belief in human agency and in the doctrine of progress, though the individual was subject to Wesley's authority, and he paradoxically exerted strong central control over his ministers and bands. Because Wesley wanted to remain in the church and did not want Methodism to be thought of as Dissent—that is, active separation from the Church of England—the identity of a Methodist was ambiguous at best. As David Hempton has put it, "The harder one looks for the essence of Methodism, the more one is convinced that there is no essence, apart from inspired innovation based on biblical ideas."[9] In fact, some people left the Methodists for other Dissenting sects to seek a more explicitly oppositional doctrine and a sharper identity that would distinguish them from the Church of England. Wesley's positioning between the two religious bodies acutely emphasizes his necessarily double stance: "In one society he was an itinerant evangelist in command of an army of lay preachers; in the other he was an ordained priest subject to a comparatively rigid ecclesiastical constitution. In one society he was required to stay put; in the other he was required to roam. In one society he was expected to preach moral, reasonable sermons; in the other he was to awaken converts to the inspiration of the Holy Ghost."[10] Thus, John Wesley positioned himself and his ministers ambiguously between the Church of England and Methodism, as well as between individual inspiration and central regulation.

In addition, Wesley's journals mediate the conflicts in the newly constructed methodized subject that largely derives from the oppressed classes who aspire to higher status, and they fashion a written, if fragmentary, technology for the accounting. Recording the history of a counterhegemonic denomination in formation, Wesley's journals and the autobiographical accounts that he extracts from his ministers aim at those who think of themselves as powerless, though the production of these disparate narratives serves the interests of the established power structures as well as those of the underclass. If Wesley appealed largely to tradesmen and artisans in his travels and sermons, his autobiographical writing seeks to outline a model for the laboring classes to follow as they become sufficiently literate to write themselves in a culture in which literacy and self-improvement through reading comes increasingly to be valued.

There has been considerable disagreement in historians' assessments of the function of religion in popular culture. Some claim that Methodism provided a cohesive work ethic that made it possible for artisans, tradesmen, and laborers to rise above economic depression, and others find in Methodism a chiliastic fervor that allowed the working classes to ignore their real economic circumstances. Michael Watts, for example, repudiates the association of the work ethic with Quakers by arguing that it was their high moral standards rather than their work discipline that made Dissenting merchants so successful, citing George Fox's opinion that Methodists' rigid scruples in commercial deals accounted for their prospering. For Harold Perkin, Methodism provides a structure of collective organization that prefigures working-class secular movements such as trade unionism by making available the necessary organizational experience and producing collective desire.[11] In contrast, for E. P. Thompson, the otherworldly nature of Methodism exerted an insidiously depoliticizing force upon the working class in its arguing for submission to authority and its urging of rigorous discipline in daily life and work.[12] Thompson states that, despite the theological pretensions of churches, the role of religion in popular culture was extremely negative because it did not help men cope with practical problems, and merely reinforced the social and political dominance of a paternalistic establishment while it taught them to look hopefully toward eternity. Thompson finds Methodism's appeal to be largely to the new industrial working class and to the poor in its arguing for the "pitiless ideology of work" (379). Following this approach, Methodism thus served the interests of manufacturing leaders in fostering submission. It held workers in line with a work ethic that required their labor yet exploited them while maintaining that poverty was a sanctified state. Methodism was responsible, in Thompson's eyes, for "a central disorganization of the human personality," for he takes spontaneity to be a natural human trait that Methodism "pollutes" (369) by inspiring hysteria, disequilibrium, and psychic exploitation.

In short, in Thompson's narrative, the poor seem to be victims of merciless mercantilists who willfully disrupt the natural and pregiven organization of the human personality. That is, the dominant ideology of the privileged remakes the natural personality of the lower classes in the interests of the propertied. If we counter this argument, however, with a more reciprocal model of power, we can allow for the tentacles of state apparatuses to be widely dispersed throughout the social formation, and for the economic to remain an important, if not the sole, determinant of social consciousness. It is not so much that the eighteenth-century working classes were urged to adopt a false consciousness as that they make use of the multiple ideological filters for experience which, as they circulate within the social space, reproduce contradictory subject positions rather than unified and essential selves. These various positions afford occasions for resistance within the very chaos that Thompson finds so disheartening, so that the disequilibrium may be less a production of the ruling class than a cultural conjunction that it harnesses for its own ends. As a major national movement of the eighteenth century, Methodism may be reconceptualized as a site of struggle over working class subjectivity in which alternative official conceptions of "self" are made available, even as Methodism also becomes a location of counterhegemonic notions of identity and subjectivity. The Methodist obsession with the state of the individual soul may well have staved off social upheaval in the artisan classes by emphasizing the psychological rather than the political and cultural dimensions of an individual's plight. By focusing on the disorientation and reorganization of an individual's interior experience, it ranks among the cultural forces that deflect attention away from larger social problems. For example, Methodism allows for extreme affective states while it also provides the language and the means to contain them. It displayed its excesses in madness and hysteria, in spite of Wesley's emphasis on putting one's personality in order through a technology of written regulation. Thus, Methodism may have served the interests of the state, the church, and the production of a self-regulating individualism, but in setting such a contradictory set of beliefs in motion, it also enables resistance to those ideologies as it also both produces and reflects a larger disorganization in the social formation more complex than individual psychological dissociation.

Being a Methodist did not require a negation of past practices so much as a promise of perpetual vigilance and constant searching, and it permitted—even encouraged—individual members to hold contradictory beliefs and engage in practices at variance with each other. The evidence seems to indicate that Methodism formulated a very malleable doctrine in the guise of rigor that allowed for a sense of cohesion in a body of believers and workers. I am arguing, then, that the Methodist journal or autobiographical narrative tolerated and mediated the conflicting beliefs and practices while it prescribed an identity that absorbed and even embraced contradiction. If Methodism satisfied "the profound associational and communal demands of people experiencing anomie (social disorganization) and social insecurity in a period of rapid social change," as Alan D. Gilbert has written,[13] it did so by emphasizing the humanist tenets of sameness in difference, of particularity in universality.

In mid eighteenth-century England, autobiographical writing gives groups of marginalized people—not only Dissenters, but women, criminals, and the laboring and middling—a voice and a story to tell, eventually making their lives a consumable product in an increasingly consumerist economy. John Wesley's autobiographical writings—prompted by his own conversion in 1739—call into being and hold in place class linkages through ideological principles for the colliers, butchers, tailors, and tallow chandlers who heard him preach and submit their brief spiritual autobiographical accounts to him, many of which he included in his published journals. This newly constructed public identity was particularly powerful in its inclusion of the humblest and poorest because Wesley claimed its universal applicability. In sum, John Wesley, in his travels and his writings, crafts a public technology of a class-identified self that stands simultaneously within and without the church, and he is instrumental in encouraging the formation and self-regulation of a unified body of individualist subjects who justify their pursuit of economic and political self-interest.

◌ॐ II

I want now to give more particular attention to this body of Methodist first-person narratives in order to look first at Wesley's experiental lens, the ideology of the genre of diaries, and then more specifically at the conversion narratives he admired and disseminated. The diary or journal is ideologically consonant with Methodism's great emphasis on the individual as part of the collective body, an association loosely formed and not requiring a declaration of identity ("I am a Methodist") but an individual subject's definite consent to belong to something. A journal connects the fashioning of an apparently spontaneous and expressive individual to the strict structure of hourly and daily entries. Wesley's journals construct a life of prayer, preaching, and social interaction based on shared spiritual understandings. Though the diaries resist the imposition of plot, they embed briefer narratives in letters and accounts of those whom Wesley has converted. The contradictions of the "self" persist, and Wesley shows very little concern about the discontinuities and repetitions of these texts. Considerable pressure, then, is placed on the narrative "I" as the connective that binds the moments and events together. If the "I" is the position from which everything should seem coherent and true, it is also the location of doubt and revision: "What the end will be, I know not; but it is enough that God knoweth." [14] In Wesley's journals, the discourses of the self, fixed in God yet tentative, cross; and the conflicting notions of self-contemplation and self-denial also intermingle. The journals document the shared experiences of persecution for a body of believers, and a "Methodist" is simply defined as one who values "love, joy, peace, long-suffering, gentleness, goodness, fidelity, meekness, temperance" (4:416). Wesley preaches the doctrines of Christian perfection, justification by faith, the witness of the spirit, and the new birth—though he is willing to acknowledge the necessity for repeated conversion: "That many of these [sanctified] did not retain the gift of God is no proof that it was not given them" (4:539).

The diary or journal gave regularity to one's labor and helped to organize the workday and -week. In a sense it served as a substitute clock and calendar as increasingly urban populations moved away from the rhythms of sun and harvest. Efficient timepieces were still too expensive for the working classes to own in the 1790s, and to be able to own a clock in midcentury would have been a mark of affluence usually attainable only by the gentry. Knowing where one is in terms of the clock and the calendar, then, was necessary in the formation of the emergent middle class, the diary an indication of participation in a middle-class practice, the development of a "timesheet of industrial capitalism." The class of workers Wesley principally addressed was urged toward greater and greater productivity. [15] Wesley, it would seem, articulated the religious doctrine of self-scrutiny along with the economic doctrine of productivity, and he made the diary a mode of producing and reflecting radical change and social disorientation, while it served as a tool for restructuring work and leisure.

By example and precept in his journals, Wesley insists on an attention to detail, a persistent energy, a rigorous work ethic, and a commitment to redeeming the moment as principles of his religious doctrine. Every minute counts: "Before I reached Kensington I found my mare had lost a shoe. This gave me an opportunity of talking closely, for nearly half an hour, both to the smith and his servant. I mention these little circumstances to show how easy it is to redeem every fragment of time (if I may so speak) when we feel any love to those souls for which Christ died" (3:83). He gives evidence of "how God overrules even the minutest circumstances" (3:373). Every moment should be used for work or edification: "My fragments of time I employed in reading and carefully considering the lives of Magdalen de Pazzi, and some other eminent Romish saints" (4:539–40). In the autobiographical texts he recommends there is a similar obsession with time: David Brainerd, an American missionary and one of Wesley's favorites, writes, "Oh how precious is time! And how guilty it makes me feel, when I think I have trifled away and misemployed it, or neglected to fill up each part of it with duty, to the utmost of my ability."[16] And in another autobiographical text, Alexander Mather evidences a restless urgency after idle moments: "Therefore I husbanded all the time, that I could save from company, eating or sleeping, to lay out in wrestling with God, for myself and the flock: so I devoted to God some part of every leisure hour."[17] Experience is to be conceptualized in the unit of a day, rather than by events judged to be significant, and it needs daily attendance and daily divine interposition (1:87)—and "evident interpositions of Divine Providence, in answer to prayer, occur almost every day" (1:92). In fact, the monotony and repetition of Wesley's journals would seem to fix a regularity to the Methodist self observing the self—that is, the "self" who *reads* as well as *writes* his own journal.

Even to the subject reading himself, time is a precious commodity not to be squandered but to be used in daily self-regulation: "And thus I give both you and myself hopes of a speedy period to these memoirs, which begin to be tedious and minute, even to myself." Conversion itself structures daily life and produces a subjectivity perpetually fixed on itself as a reader of one's own experience. In his journals and the conversions he incorporates in them and also publishes separately, Wesley, recommending specific reading practices as the most beneficial, effectively prescribes the kind of reading subject that should be produced. For example, in the preface to the 1790 edition of Thomas à Kempis's An *Extract of the Christian's Pattern*, he writes that though the pace of reading he prescribes should be regular, it must be interrupted by gaps for meditation: "Stop every now and then, to recollect what you have read, and consider how to reduce it to practice."[18] In fact he creates the concept of a "Christian Reader" in the preface to his published sermons. Urging readers to prepare for reading through prayer, he asks them to allot a specific time to it.

The books Wesley wrote and recommended fostered this kind of reading. For a newly literate population, educated at most in the rudiments of reading and writing, the publication of a book that could be dipped into was particularly important. The extraordinary amount of repetition in the journals suggests that most readers would not read it from cover to cover but would instead read it as it had been inscribed. "Open it and read where your eye falls" (4:148–49) was the way a fellow Methodist Wesley cites had advised reading the Bible, a ready and fertile source of passages that could, in opening it to any page, speak to the individual man. Wesley's published journals could be read similarly—not straight through, but randomly opened to this application of a Bible verse or that strange account or marvelous conversion. His insistence on repetition assures the reader, however, that such a passage will not be an anomaly, but will fit into a larger pattern that is providentially ordained. Similarly, the Methodist lives in the *Arminian Magazine* were published in brief installments over a period of months. Each of the issues is filled with as many as twenty conversion accounts, beginning with the first issue of the monthly periodical in 1778. At the conclusion of each installment, readers are teased with a crisis, as if Wesley is forcing contemplation on his readers, with a text that seems to call for an application of his "Christian reading" technique. The intervals of confusion and consequent heightening of interest are moments without resolution that augment the potential for the reader's transformation. In fact, the Bible, sermons, Wesley's journals, and other ministers' lives could be used as a sort of reading primer, a training text for fledgling readers to be taken up as respite from manual labor. An extreme example of this comes in a letter from Rev. Samuel Davies, who writes of the Virginia slaves, "Indeed, there are multitudes of them in various parts who are eagerly desirous of instruction. They have generally very little help to read; and yet, to my agreeable surprise, sundry of them, by dint of application in their very few leisure hours, have made such progress that they are able to read their Bible, or a plain author, very intelligibly" (4:125). Such attention to time and to the careful employment of leisure, suggests a society, extending even to its most marginalized members, engaged in redefinition and radical change in determining the apportionment of the day, the week, and the year, and incorporating reading and writing within a time span—in fact, in the production and reproduction of an attitude toward the relation of time, work, and subjectivity.

Ꮽ III

Wesley's textual manifestations of these notions of identity—a full and multilayered record of his lived experience—in diaries, journals, letters, a spiritual register, and a manuscript hymnbook continue from his conversion until death. He first inscribed many of them in shorthand and cipher, and later versions expanded the daily record of his spiritual progress and his preaching, as well as included letters from the converted.[19] The diaries purport to be private records, many of which were transcribed only intermittently rather than every day, and which, like James Boswell's memoranda, are in the imperative: "Imply," "Avoid," and the like. The second-person commands include rules and resolutions for conduct of the self. The more cryptic diaries parallel the journals. Exact records of long and busy days of devotion in which time, even to the quarter hour, is accounted for, they provide the minutes of Wesley's daily prayer, conversations, and communal gatherings: "*Thursday* 29 5 1/4 Singing, within, on business; 6:45 at Mrs. Stover's, Mrs. West, etc., prayer; 7:15 at James Hutton's, tea, conversed, Betty and Esther, Reed, Bray, etc., singing, prayer; 9:15 set out with Charles, etc.; 10 they went, prayer; 11 meditated, read, met a man, I conversed; 1 at Egham, dinner, conversed; 2:30 set out, conversed; 8:30 at Basingstoke, Mr. Knight's, Clive, Cowdry, etc., conversed, tea; 9:30 prayer, Bible, singing; 11" (2:167). Though the equation is usually reversed, on that particular day, the parallel account in Wesley's journal is briefer than the diary: "I left London, and in the evening expounded to a small company at Basingstoke." And his letter for the same day to the Fetter Lane society provides yet another representation of the day. In other words, the same experience produces at least three different accounts in its textual representation.

Distinct from the diaries yet paralleling them in the time transpired, Wesley's journals, ostensibly private documents, were issued in twenty-one relatively short parts from 1739 to 1791, in each case appearing a few years after its writing. For example, the portion covering November 1751 to October 1754 was issued in 1759; February 1755 to June 1758 was issued in 1761 and again in 1768. Wesley inserts various kinds of texts into the daily account—letters, testimonies, and sermons, among others—to provide examples for Christian conduct. The journals demonstrate the difficulties of fitting secular experience into earlier conversion models, particularly as regards the vagueness of the moment of conversion: "But I could not comprehend what he spoke of an *instantaneous work*. I could not understand how this faith should be given in a moment: how a man could *at once* be thus turned from darkness to light, from sin and misery to righteousness and joy in the Holy Ghost" (1 : 454). Like Bunyan, Wesley is perpetually troubled by his lack of *complete* conversion. Varying from the pattern of most previous spiritual autobiographies, the conversion comes at the very beginning of his published diaries, in May 1738, and yet he continues with enough details to fill seven volumes describing the activities of the converted self. He is persistent in questioning the idea of full and permanent conversion: "Of the adults I have known baptized lately, one only was at that time born again, in the full sense of the word; that is, found a thorough, inward change, by the love of God filling her heart. Most of them were only born again in a lower sense; that is, received the remission of their sins" (2 : 135).

When Wesley asks his friend Böhler if he should stop preaching until he is convinced of conversion, Böhler answers, "Preach faith *till* you have it; and then, *because* you have it, you *will* preach faith" (1 : 442). But it troubles Wesley that his experience in the historical moment of the mid eighteenth century does not match the swift and unmistakable conversions of the early Christians. He yearns for a clear and razor-sharp pattern in his own life: "I searched the Scriptures again touching this very thing, particularly the Acts of the Apostles: but, to my utter astonishment, found scarce any instances there of other *instantaneous* conversions; scarce any so slow as that of St. Paul, who was three days in the pangs of the new birth" (1 : 454). Thus, using a new mode of conversion narrative—the description and perpetual revising of the converted self—Wesley adopts a present, human, and experiential form to monitor its waverings. Wesley includes the possibility that "a man may have a justifying faith *before* he is wholly freed from doubt and fear and before a new and clean heart" (1 : 432). Wesley's journals, then, convey multiple patterns of conversion narratives in reconstituting faith to include perpetual doubt, and conversion to require constant renewal and redeclaration.

In the oral presentation of a sermon, in the theologically grounded encouragement of diary keeping, and in the publication of their own converted lives, Wesley and his ministers preached *versions* of identity that claimed scriptural authority (especially from the New Testament) and that made available to the middling sort an autobiographical story.

These newly commissioned writers described their crisis as one of having to write down their conversion experience, rather than deliver it orally; their concern is in part one of shifting from oral to written representation, as well as translating experience into new written formulas that did not rely on the allegory of Scripture.

Wesley does return to the authority of biblical passages that he selects for exegesis. In the preface to his sermons Wesley's audience is the common man, as he affects the voice that can be universally comprehended and emptied of its intertextuality: "Nay, my design is, in some sense to forget all that ever I have read in my life. I mean to speak, in general, as if I had never read one author, antient or modern."[20] He also prompts his followers to imitate his "plain" and "honest" language, and he regularly compliments these qualities in others; he adopts the appearance of spontaneous writing in the journals and insists on its originality and universal appeal. But rather than holding up biblical personages as models of a life well-lived—rather than making them into exemplars for contemporary Methodists—Wesley mandates the writing and reading of personal accounts of lives justified by faith, not simply a conversion incident. In encouraging men and women to write to him to describe relevant activities, he offers fresh public models for the production of an identity of a modest, self-denying, hard-working person who takes comfort in the similarity of his experience to those of others and its allegedly truthful representation in text.

While Wesley eventually gains confidence in the incontrovertibility of his own conversion, his seeking spiritual narratives that portray struggle suggests his recognition that at midcentury new paradigms of conversion stories were needed to structure experience and record patterns of repeated doubts and questionings. He voices this uncertainty in relation to his own conversion: "But when I set aside the glosses of men, and simply considered the words of God, comparing them together, endeavouring to illustrate the obscure by the plainer passages, I found they all made against me, and was forced to retreat to my last hold, 'that experience would never agree with the *literal interpretation* of those scriptures. Nor could I therefore allow it to be true, till I found some living witnesses of it'" (1:471–72). In his own story, Wesley offers an alternative model of conversion to indicate his many stages of false confidence in the validity of his first feeling of conversion. Dividing his account into eighteen numbered paragraphs, he indicates his serial convictions that each stage held the definitive conversion experience. Making a strong distinction between "outer" and "inner" conviction, the external recognition of God's laws prevails: "I fell, and rose, and fell again. Sometimes I was overcome, and in heaviness: sometimes I overcame, and was in joy" (1:470). Intense inner feelings did not follow his intellectual conviction until biblical passages and Luther's preface to Romans assured him "that [God] had taken away *my* sins, even *mine*, and saved *me* from the law of sin and death." And he repeatedly stresses the importance of friends in assisting with the necessary daily conversion: "To have even a small number of such friends constantly watching over my soul, and administering . . . reproof or advice with all plainness and gentleness, is a blessing I know not where to find in any other part of the kingdom" (1:160). One who is converted will evidence new judgments of *himself*, of *happiness*, of *holiness*. Thus, the fleeting sense of an inner change requires constant renewal, and serial journals become the vehicle of that imaginary self-constitution and regulation.

Other contradictory discourses display much ambivalence in these narratives about self-denial and Wesley, like his ministers, fears being "a mere *egoist*" by writing (1:86). There is, after all, something paradoxical in Wesley's protestations of self-denial as he publishes installment after installment of his journals. As we have seen, by midcentury a religious discourse of self-denial is broadly understood and widely articulated within the model of conduct and management, and it is absorbed into a more generalized spiritual identity. In *Self Examination Explained and Recommended. In Two Discourses* (1761), Samuel Clark, rector of a Dissenting congregation, cautions his readers to examine their experience and character in order to act more appropriately in the future, based on the injunction in Prov. 4.26: "Ponder the path of thy feet; and let all thy ways be established." Clark emphasizes the inner private order as the true measure of character, and constant attention to it helps in identifying "our ruling-passion."[21] This scrutiny of conduct, Clark enjoins, must be detailed if it is to be useful: "But to render this examination effectual, it will be necessary to descend to such particulars under each head, as are suited to our own case." Clark thinks of this activity, which requires regular vigilance, as an enormously difficult task, "an employment to which we are naturally averse,"[22] because the mind is unaccustomed to turning inward. In other words, character is known by attention to one's own heart rather than to the outside world, and, according to Clark, true character exists and can be recovered through daily written accounting throughout one's life. The conflict within a divided self, then, is one constructed in religious discourse and one that receives new emphasis.

A particularly common text on which sermons on self-denial are based is the text William Penn explicated in his popular *No Cross, No Crown:* "He that will come after me, let him deny himself, and take up his cross and follow me."[23] Penn is severe on the proud man who focuses on himself, calling him "a kind of Glutton upon himself; for he is never satisfied with Loving and admiring himself, whilst nothing else with him is worthy either of Love or Care" (160). In a sermon preached at Bristol at the ordination of a Church of England minister, Benjamin Fawcett cautions ministers to make Christ the pattern to copy rather than themselves: "As Christian preachers, their self-acquaintance enables them to discern the continual danger they are in, of having Christ rivalled by sinfull self."[24] Thus, the religious discourse of self recognizes the contradiction between constant scrutiny and the distraction it provides to those who should focus on Christ instead. Similarly, David Sommervail writes *The Preaching of Self exploded, and the preaching of Christ explained and enforced* to identify a whole category of preaching which he calls "self-preaching," a practice he finds both rampant and abhorrent. "Self," he writes, "is neither the source from which our sermons proceed, nor the end to which they are directed; self is neither the introduction, doctrine, nor application of our discourses, nor any part of their design.—but this is what we utterly and eternally proclaim and disavow, as intirely incompatible with the great end and design of our sacred office."[25]

By publishing his journals as a testament of faith, and thus a model for others, Wesley avoids the charge of self-aggrandizement. Yet once one volume of the serial publication is issued, his recognition as he writes the next that his "private" records will have public scrutiny surely shaped the "experience" of the later journals. This spectacle of the private is in part a reassurance that each individual's interiority may not be so dangerous, for it may be purchased and consumed. By moving to display interiority in the public arena, the journals also suggest the permeability of the edges of a "private" self that asserts its freedom and autonomy from church and state while it devises a method of self-regulation within that realm.

One textual manifestation of the free subject, then, is the private published diary that assumes a reading and writing subject who is the source and center of her or his own meaning, a meaning that can be learned by turning to one's "interior." As we have seen, the attempt to present a unified subjectivity characterized by self-scrutiny, discipline, and consistency is not without contradictions. The diary or journal serves primarily to define and maintain identity, yet the emphasis on excess feeling, as well as the proliferation of the marvelous in the "strange accounts" of Wesley's journals, especially in the late 1750s, threatens its stability. Thus, while Methodist subjects place themselves both as part of the state and outside it, simultaneously Church of England and Methodist, the enthusiastic aspect of Methodism is largely perceived as a threat to an enlightened society, and its excesses are defined as aberrant. Wesley urges journal-writers to give proper attention to emotional outbursts and apparent religious frenzies: "The danger *was* to regard extraordinary circumstances too much, such as outcries, convulsions, visions, trances; as if these were essential to the inward work, so that it could not go on without them. Perhaps the danger *is* to regard them too little, to condemn them altogether; to imagine they had nothing of God in them and were a hindrance to His work" (4:359). That is, the "irrational" or "emotional" is always intruding to subvert the fixed discipline the diary requires.

Wesley continues to solicit, and to embed in his narrative, the conversion testimonies of others. In the accounts Wesley gathers and prints, the reborn self establishes its "identity" again and again as it does in his own journal. Most of the conversions Wesley collects in the journals and elsewhere describe repeated conversions by a variety of agencies—textual, human, and divine. Zacharias Neisser was twice converted, once by human intervention, once by song; Hans Neisser was converted by his grandfather and then through a vision; David Schneider, having been converted by his parents, was then retrieved from despair by his fellow Christians; Christopher Demuth similarly found conversion through his parents and then the loud voice of God; Arvid Gradin was converted first by reading, then by Scripture. These examples, both dispersed throughout his journals and published separately in the *Arminian Magazine* and the *Christian Library*, suggest the contagion of faith, but also the perplexity of doubt and the precariousness of conversion.

Though the generic forms vary enormously in the life stories that Wesley finds appealing, certain ideological assumptions about the self persist. Wesley most admires those who make their lives into patterns of conversion in spite of the ambiguities of their perceived spiritual experience. He was early inspired by Thomas à Kempis's *Christian Pattern*, the title he preferred to *Imitation of Living*, a book he edited for publication in a tiny pocketbook edition (1790) that could easily be drawn out during a moment's leisure. (He was also moved by Jeremy Taylor's *Holy Living and Dying* as well as William Law's *Christian Perfection*.) "Pattern" is a word that recurs constantly in Wesley's journals: "I buried the body of Ephraim B[edder], once a pattern to all that believed" (4:124). In addition, he sought models in biblical passages that could be applied to daily experience: "'For this cause I obtained mercy, that in me first Jesus Christ might shew forth all long-suffering, for a pattern to them which should hereafter believe on Him to life everlasting' 1 Tim. 1. 16." Isabel Rivers has pointed out that "the *Journal* provided the preachers with a continuing pattern of a life lived out as a pilgrimage with no fixed resting place on earth; serialization effectively emphasized that Wesley's quest was never complete."[26] Forced to preach in the open air, the itinerant ministers described their lives as lacking a place. This is, however, not simply a literary trope, but, as in the case of Bunyan, a reflection of the economic condition of the largely landless tradesmen and artisan classes. For example, the self is often portrayed as a voyager on a pilgrimage, occasionally befriended but ultimately alone, rather than presented from the multiple viewpoints of the community as in Quaker autobiographies.

In addition, Wesley praises consistencies in the many autobiographies he read and published. Thomas Jackson, for example, sees the life stories of the early Methodist preachers as providing models of "holy zeal, self-denial, and enterprise."[27] And of Haliburton's *Life*, Wesley writes, "I cannot but value it next to the holy scripture, above any other human composition, excepting only the *Christian Pattern* and the small remains of Clemens Romanus, Polycarp, and Ignatius." Again, there is the emphasis on the importance of uniformity: "But the work was still carried on, by a secret and undiscernable power. . . . It was all the work of one who is everywhere, who knoweth every thing, and who will not faint. . . . And it was all an uniform work, though variously carried on, through many interruptions, over many oppositions, for a long tract of time, by means seemingly weak, improper, contrary, suitable only for him."[28] There is, then, an indication of the endlessness—yet not the futility—of self-scrutiny: "If a single man were to recount but the more remarkable deceits, with respect to the whole of his behaviour, how many volumes must he write? And if so many be seen, how many secret, undiscernable, or at least undiscerned deceits must still remain? So much truth is there couched in that short scripture, *the heart is deceitful above all things: who can know it?*" (283).

In the prefaces to the autobiographies Wesley edited, especially mean-
ingful is the spiritual regularity that Gregory Lopez and Renty exemplify.
He praises Lopez, for example: "His Life was so uniform, that by one Day
you may judge how he employed whole Months and Years."[29] Similarly,
what appealed to Wesley about Renty's narrative, one of those included
in Wesley's *Works*, was his daily pattern of self-examination: "Every day
before dinner, and again in the evening, he made an exact search into
his smallest faults."[30] Wesley emphasized Renty's capacity to align his
inner and outer selves to present a studied sameness hour after hour, day
after day. Such sameness has a philosophical base; that is, it is an imitation of Christ's pattern, as voiced in Lopez's case: "By this Exercise one
arrives at a State of Uniformity, that is, so strict an Union of our Will
with that of GOD, that our's disappearing, we have no Will but His,
which actuates, guides, and governs us."[31]

Both Renty and Lopez also receive Wesley's praise for their self-
denial. Renty prays for the strength to love God and condemn himself:
"Let us look much upon God; let us bind ourselves strictly to Jesus
Christ, that we may learn of him fully to renounce ourselves. O, my
God, when will it be that we shall eye ourselves no more, when we shall
speak no more of ourselves, and when all vanity shall be destroyed!"[32]
And Lopez also claims a guiding doctrine of self-denial: "I have not pretended to set myself up above any one, or to assume any Authority over
others. . . . And this agonizing after God, is a greater Cross, and an
heavier Self-denial, than any who have not felt it can conceive."[33] Yet
the cost of such constant attention to self had a less salubrious effect on
Renty's "personality": "But the exact and perpetual care he had over
himself, had wholly inverted his nature, and brought him to a behavior,
as well as temper, directly opposite to those he took from his mother's
womb."[34] In other words, though he aimed at self-regulation, it would
seem that its effect was the opposite of what was desired. Thus, though
the purpose of the diary would seem to be to make the self uniform,
oddly, it may embody its tensions. And as a record of self-denial, its purposes become suspect when that self-denial requires constant attention
to the self.

Conversion, to suit Wesley, needed to have a spontaneous quality, an
artlessness that attributes the experience to divine agency and threatens
established conversion patterns. The potential for subversion of these
principles is apparent in Wesley's control of the production of these exemplary autobiographical texts.[35] In fact, as Thomas Jackson's edition of

Lives of the Early Methodist Ministers points out in its preface, "No man received from Mr. Wesley an official sanction as a Preacher who could not give a satisfactory account of his own conversion to the faith of Christ. He who called others to repentance must himself have felt its sorrows,"[36] and many accounts begin with an acknowledgment of Wesley's request. This autocratic control is so extreme that Wesley intervenes in the production of some texts. Wesley tells Alexander Mather, whose account begins with his early conviction of sin at age ten, "that he had wholly omitted one considerable branch of his Experience, touching what is properly termed, *the Great Salvation.*"[37] Mather, in response, describes "an instantaneous deliverance from all those wrong tempers and affections which I had long and sensibly groaned under."[38] And in one account Mather notes that conviction arrived in 1743, in another that it *really* arrived in 1757.

Wesley devoted much of his life to disseminating lives of his contemporaries in the hope of inspiring others to imitate their example. The pattern Wesley favored in the autobiographies that he extracted, recommended, or published mimicked his own conversion. He engaged in an aggressive campaign "to counter the theological propaganda of the *Calvinistic Gospel Magazine*"[39] with alternative lives beginning in 1778, a campaign that continued well after his death until 1811. For Wesley, the *Gospel Magazine,* as well as the *Christian Magazine* and the *Spiritual Magazine,* seriously erred in demonstrating predestination rather than a doctrine of justification by faith: "That God *is* not *loving to every man,* that *his mercy is* not *over all his works:* and consequently, that *Christ did* not *die for all,* but for one in ten, for the Elect only." He wished to argue instead that "*God willeth all men to be saved,* by *speaking the truth in love.*"[40] Consequently, the conversion moment seems less important than the dogged daily attention to the secrets of the heart.

In other Methodist lives, too, the inner and outer split of the autobiographical subject—one side available for public display and evaluation, the other secret, withdrawn, often contradicting external behavior—persists. Thomas Scott, a Methodist preacher who befriended the distraught William Cowper, describes the poignant separation in *The Force of Truth* (1779): "Thus I was somewhat reformed in my outward conduct, but the renewing in the spirit of my mind, if begun, was scarcely discernable."[41] Such a divided self also frequently claims that the interior "self" is the enemy of the exterior. John Haime maintains this double consciousness, a part of him safe on the tiny spot of Mt. Etna, the other part observing his distress as "it split asunder in several places, and sunk into the burning lake, all but that little spot on which I stood."[42] It is this sense of the divided self, of the enemy within, which cannot be fully known that seems to have led Methodist autobiographers to describe a psychological disarray, and Methodism as its cause. For Thomas Scott, for example, the sense of a secret self as something apart is very strong: "I was as one, who had begun to build without counting the cost, and was greatly disturbed when I saw the favourite idol of my proud heart, my character, in such imminent danger."[43] In fact, the way that self-denial competes with the principle of self-examination in Brainerd's diary encourages the despair that brings thoughts of suicide, a phenomenon often narrowly avoided in Methodist autobiographical texts: "And especially I discoursed repeatedly on the nature and necessity of that *humiliation, self-emptiness*, or full conviction of a person's being utterly undone in himself, which is necessary in order to have a saving faith, and the extreme difficulty of being brought to this, and the great danger there is of persons taking up with some *self-righteous appearances* of it. The *danger* of this I especially divert upon, being persuaded that multitudes perish in this hidden way; because so little is said from most pulpits to discover any danger here: so that persons being never effectually brought to die to themselves, are never truly united to Christ."[44] Similarly, William Cowper, convinced that he had committed an unpardonable and unfathomable sin, writes in his private memoirs about his repeated attempts at suicide and his confinement to a madhouse on several occasions.

In most of the Methodist conversion stories that Wesley admired, the self in its doubt becomes an enemy; experienced as divided and antagonistic, the self requires resolution with itself through human agency and human speech. In spite of occasional lip service to Christ as the perfect "pattern," contemporary men more often served as inspiration in these autobiographies. Silas Told's representation of first seeing Charles Wesley is not unlike Boswell's awe at first meeting Samuel Johnson: "Look, my Lord, it comes." Told says, "Exactly at five a whisper was conveyed through the congregation, 'Here he comes! Here he comes!' I was filled with curiosity to see his person which, when I beheld, I much despised. The enemy of souls suggested, that he was some farmer's son, who, not able to support himself, was making a penny in this manner . . . but to my astonishment, he began with singing a hymn, with which I was almost enraptured."[45] Haime's sworn allegiance, then, is to Wesley rather than Christ, to God's human representative as intercessor. Thus the autobiographies also may subvert man's reliance on God in their insistence on human agency.

The subject of these serial autobiographies often claims that her or his experience corresponds to a pattern but that, because of frequent crises, physically felt and dramatically portrayed, the pattern sometimes escapes the consciousness of reader and writer. The agonies of S. Staniforth, for example, are poignantly described: "I thought the very stones in the streets, and the timber in the wall cried out against me for my enormous wickedness."[46] Staniforth's account, beginning in January 1783, comes in installments that leave him on the edge of sin, but always with the hope of permanent conversion. John Haime similarly fluctuates between faith and hopelessness; the installments end with faith, allowing the reader to pause for a month to ponder, knowing more narrative is coming and trusting in God's power to interrupt the despair. The perpetual oscillation makes the reader long for stability for Haime, and for himself. He alternates between claiming "I had no more doubt than if God had called [him] from heaven, and said, 'This is my word, and it shall stand for ever.'" But in the ensuing months his despair becomes more extreme than Bunyan's—by the fire of sin in his bones, he testifies to his astounding ability to preach in spite of the pain: "I sunk into a black despair. I could not open the Bible any where but it condemned me."[47] If Haime never reaches full and permanent resolution of his doubts, he does, nevertheless, believe that God's trials serve a good purpose and that *writing* is the only resolution.

The dramatic crises, partially erased by the religious doctrine that argues for their providential importance, offer codes for interpreting divine signals through the marvelous and spectral incidents. For example, John Haime is startled by the reaction when he throws a stick at God: "Immediately I saw in the clear element, a creature like a Swan, but much larger, part black, part brown. It flew at me, and went just over my head. Then it went about forty yards, lighted on the ground and stood staring at me."[48] The insubstantiality of the subject is to some extent reduced by the religious discourse that implies another authority—an Absolute Master Subject circumscribed within a spiritual framework that offers the soothing reassurance that the daily inconsistencies take on meaning within a larger divine plan.

In fact, it would seem that, even if the act of writing one's experience sometimes serves as a resolution of these discontinuous parts, the constitution of that "one" requires constant revision and renewal. Not uncommonly, the autobiographical narrator reflects on his narrated "self," even revising his narrative within the same text. After telling his conversion tale, Scott writes "Containing Observations on the Foregoing Narrative," as if to suggest that the gradual conversion requires an explanation and a second viewing. Only as a full believer, he declares, can he provide proper *rational* perspective on the unbelieving "I" to describe him in detail, and he concludes with an exhortation to the reader to join him in soul searching. Similarly, Silas Told tells his story twice. When a bricklayer turns him toward God, Told interrupts to retell the early years of his life, this time with spiritual consciousness. In short, in many Methodist ministers' descriptions, the conversion is gradual; the one definitive moment from which the self is permanently transformed is highly suspect; the exterior self observes a secret doubting interior self; and once the conversion is somewhat fixed, the observing self reexamines the story for revision and addenda. Thus, the unstable exterior "self" relies on the authority, however uncertain and inscrutable, of an interior secret "self." In promulgating these lives, Wesley encourages the production and reflection of specific characteristics of a writing subject who scrutinizes himself again and attempts to make that self consistent.

This massive corpus of first-person Methodist narrative constructs ideological and generic filters, through the writing and publication of Wesley's journals, the urging of others to follow suit, and in the wide dissemination of lives as Christian pattern. But that grid sets out unresolved contradictions of competing ideologies of self in the reading and writing subject it hails—contradictions that are mediated through the insistence on a Christian pattern articulated within and against the irregularity of daily lived experience. Such a practice allows for the writing of multiple versions of the self—in diaries, journals, lives, and letters—under the guise of a self that is always the same. It affects to be written only to the self, often in secret, yet it is widely published. It pretends to have no reader, yet the other later "self" reads and revises the text. It seems natural and spontaneous, in insisting that the individual is the source and center of his own meaning, when it gives evidence instead of being highly programmatic. It adopts the language of self-mastery, of being able to know the self and to tell its truths. And it insists that lives—published private lives—follow a common pattern without regard to class or economic status when the accumulation of capital and the possession of land is especially important. In forming a consistent public character for the previously marginal, illiterate, and disenfranchised, in constituting a bourgeois identity, an identity of accumulation of the textual capital of daily lived experience and self-possession for a largely trade and artisan population, Wesley's writings nevertheless empower an upwardly mobile self. This class-identified self serves the interests of emerging capital even as it threatens to subvert the self it "writes." Wesley invokes work discipline, upward mobility, and self-government as indicative of the Methodist subjectivity. In asserting that his prescribed method for living, recording, and regulating identity is guileless, Wesley succeeds in making this method seem to be "natural" to large groups of readers and listeners. He promulgates a middling common sense that, in seeming to be self-evident, disguises the very ideologies of self that operate within it.

CHAPTER FIVE

Manly Subjects

Boswell's Journals and *The Life of Johnson*

Study [to be] like Lord Chesterfield, manly. You're your own master
quite. Accustom yourself not to vent your feelings & never be querulous,
& so resemble Johnson. Study Philosophy & so have mind allways
calm. . . . reserved & polite, a man of letters & taste like Sir David, who
can see Delacour's paintings on a Saturday walk to Abbey, dine at Lord
Somerville's see Digges in Macheath at night & then sit a sober hour at
Thom's with Johnston.
     —James Boswell's memoranda, 2 August 1763

You have told me that I was the most thinking man you ever knew. It is
certainly so as to my own life. I am continually conscious, continually
looking back *or* looking forward *and wondering how I shall feel in*
situations which I anticipate in fancy. My journal *will afford materials*
for a very curious narrative.
     —Boswell to Rev. William Temple, 22 May 1789

I

 James Boswell's journal writing, more overtly self-conscious than John
Wesley's, is bereft of a generic model that would wield sufficient explanatory power to bridge its contradictions. The persistent question posed in
his journals concerns the way we can ascertain "real" identity and, especially in the *Life of Johnson*, how the coherence of public character may
be secured. When the radical instability of "self" erupts in these texts,
Boswell frequently adopts the language of the emergent science of human
nature, psychology, to tame the "self" he perceives as impossibly divided. Public and private become increasingly distinct naturalized categories, their reconciliation available in the elusive "truth" of character.

Boswell emphatically avoids imitating traditional spiritual autobiographies that render the individual moment something beyond itself. We know, however, that he was familiar with texts such as Augustine's *Confessions* and Bunyan's *Grace Abounding* and in fact read conversion narrative at an early age. In the autobiographical sketch he prepared for Rousseau, he notes that his mother spurred his interest in spiritual autobiography: "My mother was of that sect [Calvinism] which believes that to be saved, each individual must experience a strong conversion. She therefore entreated me often to yield to the operations of Divine Grace; and she put in my hands a little book in which I read of the conversions of very young children."[1] But in the main, the conventions of spiritual autobiography—the conviction of sin, the conversion through the Father's revelation and grace, and the postconversion molding of one's life to the image of Christ—do not suit Boswell's notions of reality in the journals.

Rather than assigning the authority for a reformed and unified life to an Absolute Subject, Boswell instead has recourse to classical heroic models taken from epic and drama. Making his reality into secular myth allows him to give significance to the minute details of daily life and invest them with aesthetic value. The heroic and the mythical permit him to retreat from more immediate and inarticulate feelings to generalize them into a supposedly universal paradigm of emotion. For example, one of the generic grids that surfaces in Boswell's consciousness throughout the early journals is the eighteenth-century version of the *Odyssey*, Fénelon's *Télémaque*, a tale popular during the eighteenth century for its dual themes of moral education and the search for the father.[2] One generation educates another as Telemachus takes on a series of adoptive mentors who substitute for his absent father. Similarly, Boswell's seeing *Henry IV, Part II* at Drury Lane lends dignity and epic proportion to his own struggle to usurp his father's place, his fear of incurring his father's displeasure, and his reconciliation to him. And his association of the ghost of Hamlet's father with Samuel Johnson is well-known. On 16 May 1763, Mr. Davies, actor and bookseller, "announced his aweful approach to me, somewhat in the manner of an actor in the part of Horatio, when he addresses Hamlet on the appearance of his father's ghost, 'Look, my Lord, it comes.'"[3] In these and other instances, Boswell transforms literary analogues into familiar ideological filters that are applicable to his daily existence. Boswell, then, retreats into the category of the aesthetic—though sporadically and inconsistently—to make "meaning" from the daily jottings.

In fact, however, he more often radically departs from the assumptions that govern spiritual autobiographies or classical texts. More than once, Boswell speaks explicitly of the stark differences between spiritual and secular constructions of events: "As I passed through a wood before I entered Potsdam, a branch struck my eye and hurt me a good deal. It made me think on the risk I had run of losing the half of one of my senses. I had time in the dark silence of night to ruminate on the great question concerning Providence. Should I now have said that Providence preserved my eye? But, I pray you, why did Providence permit the branch to strike me? Oh, that was a natural event. Very well, and the degree of force was natural too; so that very naturally I have not lost my right eye. For shame divines, how dare you bring in Providence on every trifling occasion? . . . Yes, the universal eye perceives everything in the universe. But surely, the grand and extensive system employs the attention of God, and the minutiae are not to be considered as part of his care; at least, we are not to presume that he interests himself in every little accident."[4] This attention to minutiae substitutes for a providential pattern: man attends to the minute, God to the universal. But the difficulty in naming experience and in locating meaning without applying the conventional paradigms persists. Meaning in Boswell's journals is constituted in vigilant attention to minute particulars, yet the experience of the present requires a perpetual reassessment and abridgment of the "essence" of experience, as well as revisioning personal history in order to make it consistent with the present or to locate its difference.

Like Bunyan and Wesley, Boswell wrote and rewrote his life in a variety of forms, ultimately revising large portions of his notes and journals into the *Life of Johnson*. Boswell's autobiographical writings reflect his commitment to translating experience into memoranda, rough notes, journals, "inviolable plan," French themes, Dutch themes, letters, and published writings. Certainly Boswell is among the first journalists to conceptualize the act of writing a diary and the formation of identity within it so that it cannot be regarded simply as a natural act; for him, diary writing requires an explanation. By the latter half of the eighteenth century, diary writing was perceived by some to reach a pinnacle of popularity as a private activity, and its publication was very much a subject for debate. Though he seldom cites other diarists as models, Boswell knows the tradition of journal keeping, an activity he believes to be a bit outmoded and old-fashioned, and he signals his recognition of that tradition in his *Hypochondriack* paper for March 1783: "A diary, therefore, which was much more common in the last age than in this, may be of valuable use to the person who writes it . . . and yet if brought forth to the pub-lick eye may expose him to contempt."[5] Throughout his writings, Bos-well self-consciously comments on the ideologies of genre that govern his writing.

Boswell frequently remarks in his journals on the frustrations involved in compressing life into text. "But it is a work of very great labour and difficulty to keep a journal of life," he continues in *Hypochondriack* 66, "occupied in various pursuits, mingled with concomitant speculations and reflections, in so much, that I do not think it possible to do it unless one has a peculiar talent for abridging. I have tried it in that way, when it has been my good fortune to live in a multiplicity of instructive and entertaining scenes, and I have thought my notes like portable soup, of which a little bit by being dissolved in water will make a good large dish; for their substance by being expanded in words would fill a volume. Sometimes it has occurred to me that a man should not live more than he can record, as a farmer should not have a larger crop than he can gather in. And I have regretted that there is no invention for getting an immediate and exact transcript of the mind, like that instrument by which a copy of a letter is at once taken off" (332). Boswell would seem to wish that language could be a complete and transparent representation of reality, and he is troubled by the distortion introduced in distilling it to text. Either life or text must be reduced. In the pages that follow, I want to consider the production of this autobiographical subject of dis-crete minute particulars in Boswell's journals and in the *Life of Johnson*, and then turn more specifically to address the political uses of the class and gender identifications of such a subject.

II

Boswell's various representations of his reality reflect linguistic and cultural confusions about ideologies of self. For example, in the later eighteenth century the notion of the ruling passion (or other versions of an essential self) competes with an equally dominant one that identity is perpetually in flux. The genre of the Theophrastan character displays some of these tensions. The attempt to conceptualize "character" and to articulate its boundaries was familiar to the eighteenth-century reader through the many editions of Theophrastus, specifically in its seven-teenth- and eighteenth-century modulations by Joseph Hall, Sir Thomas Overbury, and John Earle. This sort of character was understood to be a literary genre of its own, and it was imagined to capture the crux of a particular type of human being. In his recent history of the genre, J. W. Smeed faults La Bruyère in *Les Caractères* (1688) for his failure to make his characters coherent, unified, and consistent "by over-charging his portraits with many ridiculous features that cannot exist together in one subject."[6] Smeed adopts uncritically the language and assumptions of eighteenth-century commentators such as Henry Gally, translator of Theophrastus in 1725 who, in a prefatory "Essay on Characteristick Writings," says each trait and detail must derive from and be expressive of a whole and unified personality.[7] This insistence on the importance of innate characteristics and the unity of personality sets itself in marked contrast with the competing idea that education and experience are most formative of "character." When the grid of the Theophrastan character is laid over the lived experience of real men and women of the eighteenth century, the paradigm of the fully intelligible and nicely rounded identity that it depends upon breaks down.

The Theophrastan characters illustrate typical traits of the human species, but they are also supposed to simulate real individuals. In the eighteenth century, "character" and "identity" came to mean both a constant human nature and an individual principle, the ways in which we are the same and unlike others in our species. Personal identity implies permanence and sameness over time, a persistence in being throughout its narrative presence in spite of the changes that it tolerates or excites.[8] "Character" in these renderings is imagined to be a public construction, the material evidence of a private interior reality that reflects an individual's essence. But the Theophrastan character declines in mid-century, and this loss of the character as a model occurs at the same moment that the newly emergent genres of autobiographical writing and the novel freshly engage the question of its representation. Thus, the crisis of "character" in eighteenth-century England surfaces in part as a struggle to debate the meanings of the word and its public manifestations.

Boswell's journals of the 1760s and beyond, in contrast with the character genre, repeatedly articulate the notion that identity may be continually revised and remade. The journals register the fluctuating state of his mind, and Boswell is aware that he, as the writer and reader of the journal, may reshape that serial identity: "I wished to contain a consistent picture of a young fellow eagerly pushing through life," but he wavers in his conviction that an essential core of character exists.[9] By his own account, having turned away from being a "dissipated, inconstant fellow," he defines his "real character" instead as that of "a reserved, grave sort of man" (*London Journal*, 258). The journal form tolerates this dissonance without requiring that the "self" fit into an easily deciphered and systematically organized whole, except in the consciousness of the narrator.

The Boswell of the *London Journal* in 1762 takes care to distinguish himself at the outset from the dissolute youth who roamed the streets of London in 1760. He characterizes that first visit as "a wild expedition," whereas in 1762 he has "begun to acquire a composed genteel character very different from a rattling uncultivated one which for some time past I have been fond of" (*London Journal*, 61, 47). During his first fortnight in London, he tries to correct his image with Lord Eglinton, the rakish man of whom Boswell was extremely fond: "He imagined me much in the style that I was three years ago: raw, curious, volatile, credulous. He little knew the experience I had got and the notions and the composure that I had obtained by reflection. 'My Lord,' said I, 'I am now a little wiser.' 'Not so much as you think,' said he" (*London Journal*, 52). To *be* the person he was during that earlier period, Boswell confides, was a conscious act of construction of which he was the free and autonomous agent. Because identity is a state of mind and sensation, it simply requires, he believes, willfully possessing himself of the ideas he had at a previous time to produce a different character: "I had just the same sensations as when a boy at Culross and Valleyfield. I find it is no impossible matter to be just what one has formerly been. It is no more than having the mind filled with the same ideas" (*Grand Tour*, 116). At times, then, Boswell considers "character" to be a state of consciousness which can be conjured up at a moment's notice, and as a public production modulated through careful regulation of the minutest private details.

Another apparently competing assumption Boswell articulates in the journals is that public character, freely and individually produced, is reflective of an essential and natural "self." In an essay in the *London Magazine*, he indicates his belief that we have "real" character and "real" feelings that are often at odds with social requirements, so that "he [Boswell] can hardly recollect a scene of social life, where he has not been conscious more or less of having been obliged to work himself into a state of feeling, which he would not naturally have had."[10] Here Boswell seems to subscribe to the belief that character is a given, and that acting simply disguises it. What, Boswell asks in "On the Profession of a Player," makes one a good actor? The best player "'*lives* o'er each scene,' and, in a

certain sense 'is what we behold,'" yet Boswell retreats from the radical implication that identity would be lost in the process. He writes that
"a player is the character he represents only *in a certain degree*. An actor, then, maintains "a kind of double feeling" ("Player," 469), possessing himself of the character while he remains conscious of his own in
"real life."

But elsewhere the constancy of the individual appears less sure. In his
journal for 3 January 1776 Boswell finds both permanency and constant
change in the idea of identity: "Man's continuation of existence is a flux
of ideas in the same body, like the flux of a river in the same channel.
Even our bodies are perpetually changing . . . what then of love or hatred when we are to contemplate a character? There *must* be *something*,
which we understand by a *spirit* or a *soul*, which is permanent. And yet I
must own that except the sense or perception of identity, I cannot say
that there is any sameness in my soul now and my soul twenty years ago,
or surely none thirty years ago."[11] In the essay on acting, he vacillates
similarly between the assertion that most men possess a character and the
fear that assuming "a borrowed, fictitious, or external character, is apt to
make a man have no character of his own, except he have an uncommon
degree of firmness" ("Player," 470). Yet he allows for the possibility that
characterless men exist, "for there have been illustrious men, and perhaps our own age can find such, who had no character of their own, but
have actually been translated into various characters according to times
and circumstances" ("Player," 470) and he cites Hume's notion that man
is "nothing but a bundle of perceptions" ("Player," 470) with approval.
For Boswell, then, character is a public display of consistency, a consistency confirmed by others. Thus, the struggles among various "selves"
and between private and public representations of self dramatize the
shifting planes of discourse about the self, and the journal form allows for
gaps in the positioning of the individual in spite of Boswell's putting in
place a "free" subject who can become a public commodity.

In both life and text, public and private identity become increasingly
distinct categories for Boswell, their reconciliation available in the
"truth" of character, and any breach in the seamlessness of public character may be explained as an aberration. In contrast with the assertion of
public character, Boswell constitutes the "self" as secret, yet poised on
the troubled boundary between private and public. Boswell guarded his
journals from discovery, and he even attempted to write in cipher: "The
chief objection against keeping a diary fairly registered which [records?]

the state of our minds, and all the little occurrences by which we are intimately affected, is the danger of its falling into the hands of other people, who may make use of it to our prejudice" (*Hypochondriack*, 333). Boswell insists that the minutiae of his daily life should remain secret, and he particularly fears that his father may read the journal: "Were many people to read this leaf of my journal, they would hold me in great contempt as a very trifling fellow" (*Hypochondriack*, 129). As private texts, the journals relegate the contradictions of self out of sight. Aware of the particular historical moment that makes the *publication* of the private self possible, and even paradoxically tempting, he produces a private "self" to record. Only the select few, privileged enough to perceive the minuteness of subjectivity, ought to read such private thoughts: "Yet if brought forth to the publick eye [they] may expose him [the diarist] to contempt, unless in the estimation of the few who think much and minutely, and therefore know well of what little parts the principal extent of human existence is composed" (*Hypochondriack*, 331). "Self," then, splits between what may be surveyed and what must be hidden from view. In short, in the early memoranda and journals, Boswell attempts to confine his various public and private subject positions to two, the public as a construct, and the private as an essential core that may secretly change.

In addition to his reflections on journals and diaries, it is in Boswell's memoranda, written collaterally with the early journals, that these antagonisms between private and public are most distinctly represented. The extant memoranda begin with his London journey (1762), the Holland journal having been lost, and they are the primary material extant for 1763–64. As a substitute for prayerful self-examination, Boswell wrote the memoranda upon arising before he left his quarters, omitting them a few days each month when, apparently, his morning routine was disrupted. He jotted down memoranda (themselves written up from the earlier rough notes) as documents never intended for transcription or publication in which he adjusts his "self" to itself.[12]

These memoranda, a subaltern category of writing, name the two selves. The consistent public character fashioned in private text becomes the *retenu* or constrained, and a more disoriented interior being, the *étourdi*, or uncontrolled. When he is *retenu*, Boswell reins himself in, holding himself to consistency. But he considers being *étourdi*—dizzy, disconcerted, scatter-brained—to be his more "natural" self: "I had a free air and spoke well, and when Monsieur Rousseau said what touched me more than ordinary, I seized his hand, I thumped him on the shoulder. I was without restraint" (*Grand Tour*, 222). In these second-person singular narrations, Boswell invents a public character that is unified, an Other that is *retenu* in the extreme who acts as unquestioned authoritative master of the *étourdi*. This second-person narration, written in the imperative mode, removes itself completely from the narrative of the classic realist text.

Roland Barthes has called the second-person address "the creator's address to the creature, named, constituted, *created* in all his acts by a judge and progenitor."[13] In Boswell's second-person address, the private self is imagined as dangerous and unwieldy, and the *retenu* fastens down the *étourdi*: "Write lines soon. Have a care or you'll alter. Have a care." And "Be firm. Be manly, silent." Or "Beware. this day, labour. Swear *retenue* and manners, and seek not ease by talking; it gives it not. Try silence one week." In addition, the drinking, joking, and mimicry of the *étourdi* self must be squelched: "Return to Brown's. resume and improve; don't joke."[14] The second-person narrator apparently takes pleasure in disciplining and even policing itself. Even his own inviolable plan for behavior requires regular rereading to regulate his behavior and to confirm his identity by repetition. In constructing this consciousness under surveillance, Boswell fully enacts a technology of self in its most private manifestations.

A daily exercise in self-rectification, the memoranda become most dogmatic during the period when Boswell followed his father's directive to study for the law in Holland. The functions of the memoranda change, and the regularity of the Holland memoranda is never again duplicated.[15] By 1766 he shifts away from rigorous self-examination and its clearly delineated master-servant voices in the memoranda toward more representation of events in the approaching day. In fact, after 1769 the memoranda largely disappear, their place usurped by rough notes that later evolve into parts of the journals. That is, they shift from doing work as self-scrutiny to aiding a journalist in his task. The notes become apprentice work for the day's journal entry, and Boswell destroys them when he revises them. These memoranda, then, help produce the divided subject of the journals as Boswell's "real self," but a crucial part of what is at stake in his formulation is whether the public construction of character or the radically unstable private sensibility reveals the "truth" of identity. In sum, producing an apparently seamless public character in the later eighteenth century assumes and even requires elaborate private articulation and self-regulation.

❧ III

I want to focus more specifically now on the political functions of the conflicting notions of character operating in Boswell's journals. This is not to attempt to discern Boswell's particular psychology, but rather to unmask the way divergent ideologies of gender and class circulate in the service of a rational bourgeois "self" in these texts. For Boswell, character, clearly gendered male, is especially the possession of those of high rank during the later eighteenth century, when the greatly skewed distribution of wealth produced an increasing inequality among classes and exacerbated various tensions in the social formation. In his private journal writings, Boswell reveals his own class-consciousness at the same time that he delights in subverting public expectations of class. Adjusting his character through contact with others, he even requests from his servant a written character that will fix him in the superior position: "I said I hoped that I had been a good master. To know this certainly, I ordered him to write out a full character of me, since he entered to my service, and charged him to mark equally the bad and the good which he had observed, and to give it me carefully sealed up" (Holland, 290–91). The servant, writing ungrammatically, seems quite abashed at the request but forges ahead by remarking on Boswell's negligence in leaving personal effects about, and the ill effects of his studious habits and late hours on his health; but he also praises him for his good heart, punctuality, and kindness. His character as a benevolent master is validated textually.

Boswell, though born into a wealthy and well-connected family, slides up and down the social scale, by mimicking the class identities of the middle and the lower classes. For example, he tells of an evening spent as a member of the middle class: "I sat awhile with Lord Ankerville and awhile with Tom Davies; then dined at Dance's. My old acquaintance his mother, Mrs. Love; his wife (a pleasing girl of Lymington); and Miss Reynold, a teacher of music from Oxford, all contributed to entertain me. I had a deliberate enjoyment of that species of life which the middle ranks have in London" (London Journal, 108). Boswell toys with the idea of assuming the class-specific characters of people ranging from the Laird of Auchinleck to the lowest blackguard who roams London in search of prostitutes; but his "character" may be preserved in spite of his provisionally assuming the position of the lower classes. Though he drinks and whores, Boswell imagines himself as having, at bottom, a gentlemanly character that persistently makes itself felt. Particularly telling is his evening as a blackguard when he dressed in his "second-mourning suit, in which I had been powdered many months, dirty buckskin breeches and black stockings, a shirt of Lord Eglinton's which I had worn two days, and little round hat with tarnished silver lace." He finds a woman, identifies himself as a barber, and attempts to rape a second, more reluctant, streetwalker. "I was much stronger than her, and *volens nolens* pushed her up against the wall. She however gave a sudden spring from me; and screaming out, a parcel of more whores and soldiers came to her relief" (*London Journal*, 272–73). Boswell wins them to his side before he seeks yet another woman. The evening is a success, however, in his terms, for "notwithstanding of my dress, I was always taken for a gentleman in disguise." Because he is recognized as a gentleman, public character and its production take precedence over any private confusions about rank.

In addition to fixing "self" according to class identification, in Boswell's journals, much more than in Bunyan's or Wesley's work, "real" identity rests on sexual identity. Women not only destroy male identity but they also, through sexual license, confuse traditional class and gender hierarchies. Though largely excluded from accumulating or possessing goods, women may displace aristocratic values. Establishing legitimacy is, of course, important in securing an uninterrupted lineage. Woman's character, according to Boswell, rests solely on virtue: "I shall judge of her character from it. I shall see if she is abandoned or virtuous, I mean both in a degree,"[16] while men's character, as we have seen, involves more subtle and complex connections.

Boswell's intrigues with women sometimes interrupt class restrictions; he considers marrying a gardener's daughter, only to escape this liaison when he later regards her more dispassionately: "I am totally emancipated . . . from the gardener's daughter, who now puts on my fire and empties my chamber-pot like any other wench" (*Search*, 50). Similarly, Temple confides his passion for a servant girl to Boswell. Together the two gentlemen display an extravagant attention to the conduct of sexual activity across class boundaries in these secret exchanges. In other words, the journals function to build homoerotic bonds between friends through mutual confession of their lack of sexual self-regulation.

Producing character also requires reproducing heterosexual difference.

Though manliness may mean simply the possession of the human, in Boswell's journals it also connotes a courageous and moral masculinity that differs significantly from female fickleness. Reflection for a woman in a glass or in a journal relates to vanity, fashion, and outer adornment, while for a man it means self-scrutiny. He writes, "'And,' said I, 'as a lady adjusts her dress at a glass, a man adjusts his character by looking at it'" (*London Journal*, 230). Repeatedly in the journals Boswell represents women as laying bare the contradictions in men's public character and thus threatening masculine identity. In particular, Boswell fears that if his mind is emasculated, his private *étourdi* self will surface. He thinks of the male self as disoriented and powerless when confronted with his fantasies of specific women as whores or angels. He imagines his firm manly mind, quite unlike the more changeable female sensibility, as a solid house where lodgers come and go: "Now my mind is a house where, though the street rooms and the upper floors are open to strangers, yet there is always a settled family in the back parlour and sleeping-closet behind it; and this family can judge of the ideas which come to lodge. This family! this landlord, let me say, or this landlady, as the mind and the soul are both she. I shall confuse myself with metaphor" (*Search*, 138). The family, the fixed portion of self, reincarnates itself as a landlord and then a landlady. But once the female is introduced into the metaphor, his logic, he confesses, becomes unhinged. Boswell cannot bring the gendered metaphor to a satisfactory conclusion, for women, making him fickle, unsettle his capacity to signify: they feminize him in the sense of making him susceptible to the worst female characteristics.

In addition, Boswell's journals teem with many liaisons with prostitutes, actresses, and potential wives including Louisa (Mrs. Lewis), Thérèse de le Vasseur, Belle de Zuylen, and Mary Caroline Rudd. When Boswell engages in multiple intrigues at one time, the ensuing complications sometimes interfere with his self-definition. From the perspective of the male gaze, Boswell speaks of the dissonance between parental responsibility and his various sexual adventures: "I was shocked that the father of a family should go amongst strumpets; but there was rather an insensibility about me to virtue, I was so sensual."[17] When he has simultaneous liaisons with three women, distinguished according to class, what troubles him is that the incongruities they call forth in his identity may expose his sexual secrets. How is it possible, he asks himself, for the noted author of the *Account of Corsica* to be "the sport of a frivolous passion" (*Search*, 137). How can his public and private notions of self be at such variance, he asks himself: "Is it really true that a man of such variety of genius . . . is it possible that he was all last winter the slave of a woman without one elegant quality?" (*Search*, 44). His character, he worries, is at risk: "If she does not write to me she is certainly unfeeling, and I must at any price preserve my own character" (*Search*, 104).

With other women, Boswell's sexual exploits betray his attempt to find the perfect "woman" who will authenticate his manliness. In his liaison with "Louisa," the actress from whom he contracted venereal disease, he measures his character against hers to reassert masculine authority: "Indeed, in my mind, there cannot be higher felicity on earth enjoyed by man than the participation of genuine reciprocal amorous affection with an amiable woman. There he has a full indulgence of all the delicate feelings and pleasures both of body and mind, while at the same time in this enchanting union he exults with a consciousness that he is the superior person. The dignity of his sex is kept up" (*London Journal*, 84). When a friend remarks that Zélide possesses learning and wit, but not good sense, Boswell gleefully agrees. Denigrating her judgment becomes a matter of finding a sexual politics that will allow him to reign supreme over her: "I thought it very true, and I thought it was a good thing. For if it were not for that lack, Zélide would have an absolute power. She would have unlimited dominion over men, and would overthrow the dignity of the male sex" (*Holland*, 230). In fact, in the journals sexual activity with women other than his wife induces the dangerous but familiar state of *étourdi*: "Mem. Johnson. Think. Maintain character gained at Utrecht, nor ever rave. Mem. Father. If you whore, all ideas change" (*Holland*, 231). Clearly male "character" rests precariously on the power to maintain dominance over women. Women can unman him, and they may easily overturn the resolve of his private memoranda.

Among the women who most threatened Boswell by stealing away his stable masculine identity was Mrs. Rudd, a convicted bigamist who forged promissory notes and used her sexual wiles against wealthy men. When tried after her supposed husband and accomplice Daniel Perreau was sentenced to be hanged, she charmed the jury, became a popular heroine, and was acquitted:[18] "I told her I was convinced she could enchant, but I begged she would not enchant me too much, not change me into any other creature, but allow me to continue to be a man with some degree of reason" (*Ominous Years*, 358). Boswell grants Mrs. Rudd the power to metamorphose him so that his identity gives way to brute animality: "You could make me commit murder. [But] you would be sorry afterwards to have made so ungenerous a use of your power. You have no occasion to be convinced of your power over the human heart. You know it. I dare say you could make me do anything—make me commit murder" (*Ominous Years*, 351). Women such as Mrs. Rudd may destroy man's independent identity, and his carefully cultivated public character, through sexual power.

In Boswell's writings, there is also considerable association between women, especially from the lower class, and the savage, for both represent all that is uncivilized. The "black" lower-class women entice him to un-European behavior. His friend and adviser Temple warns him, "Now you, who think it possible for the God of nature to have a son whose blood alone can appease him for the crime a created being committed in eating an apple, do not flatter yourself that such a propitiation will atone for sins against the laws of our country and against mankind. In the vast continent of Ethiopia, where according to Diodorus men yet live in a state of nature, chastity and fidelity are not virtues, for women and children are there in common; but in our polished Europe, where we have sacrificed many of our natural rights to the peaceable enjoyment of our persons and properties, the laws of our country are our religion, and can hardly ever be violated without impiety" (*Search*, 48). Here the "savage" is equated with the female. Temple explicitly states that making women and children into property and into the vehicles for "civilized" transmission of values, allows men to attain superiority over the "savage." While some people of both sexes and all nations have "no character of [their] own on which we can depend" because of their fickle nature, the English "are truly a nation of originals, and are universally allowed to be remarkably honest" ("Player," 470). To be low class is also to be a *black*guard: "Guard against liking billiards," Boswell writes in a memorandum. "They are blackguard, and you'll have high character with Count Nassau, &c., if you don't play. Be easy and natural, though a little proud. Write out full mem. that this is your winter to get rid of spleen and become a man" (*Holland*, 22). Boswell employs the word "blackguard" loosely to mean a vagabond or scoundrel, its racial overtones obscured within its strong class designation. But in addition to its traditional application to the lowest servant of the household responsible for scrubbing pots and pans, "blackguard" also originally referred to Arab errand boys, marked as lowly by the nature of their labor as well as their origin. Real character, then, may only be achieved by male Europeans who recognize the significance of property values, and the functions that females serve within that legal and economic framework. Conventional class and gender categories, destabilized in Boswell's journals, forward the character of a manly British subject who, unlike Bunyan or Wesley, defines himself largely through sexual difference, as well as superiority to women, the lower classes, and the "savage."

In short, Boswell's journals are not a solution to the problem of forming a consistent public character that masters itself, but an indication of the exclusions necessary to produce it. The ideological gaps among conflicting notions of character, and the subject positions Boswell inhabits, make change possible but, held within the private domain, they disappear when brought to the public sphere in the unified subject. But instead of publishing his journals as such (risking full exposure of the private étourdi), Boswell incorporates the most palatable portions into biography to make something coherent of lived experience. In dealing with the life of another, he can adopt an authoritative narrative position that makes intelligible every minute particular of that human life. It is a task that he reclaims as a manly and a gentlemanly one when he restricts that narrative authority, like character, within certain class and gender boundaries. In *The Life of Johnson* Boswell figures Johnson as a universal model of self-mastery, an urban manly gentleman of letters and taste who has escaped his lesser origins to forge a consistent identity. In the *Life* Boswell produces an illusion of a shared set of values in which his friendship for Johnson, like Johnson's own powerful intellect and strongly held Christian beliefs, serves to obviate all exceptions to the general rule.

ᘓ IV

In turning his journals into biography in 1791, Boswell, unlike other eighteenth-century autobiographers, constructs a compelling narrative that displays the contradictions of identity within a vision of a coherent and fully comprehensible character. *The Life of Johnson* effects a tentative resolution to the problems of identity we have encountered in Boswell's memoranda and journals by wedding Johnson's private and public selves within it. When *The Life of Johnson* was first published, many readers praised the finished quality of the biography. This was in spite of the fact that the *Life* was also recognized to be a hybrid genre, a collection of multiple modes of representation including the *disjecta membra* (the extremities severed from the body) of school exercises, letters, diaries, and parliamentary debates (*Life* 1:109). For example, the *Monthly Review*, though criticizing the biography for its topicality, found it to be particularly well-formed: "In its present shape, Boswell's Life [sic] may be considered as one of the most complete and interesting publications in our language."[19] Another reviewer remarked on the conclusive sense of a great man that the biography produced for the reader: "His work exhibits the most copious, interesting, and finished picture of the life and opinions of an eminent man, that was ever executed."[20] In other words, these and other early reviewers may have been less rigid than the more recent readers have proved to be in trying to fit the Life into generic categories. John Wilson Crocker's 1831 edition praised the work for its combination of the "four most entertaining classes of writing—biography, memoirs, familiar letters, and that assemblage of literary anecdotes which the French have taught us to distinguish by the termination Ana."[21] The Life's most recent detractors have repeatedly criticized its excess detail, its unnecessary inclusion of Johnson's legal opinions, its unequal attention to the early and later periods of his life, and its failure of narrative line.[22] Yet the extraordinary power of the text to convey the character of Johnson derived from its hybrid nature, its intertwining of Boswell's autobiographical memoranda, rough notes, and journals, as well as Johnson's letters, diaries, and conversation, according to eighteenth- and nineteenth-century readers. Its heterogeneity could always be explained in the convincing unity of Johnson's personality.

One of the difficulties in reading The Life of Johnson that has set recent criticism on a circular course is the persistent opposition between truth and art; but the argument over whether the Life is fiction or biography is completely exhausted and ought to be abandoned.[23] Certainly formalism was itself a reaction to a naive historicism that wanted to attribute a simple referentiality to texts. But rather than escaping to formalism with its self-enclosed texts that may be read without access to history or the material conditions of production, the emphasis is better placed on the complexities of the relationship between fact and representation, and the seductive power of the ideology of genre that molds it. The question as to whether the Life is true—that is, whether it offers an accurate picture of Samuel Johnson—is indeed the question Boswell posed (and urged readers to answer affirmatively) in his insistence that he had run over half of London in search of the facts. But an alternative way of regarding the text is to ask what ideological positions the reader of the Life has to occupy in order to assign coherent structures of meaning to a human life. The argument is advanced here to open texts to expose the struggles for power over the forces that will define the class and gender of character at particular moments of history. This mode of regarding autobiographical and biographical writing, then, intervenes in the assumed generic codes to mark the way that the dichotomy between truth and art is a historically bound division.

In the later eighteenth century, journal writing provides a new discursive model for biography, one that incorporates the fully displayed and conflictual private life as explanation for the public man. Among the patterns that Boswell transfers from his journals to the *Life* are its chronological order and its arrangement according to Johnson's age (the constant visual reminder at the top of the page—*Aetat*), and the promise to reveal Johnson's interiority in the absence of his own autobiographical account, an emphasis that succeeds in establishing the reader's sense of his divided and contradictory "self." Boswell justifies including the "innumerable detached particulars" as relevant because they all "relate to a distinguished man" (*Life* 1:33); it is the unified individual verified by the omniscient Boswell that gives the details relevance. Similarly, Johnson's productions are defended for their relatedness, his *Adversaria* as an example of the fertility of his mind (1:205) and all 208 numbers of the *Rambler* as "one uniform vivid texture" (1:217). A human life and consciousness are, then, sufficient justification for yoking together the "strange succession" of contradictory qualities (4:426) and the "strangely mixed scenes of human existence" (1:10). The ideology that each individual personality participates in the larger community binds the puzzles of Johnson's identity together through his "inflexible dignity of character" (1:131); his spheres of outer and inner life are sharply distinguished only to be erased in the substitute emphasis on his morality, faith, and commitment to Truth.[24] The point, for Boswell, is to make Johnson exemplify the Christian and classical humanism that would allow all readers to associate themselves with his struggles and to place themselves within those timeless values in order to participate in the aesthetic.

The Johnson presented in the *Life* personifies the humanistic belief in the sameness that makes him like all other human beings, the difference that guarantees his individuation. The *Life* provides the illusion that anyone, regardless of class or gender, may imitate Johnson's character to share in the plenitude of being a fully comprehensible biographical subject. The *Life*, then, pressures the reader to respond to her or his incorporation within the existing social formation, and yet to believe she or he is free to draw conclusions about Johnson's character. Readers, located in history in various acts and moments of reception, participate in the production of the text as well. A biography is always narrated; Samuel Johnson, as Marshall Waingrow has reminded us, "will always be somebody's hypothesis," and, I would add, that hypothesis is always the product of specific historical and political constructions.[25] In the *Life*, Boswell repeatedly uses the metaphor of the reader as jury who will have to judge which of the contradictions in Johnson is to be granted priority as he defends a man who has been much maligned. Boswell acknowledges and places in the foreground these contradictions, even granting his reader the possibility that "at different times, he seemed a different man," though not in any *essential* way (4:426). Boswell's success in the *Life* with many eighteenth-century as well as twentieth-century readers is in no small part due to the text's prodding the reader to *contend* with the anomalies in order to resist letting them dominate as the lasting impression.

Boswell's *Life* assures readers of their own essential human qualities as they are positioned to make something intelligible of Johnson's private interior life within his public character, a private life that finally does not paralyze him with doubts. The *Life*, then, takes the risk that the reader will "discover" himself in the biography and respond to his incorporation into existing social relations, and yet believe he is free to draw his own "original" conclusions. Among the characteristics of the young Johnson given full play are an "unsettled turn of mind" (1:49) and "that aversion to regular life" (1:63). Though Johnson's contradictions are made his most dominant characteristic, the reader learns to admire them as an indication of his complexity and genius. In the most "difficult and dangerous part" (4:398) of his task, Boswell concludes the *Life* with a "character" of Johnson which he produces under some duress: "The character of Samuel Johnson has, I trust, been so developed in the course of this work, that they who have honoured it with a perusal, may be considered as well acquainted with him. As, however, it may be expected that I should collect into one view the capital and distinguishing features of this extraordinary man, I shall endeavour to acquit myself of that part of my biographical undertaking, however difficult it may be to do that which many of my readers will do better for themselves" (4:424–25). As he has done throughout the *Life*, Boswell here contrasts Johnson's strong Christian faith with his independent spirit; his temper with his benevolence; his powerful intellect with his tendency toward melancholy in the concluding character. Because his contradictions are explicable and their insertion into the public naturalized, Johnson somehow becomes the

locus of stable meaning, himself the personification of "truth," the embodiment of an authoritative, moral, and Christian omniscient presence
on earth, the secular Absolute Subject. The character and the *Life* end
with an implied reference to his singular narrative authority as the authentic biographer of Johnson: "From a spirit of contradiction and a delight in shewing his powers, he would often maintain the wrong side with
equal warmth and ingenuity; so that, when there was an audience, his
real opinions could seldom be gathered from his talk; though when he
was in company with a single friend, he would discuss a subject with
genuine fairness: but he was too conscientious to make error permanent
and pernicious" (4:429). Yet the anecdotes mentioned in the early pages
of the *Life* were forwarded as "characteristical" of Samuel Johnson, as if
his essence, in spite of the contradictions, was fully recoverable. The
Life, then, turns the contested terrain of tangled subjectivity into a comprehensible and absorbable character. In short, Boswell acknowledges
the affinity between a deceptively classless and genderless position from
which to read the *Life* and Johnson's character to construct a coherent
narrative of the public man that elides his inconsistencies.

Boswell situated the publication of *The Life of Johnson* within the context of competing lives, Hester Thrale Piozzi's *Anecdotes of the Late Samuel Johnson* (1786) and Sir John Hawkins's "official" *Life of Dr. Johnson*
(1787). Boswell's corrections to Thrale and Hawkins in the introductory
and concluding sections of the *Life* carefully reweave the connective
tissue of Johnson's character that these other versions threatened to tear
apart. He chides Hawkins for including (in contrast with his own life)
irrelevant and inaccurate data. His tactic for refuting Hawkins is, in large
part, to dismiss his work for its "dark uncharitable cast" (1:28). Hawkins
is held accountable for his hints of Johnson's arrogance and temper, his
allusions to mad melancholy, and his "misreadings" of Johnson's sexuality as uncontrolled. Boswell insists that Johnson's melancholy is an inherited malady, "a defect in his nervous system" that does not disturb the
entirety of Johnson's mind. Unlike madness, "a disorder by which the
judgement itself is impaired," melancholy "affects only the imagination
and spirits, while the judgement is sound" (1:65–67). To argue otherwise would be to admit the inexplicable into Johnson's character and
might subvert Boswell's claims to its ultimate unity.

But Boswell unleashes his greatest textual fury on Hester Thrale. Her
work provides the "slighter aspersions" (1:28), but she is condemned for
showing Johnson as "extremely deficient in affection, tenderness, or

even common civility" (4:346). She displays the private interiority that could give the lie to Boswell's version of Johnson's public character, and he reasserts masculine narrative authority over the minute particulars. From the first, Boswell wishes to distinguish his work from a mere compilation of anecdotes that by some accounts is perceived to be a feminized mode in the later eighteenth century. One could read *The Life of Johnson* in order to prove Boswell's or Johnson's misogyny, or to determine whether Hawkins or Thrale wrote the more accurate account of Samuel Johnson. Thrale's *Anecdotes*, for example, are often regarded in psychological terms as her vengeance for Johnson's unwillingness to accept her marriage to Piozzi, a sign perhaps of his sexual jealousy. But it is worth considering what political effects beyond the personal and idiosyncratic we can assign to Boswell's vendettas against Thrale in the *Life*, and what they can tell us about gendered relations at the end of the eighteenth century.

A crucial part of Boswell's version of Johnson's "real" character must lie in his unequivocal manliness in the face of the assault on it by Hester Thrale, a writing woman who dares to print her intimate knowledge and who attempts to usurp male authority regarding the *truth* of Johnson's character in her *Anecdotes*: "As a sincere friend of the great man whose *Life* I am writing, I think it necessary to guard my readers against the mistaken notion of Dr. Johnson's character, which this lady's 'Anecdotes' of him suggest; for from the very nature and form of her book, 'it lends deception lighter wings to fly'" (4:341). In Boswell's animadversions on Mrs. Piozzi near the end of the *Life*, Boswell accuses her of exaggerated attention to Johnson's peculiarities. Piozzi's allusions to moments of madness, of rudeness, and of thoughtlessness pollute his vision of a whole Johnson whose private and public lives, while sometimes disjunctive, may be adequately explained.[26]

In the *Life* the distance between the Scots aristocrat and the English commoner is collapsed into their union as men of letters, a category that by definition excludes women of any class. The Johnson of the *Life* is a man of letters, a literary eminence who, as the son of a bookseller, removes himself from dealing with books as mere trade. Boswell grants Johnson this right to advance from low origins to national prominence because of his genius: "Though from my very high admiration of Johnson, I have wondered that he was not courted by all the great and all the eminent persons of his time, it ought fairly to be considered, that no man of humble birth, who lived entirely by literature, in short no author by profession, ever rose in this country into that personal notice which he did" (4:325–26). The ideological field of the *Life* makes possible a reading in which Boswell and Johnson's friendship, the relationship of two males, enables the trivialization and dismissal of "woman." Thrale, associated with the "namby-pamby rhymes" of children, trifles in gossip in contrast with Boswell's scrupulous pursuit of truth. In addition, he contemptuously draws attention to the contradictions within Thrale's *Anecdotes* to demonstrate the absurdity of her claim that Johnson could behave so differently on one day or another: "I am sorry this lady does not advert, that she herself contradicts the assertion of his being obstinately defective in the *petites morales*, in the endearing charities of social life, in conferring smaller favours" (4:344). Similarly, he reasserts his authority by claiming that he heard her argue just the opposite. Boswell even resorts to using Sir John Hawkins against her notion of Johnson's character. "Poor Thrale!" Hawkins writes, "I thought that either her virtue or her vice would have restrained her from such a marriage [to Piozzi]. She is now become a subject for her enemies to exult over; and for her friends, if she has any left, to forget, or pity" (4:339). The *Life*, then, struggles to inhibit one woman's challenge to patriarchal dominance over the authorized version of public character.

The early sections of the biography emphasize Johnson's class pride, his unwillingness to accept charity, and his manly independence (1:246). In constructing the character of Johnson, these early portions of the *Life* carefully separate Johnson from the taint of his friend Richard Savage, a bastard who maintained he was the unacknowledged son of the Countess of Macclesfield, contrary to the apparent facts of the case. Class is paramount in this narrative maneuver, for though the details of the case remain obscure, Savage may well have been only an aspiring shoemaker's son who invented the lie of aristocratic birth to improve his fortune.[27] Boswell is also at pains to insist on Johnson's masculinity, his rigorously gendered identity. Johnson's childhood tantrum against his schoolmistress, for example, is presented as a triumph of male independence over female authority. The nearsighted child Johnson "was obliged to stoop down on his hands and knees to take a view of the kennel before he ventured to step over it. His school-mistress, afraid that he might miss his way, or fall into the kennel, or be run over by a cart, followed him at some distance. He happened to turn about and perceive her. Feeling her careful attention as an insult to his manliness, he ran back to her in a rage, and beat her, as well as his strength would permit" (1:39). As we have seen in Boswell's journals and the *Life,* "woman" is figured as a danger to masculine autonomy, and, at the same time, establishing this sexual difference is crucial to the formation of manly character.

Boswell inscribes sexual difference to make "manly" synonymous with human nature, character, and a physical violence in defense of one's dignity in spite of, for example, the teacher's solicitude. Similarly, Johnson's writing is the "expression" of that nature. His language, Boswell writes, "must be allowed to be too masculine for the delicate gentleness of female writing" (1:223); it possesses "manly force" (1:123), "manly dramatick criticism" (1:181), "manly and noble sentiment" (1:215), "manly fortitude" (4:326), and an exemplary and disinterested masterly style. Making "manly" highly desirable has the effect, then, of excluding women's writing from the best writing.

Near the end of the eighteenth century, the Isaac D'Israeli who reflected on diary also argued strongly for female difference in his claim that women are superior to men in politics and religion because of their personal charms. In an essay on woman's character he declares that women cultivate excellent skill in psychological observation. That differential ability, however, is firmly linked to inferiority and the necessity for male domination. Women, then, are perceived to specialize and excel in the private and subjective domains, at the same time that they are denigrated for their expertise in this "contemptible science":

That the female character may excel the masculine ability, in what is termed a knowledge of the world, and that there is a sexual distinction in this contemptible science, is a fact, which an observer may discover in his private circle. Bruyere is a character more extraordinary among men, than it would be among women; for I am persuaded, that there are many female Bruyeres not accustomed to write down their observations, and pourtray the characters of their acquaintance. Women, of even a mediocrity of talent, excel in the knowledge of their circle; and we may account for this curious circumstance, on the principle of their stationary situation in society, where their opportunities for observation are more frequent, and where their perception becomes more exact, by an attention, which . . . is never entirely suspended. . . . Many experience, and some acknowledge, what Rousseau relates of his Theresa. This woman, whom he describes otherwise as heavy and dull, afforded him excellent advice in the most trying occasions.[28]

In this passage D'Israeli explains La Bruyère's talent in dealing with character by feminizing him, and the fear of femininity surfaces in Boswell's journals. There is something inherent in women that gives them special and privileged insight into private character. And clearly such talent is not a mark of class (Rousseau's Theresa was also his servant) or intelligence. Instead, D'Israeli argues, it is "the peculiarity of her situation," her fixed position, that enables her to be superior in conversational and epistolary skills. If women were to cross-dress or become men, "the wandering and active sex," they would only diminish themselves; their advantages derive from their forced attention to delicacy and sensibility: "By becoming [man's] rival, she would not only lose that feminine sweetness, that amiable debility, and that retiring modesty which lend so much eloquent persuasion to her actions, but what would not be compensated by this violent and unnatural change, she would lose her actual position in the social order which imparts her present superiority, by enabling her to detect the secret foibles of man."[29] In short, women's space is stationary while men's is mobile, their natural difference the occasion for misogyny and the justification for domination. Woman's "natural" situation demands her oppression.

Boswell, enlisting the authority of "the Great Cham" against Thrale, insists that women, who may have special access to private character, must suppress their special knowledge. Men of a certain class and nation have access to the truth of character, and they control its private representation and public dissemination. The powerful effect of Boswell's journals and The Life of Johnson, then, is to reassert a gender and class hierarchy and, in so doing, to invalidate reader positions that do not assert the obviousness of this hierarchy. Thus the Life asserts Johnson's manly prose and authoritative male character against the onslaught of female readers and writers in late-eighteenth-century England to reclaim the category of literary character and its artful representation for men. Men are the sole authorized venders of the private biographical subject and its ideology of genre.

In short, one use of The Life of Johnson is the reclamation of the masculine domain of English literature from the encroachment of female and other newly literate readers and writers within the public arena. But a materialist feminist criticism is committed to disclosing and resisting such strategies at this time when it is crucial to open texts to the power struggles that define subjectivities. Restoration and eighteenth-century women are among those on the margins who found leverage for resistance to their co-optation by becoming the autobiographical subject rather than the object of the textual representation of their lives. These women, including the spiritual autobiographers, scandalous memoirists, and diarists discussed in the pages that follow, are among those who most forcefully claim access to sexually bounded territory and legitimate alternative subject positions across class and gender lines as readers, writers, and interpreters of the "real."

CHAPTER SIX

The Gender of Character

❦ ❦ ❦

*At dinner our conversation first turned upon Pope. Johnson said, his
characters of men were admirably drawn, those of women not so well.*
—Boswell's *Life of Johnson* (1791)

*I confess that the female character has seldom been heard on the public
scene, as the prompter of a theatre; or as rarely been visible as the scene-
shifters. But miserable were that philosophy which confounds invisibility
with non-existence; the female character, like some other objects, derives
all it's influence from concealment; in politics, woman is terrible.*
—D'Israeli's *Miscellanies* (1796)

❦ I

For Bunyan, Wesley, and Boswell, the "male" is usually synonymous
with the "human," and the gender implications of their multiple and
contradictory identities arise with less insistence than they do in wom-
en's autobiographical writing. The humanist tenet that man's nature
remains the same in spite of gender or class is a commonplace that is
repeatedly voiced as self-evident during the period. "Human Nature (as
daily Experience shews us) is, in the general, alike in all, from the Prince
to the Peasant," writes James Nelson in an exemplary statement, for "the
same Weaknesses attend us; the same Passions torment us; the same Diseases kill us: all are the Work of ONE GREAT ARTIST." [1] The male category,
usually assumed to be universal and dominant, is more easily traced in its
permutations, and the category of "woman" manifests itself more subtly.
"Man" and "woman," culturally produced divisions that reciprocally shift
their nuances of meaning through time and place, are newly represented
in the language of the proliferating autobiographical practice of the eighteenth century. For instance, in contrast with men, women autobiographers frequently call attention to the oddity of their activity, the

strangeness they find in speaking about identity and experience to potential readers, if only themselves. These uneasinesses testify to the special
status that gender gives to their writing and to their situation, but determining the nature of that special status has led to a variety of pitfalls, and
it deserves more careful delineation.

Most historical and critical studies of autobiographical writing in the
eighteenth century ignore women's writing or treat it as inferior to the
male corpus. Consequently, a canon of women's autobiography for
the eighteenth century is only beginning to be established, and few of
the women who wrote in the first person recognized their own participation in an emerging female tradition. Most recent critical studies, rather
than admitting women into the canon, clearly assume the autobiographical self is male, and women's participation in the genre is an addendum
to it.[2] Recently a corrective to this androcentric model has begun to
emerge. Domna Stanton, for example, criticizes the erasure of women's
texts from the history of autobiography, and argues for a female subject
rather than a centered self. And Sidonie Smith attempts to formulate a
poetics of women's autobiography by extrapolating from several sample
English and American texts. But only Patricia Meyer Spacks, in a series
of articles and books, has probed women's life-writing in the period in
any detail.[3]

Discussing Laetitia Pilkington, Charlotte Charke, Lady Mary Wortley
Montagu, Hester Thrale, and Fanny Burney, Spacks proposes that wom-
en's first-person texts share a self-representation of weakness, a "dichotomy between public passivity and private energy" that splits them into a
double positioning. Society, Spacks concludes, "makes women dwell in a
state of internal conflict with necessarily intricate psychic consequences"[4]
that would seem, in her formulation, to suggest a constant difference in
women's consciousness that manifests itself in certain repetitive themes.
Spacks focuses on these patterns without drawing generalizations for
women's autobiography or developing her concepts theoretically, but she
significantly reformulates the canon to include women's texts as part
of the history of eighteenth-century self-writing. The territory of Restoration and eighteenth-century female autobiography might comprise,
then, seventeenth-century gentlewomen; spiritual autobiographers, including Quaker, Baptist, and Methodist journalists; apologists (usually
called scandalous memoirists) beginning in the 1740s and extending to
the early nineteenth century; the noteworthy diarists and letter writers
such as Montagu, Thrale, and Burney; and writers of numerous unpublished diaries and letters throughout the century.

In considering issues of gender theory and history, I want to focus on several areas where productive work has gone on and where major theoretical quagmires have developed. Particularly important for the study of women's autobiography is the articulation of a feminist theory and the problems of biologism which forming a separate female tradition raises. In addition, there is the problem of reducing questions of female oppression to the economic, and I have posed some alternatives to this severely limited notion of ideology. A post-Althusserian concept of ideology as a conflictual grid of available meanings, materially produced and with material effects, helps, as we have seen, to extricate us from the rigid distinctions between base and superstructure and enables us to look instead toward various shifting ensembles of practices in particular social formations. We can look at the contradictions and interrelations among the economic, political, and ideological practices that (re)produce sexual difference rather than separate gender hierarchy and its effects within patriarchy from economic systems such as capitalism. This dual systems theory, simplifying the relation between class and gender to a causal relation in which one determines the other, fails to find ways of talking about their connections.[5] In fact, women's autobiography can be thought of as a particular crux for drawing out the implications of these problems, and for pointing toward new conclusions about gender theory and for women's studies.

The problematic of whether women's autobiography constitutes a separate tradition from men's may be thought of as the problem of women's studies in miniature. Is it better to be separate and marginalized, or to be lost in the more powerful and dominant mainstream? Women's autobiographical writing has most often been seen as a relatively pure form of writing where women could raise their consciousness and define an identity.[6] There they could develop a distinctive voice that reflected their unique historical situation and their exclusion from universal categories of human nature. But in attempting to mark that voice and resist incorporation into generic (male) definitions of self, women have also found themselves caught in the trap of the biologism and essentialism that trivialize the issues of gender and segregate them from the problems of class and race.

Whether, in fact, women writers have their own tradition, metaphoric rooms of their own, has long been a crucial question for feminist studies. Among those who have defined such a gynocentric space is Elaine Showalter, who identifies it as a female wilderness or wild zone: "Spatially it stands for an area which is literally no-man's-land, a place forbidden to men. Experientially it stands for the aspects of the female life-style which are outside of and unlike those of men."[7] For Showalter, in an extension of this formulation, the problem in speaking and writing such an imaginary space is that woman, placed within both traditions at the same time and denied the "full resources of language," has been suppressed and silenced; the insufficiency is not in language but in its repression. But American feminists such as Showalter and others have been loath to people this "woman's land" with the traditional woman who, somehow closer to nature, can only represent the opposite, or absence, of what is valued in the dominant male culture. French feminists such as Luce Irigaray, Monique Wittig, Annie LeClerc, Julia Kristeva, and Hélène Cixous also seek to delimit and define female spaces. Revolutionary and utopian, woman's space is unspeakable and mysterious. For Cixous, for example, it is a "*Dark Continent*" that is "*neither dark nor unexplorable.*"[8] This territory that will dislocate and explode male discourse is "without" male discourse, a place that issues forth from the body of woman's difference—from breasts, vagina, and womb. While American feminists have been criticized for the value they assign to female experience, French feminists have been accused of creating new prisons for women in their bodies. What these diverse critics seem to agree upon is that women's spaces are largely unspoken, unwritten, and unrepresented ones that have not yet been described. All would seem to be trying to define and name a peculiarly female voice.

More recently, Alice Jardine has attempted to negotiate a theoretical common ground between American and French feminism. The conflict between these theories, as she outlines it, lies in their different emphases on the graphic or the corporal, the *written* body or the written *body*: "To refuse 'woman' or the 'feminine' as cultural and libidinal constructions . . . is, ironically, to return to metaphysical—anatomical—definitions of sexual identity"; but the contrary reduces woman to the symbolic ("a semiosis of woman") and again erases political and historical woman, marginalizes her, and requires her absence. Jardine thus positions herself between the American feminists' attempt to recover women's real selves and experience, and the French feminists' recognition that questions direct access to self or reality.[9] What Jardine fails to take account of, however, in her quest for the truth about "woman," is the very constructedness of the female in its historical and cultural specificity, and that even woman's body must be read as the product of discourse *and* of material conditions, a historicized site for the inscription of gender.

Contemporary psychoanalytic theories of identity, notably those of Freud and Lacan, have been much analyzed and revised by feminist theorists who labor to define a gendered subjectivity.[10] As I have noted in discussing more broadly the problem of the autobiographical subject, for Lacan, subjectivity begins at the moment of the infant's separation from the symbiosis with the mother. This moment is marked by the infant's taking up language; it is a moment of difference when all that is not articulated is excluded. Language, the argument continues, inevitably reflects loss and the desire for regaining what cannot be spoken or signified. Lacan differentiates between the infant's experience of his mother and father to theorize sexual difference in its relation to identity. Lacan suggests that "mother" is a signification or metaphor rather than a real material being, and thus "mother" becomes a code for the child's unattainable atonement and unity with her. Consequently, the separation from the mother is the foundation of desire.

But for materialist feminists, an approach that attempts to draw universal gender distinctions cannot be reconciled with the shifting relations of reproduction through history. Lacan fails to make diachronic distinctions in the categories of mother, father, and child, and assumes that his family drama is played out regardless of the particulars of specific sociocultural situations. Thus, Lacanian theory does not seem to consider the political effects of male domination in the interest of changing them or to entertain the possibility of a nongendered society; it does not connect signification to the material conditions of lived experience through history. Feminist theory, in addressing the political implications of Lacan's claims, can acknowledge that his theory and the uses to which it can be put are themselves situated within the ideological, for Lacanian approaches cannot account for the varieties of consciousness spoken and written within various social relations and over time except as they relate to a universal signification of gender difference. Within such a frame, the female subject in women's autobiography ("autogynography" is the term Domna Stanton coins) is always different from men's because of women's otherness and their absence from the social order.[11] This subject attempts the impossible act of self-possession, and yet the female signature also would seem to liberate women as they seek textual identity. Stanton is appropriately uneasy with this resolution in contradiction when she registers her "illogical belief that the gender of the author did make a difference, at this discursive point in time."[12] Moving us toward recognizing the incongruities in female subject positions, Stanton falters when she attempts to identify the distinguishing characteristics of autogynography because the universality of the Lacanian paradigm and its derivatives remain abstract in their application. Sidonie Smith, too, raises important questions about the study of women's autobiography within French and Anglo-American feminist criticism. Smith recognizes the inadequacy of traditional models of the self in autobiographical criticism, but she falls into transhistorical snares when she vacillates between asserting a "poetics of women's autobiography" and declaring that she will offer "no comprehensive theory of women's autobiographical writing."[13] Both Smith and Stanton, then, usefully complicate the concept of "self" but are hampered by their inattention to the political and economic purposes that difference serves in women's autobiography and the particular historical conditions in which certain textual practices erupt.

Theories that speak about women's voices must be grounded instead, I think, in particular and local instances of autobiographical writing within a systematic theory, provisionally held and subject to critique, if we are to avoid the generalizations that contribute to a gendered oppression by insisting that writing emerges from biological difference. Materialist feminists—who emphasize the material base of oppression as well as its signification in language—have debated these issues in relation to literary texts by questioning the relevance of the author's gender and of experience to their representation in text, and whether a given work can be said to possess an inherent ideology of "sexism" or "feminism." Michèle Barrett resists separating feminist art from women's experience, and she calls attention to the way that an aesthetic or textual artifact can be a location for an ideological struggle that displays its material effects.[14] That is, the same object or text may, for example, be appropriated for sexist or for feminist purposes. Images do not necessarily hold within themselves an ideology of feminism or antifeminism, but their reception as one or the other may be acknowledged as an important part of the production of their meanings. Barrett does not, however, take sufficient measure of the way in which the reading of these artifacts may vary over time.

Similarly, Rosalind Coward has pointed out that women's novels are not necessarily feminist texts. Defining feminism exclusively as a shared *politics* rather than a shared situation or tradition, Coward attempts to keep women's writing distinct from their lived experience: "Feminism can never be the product of the identity of women's experiences and interests—there is no such unity. Feminism must always be the alignment

of women in a political movement with particular political aims and ob-
jectives."[15] Coward usefully stresses the importance of effective political
practice, but her distinction between text and experience is difficult to
maintain if, as I have argued, discourse, itself positioned within power
relations, is considered to be both productive and reflective of material
practices that intervene in the construction of the "real." For example, a
female autobiographical tradition can exist only when women begin to
write, and to read other women's autobiographical writing. This requires
a literate body of female readers, and, in order for such autobiographical
texts to reach a relatively wide audience, they must be published and
made available to other women readers. In England these conditions first
began to be met when Quaker women's journals and testimonies were
disseminated in the latter half of the seventeenth century, and in the
later publication of scandalous memoirs in the mid eighteenth century.
This attention to particular historical moments allows us to resist temptations to read the history of women's autobiographical writing as a separate and self-contained reflection of the essence of woman.

Some feminist theorists have come close to claiming that women's experience intrinsically lends itself to private autobiographical writing in
diaries and journals. Certainly many Restoration and eighteenth-century
women found the diary, journal, and serial autobiographical forms particularly congenial for speaking on the cusp, for fashioning liminal selves
that could not reach closure without confirming the kinds of inferior female selves urged by male hegemonic and misogynist discourses. When
we write ourselves and our experience, the language we use derives from
our own subjectivity, but that subjectivity is constituted in social relations. Eighteenth-century women who represent their subjectivity were,
however, caught in mimicking the dominant ideologies of themselves.
Their self-fashionings were inevitably bound up in cultural definitions of
gender—those assumed, prescribed, and embedded in their consciousness—as well as in their subversive thoughts and acts of resistance to
those definitions. Eighteenth-century writing women positioned themselves all along the feminist and antifeminist spectrum from the discourse
of inferiority to the assertion of equality. Some eighteenth-century
women speak as harshly as men about the sex, and others shift positions
rather arbitrarily during the course of their lives. They may assume a
position that implies moral or spiritual superiority, they may speak their
own denigration and collude in their subjugation, or they may attempt to
disrupt the ideology of gender by disguising themselves as males. Some

eighteenth-century women's diaries, memoirs, and autobiographies incorporate that ideology to reproduce it, while others challenge it with an
alternative discourse. This concept of a particular ideological formation
helps to negotiate traditional dualisms between the individual and the
social, to mark the way gendered subjectivity produces and reflects the
systems of sexual difference in eighteenth-century England.

The question becomes, Whose interests are served in constituting
gendered subjectivity in certain ways, and in maintaining the power relations of heterosexual division? The ideology of female character moves
beyond discursive or signifying practices to the lived experience of social
relations that is produced, reflected, and reproduced in gendered subjectivity. Individual autobiographers are positioned by ideology—particularly bourgeois ideology at midcentury—to believe that they are free
agents who create their unique character and who construct positions of
subjectivity that will cohere. Specific ideologies, situated within history
and culture, compete for dominance and serve to mask the contradictions within given discourses and domains of "meaning." Ideology, rather
than simply reflecting dilemmas of character in the lives of the autobiographers of the period, camouflages the conditions of production of
those lives to constitute the "real" and disguises its incongruities between
competing, apparently coherent, systems. That is, any given autobiographical narrator may be held in place by multiple and variant systems of
signification. By midcentury ideologies of character compete to produce a
recognizable category of woman's public representation of her interiority.

If "women" and "men" are categories produced by social, historical,
political, and economic factors, then individuals are less the source of
their own meaning than the place where clashes to control meanings of
words occur. Women's self-writing in Restoration and eighteenth-century England ventriloquizes dominant ideologies of gender and class
while it allows alternative discourses of "experience" to erupt in the gaps
between subject positions. Woman's subjectivity is not a given that pre-
cedes entrance into the social formation or can be defined outside of it,
for social relations are always implicated in the production of private
interiority and public character. Thus, women's commonplaces—the
places where meanings meet—escape universal categorization and are
subject to ideological uses that shift and change over time.

Turning from the question of a separate female voice, I want to concentrate on another of the problems that troubles studies of eighteenth-
century women's autobiography. How is it possible to wed economic

systems, specifically capitalism, to the problems of sexual oppression, specifically patriarchy? Dual systems theorists have argued that *both* are separate systems, each as important as the other, and, in functionalist models, that patriarchy or capital is the determining cause. Such notions would attempt to keep the economic class system distinct from the sex/gender system. Dual systems theories often rely on the traditional Marxist concept of ideology as "false consciousness," which restricts them to a definition in which hegemonic forces urge a misrepresentation of reality upon oppressed classes. This idea of false consciousness, then, is an element of subjectivity and the psyche that may seem separable from reality. But critics of dual systems theory note that it is a defect of traditional Marxism, not of the economy itself, that it says little about gender.[16] Thus production of all kinds is so implicated in the gender system as not to be separable from it.

Other versions of this theory have argued that gender oppression is an *effect* of capitalism—that is, that it emerges at the point of capitalism's emergence and that one system has a causal relation to the other. Following Engels, they claim that a crucial point of entry of the state into the personal, of capitalism into social relations, is the bourgeois family.[17] While the insertion of the state into policing the ideology of the family is especially relevant to the eighteenth century, the difficulty with this line of argument is that patriarchy and capitalism cannot be easily seen as mutually productive of each other, or engaged in a reciprocal relationship, but one becomes the source of the other.

An alternative way of regarding gender considers patriarchy to be a historical, rather than a natural, category that is complexly knotted into the economic and political. Giving historical specificity to both terms helps avoid putting either the economic (capitalism) or sexual relations (patriarchy) as the first cause or one as always determined by the other. In her recent consideration of patriarchy, Gail Omvedt believes male dominance emerges at the historical moment of the capitalist state so that a clear and tenacious system of hierarchical gender relations is set in place.[18] For Omvedt, "women" produce *life* in a private and suppressed sphere while "men" produce *things* in a public and powerful sphere. But Omvedt also argues that the production of life, women's role, goes on outside the capitalist mode of production so that gender oppression crosses with class exploitation. This analysis bears especially on the gendering of character and identity in eighteenth-century England where class and gender intersect. In addition patriarchy, as Veronica Beechey has argued, is not directly derived from capitalism,[19] and the biological category of woman does not ensure oppression by men across class or at all historical moments. Neither patriarchy nor capital is the sole determinative cause for exploitative sexual relations, for it is possible to conceive of patriarchy, like capitalism, as oppressing biological men as well as women, unevenly and unequally without necessarily following gender patterns, especially as men and women inhabit more than one class position. Thus, any theory of patriarchy is most useful if it examines its particular forms within the various modes of production so that the relations between patriarchy and capitalism are made historically explicit. Comprehensive narratives may still be woven.

Women's autobiographical writing, when conceived of as a private expression of the individual, is often assumed to be outside the state and the economy, even in its published modes. This insistence on a public/ private split with the emphasis on personal and emotional life elides the way that the production of a rich and complex inner life is itself a political practice. As newly literate women become the subject and object of their own scrutiny, they adopt stances within gender ideologies. Most eighteenth-century women wrote privately, never submitting their texts to public scrutiny. Women are largely explained through discourses that restrain them to private modes of being while men are gendered public and political. Private diaries and journals record female "experience," removed from public sight yet permeated by the larger cultural and political notions of "reality." In other words, the edges of the public/private dichotomy become very hazy when we consider the way generic filters shape perceptions of experience, and, equally important, the way many diarists assumed that their writing would be published after their deaths. Some few eighteenth-century women published their lives while they were still living. Some made use of them in a political way to defend their individual "character" by requiring a change in the public perception of their lives, in believing their text would bring about moral or spiritual change in the reader, or by launching a challenge to existent female models.

Patriarchy in eighteenth-century England, then, may be defined in economic, political, and ideological terms. For example, oppression and exploitation of women dictate their being allocated significantly less as wage laborers, and this idea persists within the bourgeois family, where domestic work contributes to the family's well-being but is without monetary compensation. In addition, patriarchal hierarchies pervade institutional practices so that male dominance operates at the ideological level in prescribing women's imaginary relation to lived experience. A crucial activity, then, is to locate the discursive practices and the material conditions of "woman" in the period, to identify their disguises within dominant ideologies of institutions. In private and public autobiographical texts, patriarchy and its ideology of the female second sphere are inscribed as much as they are resisted.

Seventeenth-century gentlewomen intimated through their choice of content that their husbands' lives superseded theirs; they defined self by relationship. Often recently impoverished, they wrote their autobiographical accounts for a group of intimates, but the accounts were seldom published until the nineteenth century. Lucy Hutchinson's memoirs were published in 1806, Anne Clifford's in 1817, Ann Fanshawe's in 1829, and Anne, Lady Halkett's, in 1875.[20] As we shall see in specific instances, the religious women's accounts bear remarkable similarities to each other and to the male texts they imitate. They frequently adopted the mode of discourse established by their (male) religious leaders—Fox, Bunyan, Wesley—or found their voices usurped by husbands or fathers who formed their biographies into the expected shape. They inscribed themselves, or were inscribed, in the familiar patterns of awakening, conversion, and ministry, their "selves" shaped in imitation of Christ and his (male) disciples. These women learned what sorts of lives to lead and to write principally from hearing and reading men's lives, from the cultural practices that confined their subjectivity, and from the religious doctrines that forced closure on ideas about identity and selfhood. In the conversion narratives and diaries, women explain their interest in public speaking as divinely ordained and inspired, their wish to travel as the will of God. Some women spiritual autobiographers argued against a gendered hierarchy within the dissenting sects, and thus threatened the established patriarchy of church and state.

As scandalous memoirists, women proclaimed their economic and sexual victimization, recognizing their otherness within existing relations of production and attempting to escape their position as commodities to be exchanged through *public* display of that gendered subjectivity. The scandalous memoirists function, in large part, outside the family. Excluded from it, they also pose a threat to it. These women threaten to disrupt the intricate power relations of capital and patriarchy, while they also believe themselves to be freely constructing their textual representations of that interiority. In addition, reproduction and motherhood were given little attention in representations of their subjectivities, and the offspring of their sexual liaisons were usually treated as incidental to the narrative. Hester Thrale, on the other hand, embraced motherhood and the family, taking her own identity from kinship ties and defining men and women as happily distinct. Privileged bourgeois women such as Thrale voice ambivalent pleasure in their private autobiographical writing about their domestic role as dutiful wife and devoted mother. Thrale finds resolution of that ambivalence in the ideology of romance that comes with her second marriage to Gabriel Piozzi but that consequently forces a divorce from her daughters and from her accustomed social milieu. Women autobiographers in the eighteenth century, then, speak in the codes and language that are available to them in texts that imitate and reflect the autobiographical subjects of the male hegemonic social formation.

☙ II

I want to turn now to aspects of legal, medical, and educational discourses that were most relevant and influential in the formation of a secondary and privatized female interiority in an increasingly dominant capitalist economy as class and gender relations intersect. In the pages that follow, the power, property, and social relations figure importantly as they constitute the "real," and thus the materiality of gendered ideology, in eighteenth-century England. As the emergent credit economy requires consuming subjects, it produces "women" who are variously positioned in relation to the means of production. There are, however, significant points of sexual difference, as that is constructed in history, between male and female autobiographical expression, for eighteenth-century women have access to different regimes of truth, and they take oppositional stances that recoil against representations of themselves in official texts and ideology. Subjects, called into being by several contradictory ideologies at once, may expose contradictory aspects of an ideological formation that were previously invisible.[21] Resistance and change occur at the point of contradiction between the available subject positions, when it is not possible to elide the gaps, and when those elements, previously excluded from frames of intelligibility, are recognized, so that in the continual struggle between languages and ideologies, in the process of the struggle for power, resistance propels a move to new positions that will explain the contradictions.

Thus the dominant ideology, an ensemble of discursive and material practices, changes in response to being an ideology *in* history, and its seams and fissures may be exposed. Suppressed ideologies, or ideologies newly imagined, make possible fresh positions that contest the dominant ideology, yet they are themselves situated in history and politics. Autobiographical writings in the Restoration and eighteenth century make it possible for women, writing privately, to read themselves and their lived experience, and to articulate contradictory positions. Thus, they smooth over the gaps, exaggerate them to make them the site of resistance and change, or retreat into madness, sickness, and silence. For Quaker autobiographers, the chief point of resistance lies in the arguments on women's preaching, the claim to have a public voice, yet, at the same time, a voice on behalf of a patriarchal God. Whether itinerant female spiritual autobiographers drew on their sects for economic support or contributed to a group's economic well-being, for the first time women had to be figured into their community's accounting as they exceeded their prescribed functions. Authorized to escape the restrictions of the bourgeois family *only* if allegiance to God required it, these occasional exceptions to male domination made oppositional stances even within religious ideologies possible. The women who wrote scandalous memoirs, often displaced from rank and status expectations, possessed little property except themselves, as they produced an urban consciousness that especially encouraged individualization. Their bodies, complexly inscribed as the location of sexual difference and desire, are perceived as violating the bourgeois family. For scandalous memoirists, the resistance point lies in the urge to correct public constructs of their fall as the pivotal and definitive moment that gives meaning to their "character"—in the cultural construction that makes a woman lose her reputation if she is known to be sexually active. Defining their "character" in the public domain, such women both celebrate and apologize for their behavior.[22] Charlotte Charke, Laetitia Pilkington, Ann Sheldon, Elizabeth Gooch, George Anne Bellamy, Margaret Leeson, and others have in common the fact that their self-writing finds its genesis in an accusation. Each text vindicates the apologist from blame, while, in contradiction, it attempts to transform the very moral and social system that requires explanation.

In contrast, for Hester Thrale, the crucial point of difference from men rests in formulating the identity of a bourgeois mother, the educator of her children and the caretaker of their health, as well as a wife to a

brewer and the frequent hostess to Samuel Johnson. For Thrale, resistance to these prescribed identities came in insisting, however ambivalently, on the importance of the "unimportant." Thus, in the period
when women first began to publish what had previously been assumed to
be private, the question of the conditions under which women's identity
should have public status becomes more complex. With increasing subjection to a broader public surveillance and increasingly held publicly accountable for their transgressive activities, women's lives have special
fascination for the newly literate and middle-class reading public. As the
legal and medical institutions intrude into the previously private, Hester
Thrale "manages" the labor power of servants, wet nurses, and teachers
for her children; without being directly engaged in her husband's trade,
she seems removed from the relations of production. The sexual division
of labor is reinscribed as she procreates, manages the home, and serves
the interests of patriarchy and of capital as a consuming subject. But
within the inconsistencies of the prevailing practices, there is space in-
side autobiographical writing to contest eighteenth-century versions of
male dominance.

In particular, eighteenth-century women's autobiographical texts take
cognizance of the contradiction between producing difference from men,
and insisting on the equality of that difference. This is particularly slip-
pery territory, from a materialist feminist perspective, because the merest
hint of inherent difference opens the possibility of complicity in the gender hierarchy. Mary Astell, for example, takes great pains to insist on
women's difference as writers in order to keep them from being subsumed
under the masculine. Women ought not to be dismissed as acting "above
their sex," she writes, "since the Men being the Historians, they seldom
condescend to record the great and good Stations of Women . . . by
which one must suppose they wou'd have their Readers understand, That
they were not Women who did those Great Actions, but that they were
Men in Petticoats."[23] Though Astell argues strongly against the tyranny
of Custom as oppressive to women, she reinscribes the sexual division of
labor to insist that children's education and care are their primary responsibility. Nature, then, requires women to breast-feed and nurture
their own children: "And if Mothers had a due regard to their Posterity,
how Great soever they are, they wou'd not think themselves too Good to
perform what Nature requires, nor through Pride and Delicacy remit the
poor little one to the care of a Foster Parent."[24] Thus Astell, in affirming

women's natural equality with men, falls prey to the perils of difference without working out the avenues that might empower women.

Similarly, Astell addresses a female reading audience and exposes the oppression of (upperclass) women in unhappy marriage but largely confines her proposal for relief to the private sphere within this framework. Astell radically proposes that women bond together to detect their mutual interests, and she urges women to possess themselves of a self. At a time of currency for Locke's argument that identity was consciousness— that "a thinking intelligent Being, that has reason and reflection, and can consider it self as it self, the same thinking thing in different times and places"—Mary Astell insists on women's right to reflect on self rather than the body or its adornments. The establishment of a Protestant monastery, a temporary haven for unmarried women or the victims of unhappy marriage, would allow them to find an individual identity, Astell writes: "Your Glass will not do you half so much service as a serious reflection on your own Minds, which will discover Irregularities more worthy your Correction, and keep you from being either too much elated or depress'd by the representations of the other. . . . No solicitude in the adornation of your selves is discommended, provided you employ your care about that which is really your *self*" (141). Subject to their husbands, women could escape domination only by removing themselves to a private place to attend to self and to base that self on virtue, honor, and education rather than property, name, or heredity. Removed from commerce and business, they could "stand still and reflect on our own Minds" (148). Recognizing themselves, they could distinguish themselves from beasts to claim a self that participates in universal human nature "that Women may no longer pass for those little useless and impertinent Animals, which the ill conduct of too many is caus'd 'em to be mistaken for" (152). In such a retreat, women could escape Custom, tyranny, and the distractions of the world, all synonymous with patriarchy. Thus Astell asserts that a free space of the self may be realized for women, and women are urged to regulate themselves in this newly constructed territory that is ostensibly free from patriarchy. But Astell cannot cope with the full force of the problematic. Even such a "free" space is permeated by the ideologies of the culture that tolerates it, and women who rejoin the commerce of the world are paradoxically urged again to relinquish that hard-won "self" to the gendered hierarchy of husband, father, and king.

If gender becomes increasingly differentiated in defining character and identity for Astell and other early feminists, it also takes on new significance in a sexually differentiated biology. Male dominance is inscribed on the female body as male doctors increase their observation and regulation of it. In medical descriptions, a woman's body is a locus of explanation for her character. For example an anonymous essay, "Of Women and their Vices, with Instructions for their Behaviour in general," binds the female body to an inferior nature: "The Weakness of Womens Natures, attended with over-much Heat and Humidity, makes them in general (tho' the Women naturally virtuous, are very numerous) more inclinable to Vice, than the Men, the nobler and more substantial Part of the Creation; but their Education, Dress, and Way of Living makes it less in their Power to practice, tho' it contributes to Pride, which is natural in the Whole Sex."[25] The medical treatises from midcentury on demarcate women's biological inferiority, but because most of these treatises were in Latin, the woman who could read those doctors' descriptions of her body is indeed rare.

Hysteria is frequently codified as the only disease that exclusively attacks women in the eighteenth century. With the hystericization of women's bodies, as Foucault has called it, the female body becomes "the inscribed surface of events (traced by language and dissolved by ideas)."[26] According to eighteenth-century medical authorities, hysteria, the woman's disease as distinguished from male hypochondria, is as elusive as woman's nature, for it is "extremely difficult to give a general character or definition of it." William Perfect in Cases of Insanity makes the distinction unequivocal—"the Hysteric Passion, A Disorder peculiar to the Fair Sex, differing in most cases very essentially from the Hypochondriac Affection, both in Cause and Situation"[27]—and he provides case histories of the treatment of madness that keeps hysterics and hypochondriacs clearly segregated according to sex. Difference, then, is located in the reproductive organs and in the way that diseases manifest themselves in changes in "character" and identity.

Some doctors, of course, did assume both men and women were the same. Richard Blackmore, in A Treatise of the Spleen and Vapours: or, Hypochondriacal and Hysterical Affections find the symptoms to be largely identical in both sexes, though in "the Female Sex, in a higher Degree or in a different Shape and Appearance from the same in Men."[28] Robert Whyte, who was unlike many of his contemporaries in thinking that hysteria and hypochondria displayed the same symptoms, nevertheless writes that "WOMEN, in whom the nervous system is generally more moveable than men, are more subject to nervous complaints, and have them in a higher degree." [29] And William Cullen also believed the diseases to be of varying intensity according to sex: "These affections have been supposed peculiar to the female sex; and indeed they most commonly appear in females: but they sometimes, though rarely, attack the male sex; never, however that I have observed, in the same exquisite degree." [30] In addition some texts consider this essentialized female body to be the source of aberrant behavior. John Astruc, in *A Treatise on All the Diseases Incident to Women* (1743), speaks of the convulsive nature and plethora of women; and Alexander Hamilton, in *A Treatise on the Management of Female Complaints* (1795), notes that "women, it has been observed, are more irritable than men." [31] Hysteria, then, was thought of as *excess* arising from the uterus or site of female difference, a plethora that had to be relieved. In other words, these diseases help fix the associations between a woman's character and her body.

It is precisely this biological divergence that Feyjuo y Montenegro disputes in *An Essay on the Learning, Genius, and Abilities, of the Fair-Sex*, a neglected feminist text. [32] There is, he maintains, no significant difference between the sexes. Yet he entertains the possibility of difference in order to draw new conclusions that dismiss the implications usually drawn. If any difference exists, he writes, it would have to be "an *entitative* disparity of souls, or a different organization, or different temperature in the bodies of both sexes"—but he then goes on to demonstrate that, even in the unlikely event such differences could be proved, difference is not a legitimate excuse for dominance. After discounting the possibility of a difference in the equality of souls, and arguing that even if women's brains are smaller it is of no consequence, he limits difference to the reproductive organs and diminishes the importance of biology, "women being of a different formation from men only in those organs which nature has appointed for propagation, and not at all in those appertaining to reason" (115). Thus, for Feyjuo, there *is* a difference, but he does not think that woman's reproductive capacity can be a logical rationalization for a gendered hierarchy of identity.

Feyjuo's remarkable document places great emphasis on the woman's body and defends a physical equality of brain, body, and soul between men and women. In fact, Feyjuo makes a counterargument for the superiority of women's brains as potentially more flexible, better able to form "better perceptions of the objects" (141). Similarly, Feyjuo validates a material difference between women and men in the amount of moisture present within their bodies, and perhaps in their brains, for women are equally "penetrative and profound," a situation that could not prevail if moisture weakened the brain: "Therefore let not moisture any longer labour under the unjust reproach of being incompatible with wit; and be it allowed as a certain truth, that no such argument can afford any satisfactory proof that women are inferior in reason and understanding to men" (141). Contradictory arguments that women's brains are softer or more impressionable must also be strongly resisted, he indicates. But Feyjuo's views are strikingly atypical rather than representative in the contest over difference and dominance. Lucy Aikin's vigorous argument for the corporal inequality of men and women in 1810 gives evidence that the contradiction between nature and custom remained current: "As long as the bodily constitution of the species shall remain the same, man must in general assume those public and active offices of life which confer authority, whilst to woman will usually be allotted such domestic and private ones as imply a certain degree of subordination." She adds, "Instead of aspiring to be inferior men, let us content ourselves with becoming noble women: . . . but let not sex be carried into every thing."[33] These discourses defining a second lesser sphere based on woman's bodily nature intersect in autobiographical writing to produce the category of woman and to maintain the categories of sexual difference and domination within her consciousness. Character, then, is inscribed in women's bodies, and gendered subjectivity is produced within a male dominance that requires systems of heterosexual difference and desire.

III

I want to focus now more specifically on some of the interconnections and contradictions within class and gender in representations of women's identity in eighteenth-century England. Women's being thought of, in Pope's words, as "a contradiction still," links these problems, for the concept of woman's public "character" becomes a way to attempt to rid women of contradiction and to resolve ideological struggles both by canceling women's relation to capital and by idealizing their lesser status. Women seldom figure in eighteenth-century discussions of the relationship between class and character; instead it is usually assumed that women take on the class of their father or husband. But class affords a way of making distinctions, among women as well as against men. Cutting across patriarchal ideologies allows us to differentiate, for example, among the bourgeois women, the itinerant women preachers who were also artisans, and the pauperized seduced maidens.

As E. P. Thompson has argued, eighteenth-century class structures are kept in place by implicit reciprocal relations between the gentry and the plebeian class. For Thompson, when the middle and professional classes begin to recognize themselves as such in the later years of the century,[34] class serves to integrate residual fragments of an older order into a newly recognizable category: "It is in class itself, in some sense a *new* set of categories, rather than in older patterns of thought that we may find the shaping cognitive organization of plebeian culture."[35] Autobiographical writing provides an important place where we would expect to find this "shaping cognitive organization," and, to the extent that women in the classes were literate, these new categories surface in texts. But, as we have seen, class is more than cognitive, having material existence in economic and political conditions rather than being simply a state of consciousness, and subjectivity has material effects.

Eighteenth-century women, most frequently given their class designations because of their relationships to men, may occupy a precarious position easily revoked by separation, dispossession, or death. Women also act to sustain certain class identification. Middle-class and upper-class women benefited from the work of other women without being sensitive to their participation in exploitation. Though wives of laborers were certainly expected to work to contribute to the household, foreigners noted the luxury and leisure of the married female of the middle class and the way that women of the upper and middle classes employed women servants or children to assist them in the domestic routines of washing and child rearing.[36] Their work lasted long hours, though work was irregular and often determined at the whim of the employer. Such bourgeois women are positioned in contradictory situations as in the case of Hannah More who, as a privileged lady, balked at Ann Yearsley's wish to buy the hogwash from her kitchen and appropriated to herself the capital raised from collecting subscriptions to Yearsley's book of poems. Ann Yearsley, the "Milkwoman of Clifton," filled her brief autobiographical narrative with anger at her exploitation and at the character assassination engaged in by her patron Hannah More. Yearsley, infuriated at the injury to her public character, writes the narrative as a preface to her poems in self-defense against her patron's abuse: "Here let me close this true but unpleasant narrative, with the humble hope of your forgiveness, for obtruding on your attention so insignificant a tale: but, as character is more precious than life itself, the protection of that alone compelled me to the task."[37]

Women's legal and political "selves," of course, were largely subsumed within men's. Women were excluded from the vote, and thus from the body politic, though gentlemen, as well as some freeholders and burgesses, could participate in elections. In addition to women's being unable to vote, their legal situation varied throughout the century according to marital status and class. Defining women's identity in relation to men, Blackstone's *Commentaries on the Laws of England* describe a woman held in place by a domination based on gender that uses the necessity for protecting her as its excuse: "By marriage, the husband and wife are one person in law: that is, the very being or legal existence of the woman is suspended during the marriage, or at least is incorporated and consolidated into that of husband: under whose wing, protection, and *cover*, she performs every thing; and is therefore called in our law fresh and *feme-covert*, . . . is said to be . . . under the protection and influence of her husband, her *baron*, or lord."[38] Blackstone goes on to indicate that under civil law, women have the right to possess estates and contract debts, "but, though our law in general considers man and wife as one person, yet there are some instances in which she is separately considered; as inferior to him, and acting by his compulsion" (1:444). Similarly, women are defined as the inferior parent and thus are excused from providing for their children because they act under serious natural and legal disadvantages. Patriarchy, then, encompasses and obscures the contradictions between qualification and subjection, but explains woman's inferiority by means of her inherently weak nature. In other words, the dominance of the husband over the wife in the domestic sphere is maintained to ensure deference to law and order that will be mimicked in the larger society.

A woman's subjection to her husband's correction and chastisement, "within reason," is made parallel to a man's correcting his servants and children. That is, she is an inferior who yields to superior male wisdom. In addition, class-specific references appear within Blackstone concerning domestic arrangements. First, the *Commentaries* indicate that restrictions on marriage among the lower class are undesirable because they prevent growth in population and encourage debauchery (1:438), particularly interesting in light of the fact that about a third of England's eighteenth-century marriages were begun when the bride was already pregnant, and the proportion of pregnancies increased toward the end of the century.[39] Second, Blackstone argues that the law should be more lenient on "the lower rank of people, who were always fond of the common law," and lower-class husbands should be permitted to restrain their wives if they misbehave. That is, under Blackstone's interpretation of the law, lower-class women are subject to stricter patriarchal dominance than women of the higher classes. These restrictions were particularly insidious in the laboring classes where the household could seldom survive without the employment of wife and children, their labor exploited but their legal rights curtailed. In brief, the category of "woman" intersects with the category of class legally to place women in various classes in contradiction with each other, the lower class of women the special prey of both sexes.

Further, in Blackstone, woman's space—the realm in which she has some authority separate from her husband's—is legally confined to a brothel or a constricted domestic space "that a wife may be indicted and set in the pillory *with* her husband, for keeping a brothel: for this is an offence touching the domestic oeconomy or government of the house, in which the wife has a principal share" (4:29). Her territory is restricted, then, to the marginal and private arena where she serves men's needs. Under criminal law in the eighteenth century, a woman was excused from the penalty for a crime if she was following her husband's command. Thus, the inequalities of the law for women were justified as necessary for the protection of the fairer and weaker sex, for "even the disabilities, which the wife lies under, are for the most part intended for her protection and benefit. So great a favourite is the female sex of the laws of England" (1:445). In short, female prerogative is granted, but it is sufficiently qualified so that the resistance to the dominant legal ideology of "woman" must be exercised in the realm of the invisible.

Eighteenth-century women were especially likely to be among the poor and the victimized, according to Dorothy George in her unsurpassed study. "There can be little doubt that the hardships of the age bore with especial weight upon them," she writes. "Social conditions tended to produce a high proportion of widows, deserted wives, and unmarried mothers, while women's occupations were over-stocked, ill-paid and irregular."[40] In the later eighteenth century, women were also the principal victims of lotteries, even purchasing portions of tickets with their last pence. In the Second Report of the Committee on Lotteries for 1808, the committee remarked on the special tendency of women to suffer from gambling on the lottery: "We frequently have females come to us when the head of the family has lived in credit and reputation and all of a sudden they are in ruin, the husband gone, the children in rags."[41] Ruined women, fallen from class privilege or male protection, were commonplace, and it seems very likely that the pauper class included more women than men.

The welfare of the working-class family depended on the wages of wife and children, even though their wages were much lower than men's. Eighteenth-century women of the lower classes produced life, but they also produced wages essential to the survival of the family unit. Employed as both day laborer and housewife, such women had more work and a lesser status than their working-class husbands. Women field workers found themselves making approximately half the wages of their husbands, particularly at harvest time when engaged in weeding or raking, yet that half-wage was crucial to the family's survival.[42]

These working-class men and women constituted the overwhelming proportion of England's population in the eighteenth century—approximately 80 percent.[43] In his autobiography, the tailor Francis Place indicates that weavers were kept at low wages because wage setters knew that the wife and children could also be forced to work at the trade.[44] Even within given trades, there were hierarchies based on gender. Those women who labored in trades such as watchmaking, silk weaving and shoemaking frequently were given the least-valued tasks and paid the lowest wages. Girls of six or seven years of age also became apprentices, sometimes to married women, sometimes to men, to assist in trades or to learn about domestic labor.[45] Women were often assigned a particular portion of the production of a commodity for which they were responsible, such as the watch-springing and lining in making timepieces (175). Women shoemakers made the least of all those who worked on shoes, and they were assigned particularly to shoe closing and binding. Dorothy George remarks, "Among women the lowest grade of workers seem to have been the cinder-sifters who worked at Tottenham Court and probably in all the outskirts of the town" (158–59). In fact, she indicates, "When we reach the level of the 'labouring poor' it can almost be said that there is no work too heavy or disagreeable to be done by women, provided it is also ill-paid" (170). Women sold dog and cat meat, and served as slaughterers for butchers. Charlotte Charke, the actress who also wrote plays and memoirs, hawked sausages, but considered fish hawking too low. Such women contributed to the perpetuation of the laboring class exploitation by performing unpaid labor for the well-being of the household or by supporting themselves and their children. But they were positioned through their labor as different and lesser beings, inhabiting a second sphere of existence. These class and gender ideologies intersect to produce female character and subjectivity, neither one in eighteenth-century England the single determinant of exploitation by a more dominant class or by the patriarchy that oppresses them all.

❧ IV

At midcentury a disintegration of preexistent categories of gender and character became particularly pronounced within an emergent capitalism. It was no longer so immediately apparent that the relationship of the sovereign to his subject was also the hierarchical relationship of husband and wife, as the powers of the monarchy were increasingly limited and dispersed in the wake of Walpole's administration and fall. Men and women had available to them unprecedented modes of proclaiming and disseminating the intimate details of their lives, and they give evidence that new experiences could not be subsumed within the available types and old generalizations.

This crisis in making character, bound up with issues of gender, marks a historical moment of definition and maintenance of separate domains for each sex as the middle class begins to recognize itself and to require more rigid divisions of labor based on sex to reproduce itself. From our present vantage point, we can reconstitute eighteenth-century character in order to understand the ways Pope, Fielding, Johnson, and the anonymous tracts on character attempt to fix gendered character when traditional notions about it are disintegrating and taking new shape in relation to the formulation of a bourgeois identity that comes to recognize itself. By midcentury gender differences become increasingly clarified, and texts such as Pope's *Moral Essays* (1731–34), Fielding's "Essay on the Knowledge of the Characters of Men" (1743), and Johnson's *Dictionary* (1755) function to identify and to regulate gender difference with a special explicitness and vigor. When Samuel Johnson defines "character" in the *Dictionary*, the familiar misogynist quotations from Milton and Pope on women's character figure prominently among the eight definitions he supplies. In the first and most familiar definition, character is a "mark; a stamp; a representation." It is the distinctive aspect that separates one from another, and, predictably, *Paradise Lost* provides the exemplary text: "In outward also her resembling less / His Image who made both; and less expressing / The character of that Dominion giv'n / O'er other Creatures" (8:543–45). "Character" is also defined as a letter of the alphabet and the manuscript hand in writing, but most relevant to our purposes, it is "an account of any thing as good or bad," "the person with his assemblage of qualities," and finally "personal qualities; particular constitution of the mind," which Johnson illustrates in the *Dictionary* with the first two lines of "Epistle to A Lady": "Nothing so true as what you once let fall, / 'Most Women have no *Characters* at all.'" Female character, contrasted with men's character, is thus lesser or the negation. Here the definition extends to the universal, the way that individual members of one gender are like each other, as female character is asserted to be unified while it is also unmarked or without identity. Women, as Pope writes in the argument to the "Epistle," can be "contradistinguished from the other Sex" as "inconsistent," "incomprehensible," and yet more "uniform and confin'd."[46] In short, female character with its combining of uniformity and uncertainty, its insistence on sexual difference and inferiority, poses an especially problematic crux for ideologies of character and identity in the period.

At the same time that women were encouraged to accept public perception as their "character," they were discouraged from "knowing" their own character or recognizing their intelligence. Feyjuo y Montenegro's feminist treatise mentioned earlier concludes in noting that men often fear women's self-knowledge because "it may . . . occasion many mischiefs, as fomenting the pride and presumption of women." His work argues instead for the benefits of women's knowing their own character: "Therefore, as women's knowing what they are does not lead them to entertain any overweening conceits of their accomplishments, it cannot puff them up with vain-glory or presumption."[47] In other words, to "know" one's character—to assert and recognize one's own specifically female identity—paradoxically threatens the possibility of maintaining the heterosexual gender system.

In "An Essay on the Knowledge of the Characters of Men," Fielding excludes women as he constructs a closed masculine system in which reader, author, and subject are male. Defining sexual difference is possible, Henry Fielding claims, though when pressed to articulate its female component, he leaves the equivalent of Sterne's blank page in describing Widow Wadman. In Fielding's essay, as in the anonymous *Characterism, or the Modern Age display'd: being an Attempt to expose the pretended Virtues*

of both Sexes; with a Poetical Essay on each Character (1750), true character can seldom be assessed from external appearances: "The whole World
becomes a vast Masquerade where the greatest Part appear disguised
under false Vizors and Habits; . . . a very few only shewing their own
Faces."[48] Fielding summons his readers to place character in the public
domain and make it an object of scrutiny. His essay calls into being a
reader and spectator who must hone his skills as an interpreter and observer of "human nature" in order to distinguish the external manner
from the interior truth. Private subjectivity, then, holds the truth. But
Fielding openly ignores "the Fair Sex, with whom, indeed, this Essay
hath not any thing to do." He asserts that drawing female character requires a separate skill, "the Knowledge of the Characters of Women
being foreign to my intended Purpose; as it is in Fact a Science, to which
I make not the least Pretension"(1 : 161). Even for so discerning an observer as Fielding, female character remains complex and elusive. In
other words, both Pope and Fielding give precedence to gender over
class, to sexual hierarchy over economic relations, in the formation of
character.

Similarly, in *Characterism*, gender is more significant than class in determining identity. Neither male nor female character is easily known,
but by implication the disparity between exterior and interior is greater
for women than for men. Unlike Fielding's text, *Characterism* divides the
characters evenly between the sexes: the first of two parts is on the ladies,
the second on gentlemen. The male characters are defined by profession:
the "Ambitious Clergyman," the "Corrupt Statesman or Complete Cour-
tier," the "Avaritious Lawyer." In contrast, personality or character traits
identify the women—the "Inquisitive Lady," the "Jealous Lady or Dis-
satisfied Wife," the "Hypocritical Lady," the "Great Man's Prostitute or
Actress." The "Female Pedant," for example, is defined as constituting a
third sex. She "has only, by her much reading spoil'd a good Pudding-
maker, and neglected those useful, tho' humble culinary Arts, more
properly adapted to a female Genius, to make herself that prodigious un-
couth kind of a Hermaphrodite, a deeply-read Lady" (13–14). Gender identification for a woman depends on not reading; that is, to be
"woman," one apparently must not read. Reading removes woman from
the kitchen and the boudoir.

In *Characterism* there is also an assumption of the dualism of character, and inner life is its indicator. Predictably, the women in *Characterism* are criticized for the dissimilarity between their interior and exte-

rior, "looking as innocent as Angels, whilst the *Devil* himself has an *Asylum* under their Petticoats." The truth of character for both sexes is internal, and the exterior is a falsification or a disguise. As this split between inner and outer emerges, the importance of believing that an interiority exists and that it serves as a code to the "real" character takes on greater significance. The split is even greater for women than for men. The key to real character is the construction of a secret interiority, and true character is difficult to ascertain. That is, it becomes increasingly important for women to produce a private subjectivity that corresponds to public perceptions of character, and the first-person autobiographical narrative becomes its legitimate public expression.

For eighteenth-century women, character extends beyond its semiotic rendition to have material effects in the world.[49] Women's real lives are made or irremediably ruined because of their public construction. In this context, taking up the public position as subject rather than object for the first time in autobiographical writing, eighteenth-century women construct a public secular character when "women" ostensibly have no character at all. In short, a woman must possess herself of both generality and individuation; she must be both a "woman" and, at some level, characterless. Personal identity becomes public in an unprecedented way, and the consequences for women could be particularly devastating. A complex relationship develops between women's entry into the public sphere, through publication, publicity, and sexual representation. Some women publicized themselves in part *because* they became illicitly sexualized; hence the two forms of transgression coincided. Such a woman must make her "character" cohere when her unorthodox experience may not fit the codes available to her and to her reader.

Gendered subjectivity and its public manifestation as "character" emanates not only from difference, variously defined, but from division, oppression, inequality, and an internalized subordination. These textual representations of woman's character both produce and reproduce the material ideologies of the period in a reciprocal relationship with them. "Woman," then, in eighteenth-century England, is both victim and victimizer, and women's autobiographical writings set out the contradictions of their multiple positionings, often without the ideology of genre, of self, or of the aesthetic to bind them into unity. Thus, gender ideologies are not the particular property of one class or gender but are in perpetual revision and contradiction, subject to co-optation by particular economic and political programs. The word, the text, the discourses of identity, and gender ideologies vie for dominance as the definitive order of intelligibility. Autobiographical writing by women, public and private, places these ideologies in text to articulate gender difference and to formulate gendered identity in its many revisions. The writings also provide potential ground for resistance to prevailing ideologies of gender and its intertwinings with class as articulation reveals the material excesses beyond "woman." Eighteenth-century women's diaries, journals, and published memoirs allow readers and writers to imagine alternative identities as they (mis)recognize the inadequacies and inequalities of current ideologies. Specific women's texts may be read then, as I will do in the chapters that follow, as the reiteration and contestation of these matrices, interrelated and interactive, subject to particular historical conditions and always in formation.

"Of Woman's Seed"

Women's Spiritual Autobiographies

She found it of singular Advantage to herself, to observe this Method;
and would often say, that were it not for her Diary, she should neither
know what she was or what she did, or what she had.

—Elizabeth Bury, An Account of the Life and Death of
Mrs. Elizabeth Bury (1720)

She [Dafeny Lightfoote], fearing her husband's displeasure for leaving
him soe long, returned home, and by her I sent my owne Booke of my
Life . . . , that Dafeny carried, which did abundantly please and sattisfy
her, and said that "it was not writt as if a weake woman might have don
it, but might have become a devine," tho' she knew the contents to be of
my whole life to that time.

—Alice Thornton, The Autobiography of Mrs. Alice Thornton (1668)

I

The public declaration by women of their characters comes into existence only at the point when newly literate women gain access to print,
and when the culture begins to believe there is something about women's
lives that is worth consuming. In England these conditions are met in
the large numbers of early spiritual autobiographies written by sectarian
women, especially the Quakers, Baptists, and Methodists. In spite of
their considerable political activities in defense of their beliefs, women
spiritual autobiographers closely resemble men in the kinds of religious
details they find significant enough to record and in the generic definition the autobiographical writing takes. The published texts largely reflect prevailing ideas about gendered identity, and the religious ideologies that inform them. Though they attest to the sexual differences that

were assumed by both sexes, there are, however, points at which shifting concepts of identity present a space to contest their self-evident nature. In spiritual autobiography, public and private as well as individual and collective, notions of gendered identity intermingle; for women, personal narrative also provides an occasion for confronting the particular ways in which their claiming public territory for speaking and writing violates social conventions of long standing, though medieval autobiographical writing by women also exists.

Even illiterate women wrote their lives. The preface to Elizabeth West's *Memoirs or Spiritual Exercises of Elizabeth West: Written by her own Hand* indicates that she was illiterate, and, because the text also indicates that the publication was copied exactly from the manuscript, we must assume that she dictated it to a friend.[1] But, in large part, the practice of women's writing themselves into texts proliferates when literacy and learning reach past the few aristocratic chroniclers to the middle ranks of society. It is noteworthy, for example, when Quaker Mary Mollineux writes that, in learning Latin, Greek, and arithmetic, she was tutored by her father "to more Learning, than is commonly bestowed on our Sex."[2] Instruction was largely conducted in Latin and Greek in England until midcentury, and women had little chance of entering the Dissenting academies.

Certainly many women privately kept their own spiritual narratives and diaries, but throughout the eighteenth and into the nineteenth century, women's literacy lagged far behind literacy rates for men though it continued, of course, to increase. In fact, it is not clear just what relationship exists between the ability to sign one's name and the level of literacy skill that was achieved by men and by women.[3] Assessing the level of women's literacy is further complicated by the fact that women certainly memorized and dictated when they could not write fluently, and they absorbed texts that were orally transmitted and circulated within the family even when they could not read at a high level of competence. But even if we treat recently compiled literacy data with skepticism, we can determine that the trend toward teaching women to read and write never matched the trend toward male literacy. During the 1750s, only about a third of women and 60 percent of men were able to sign their names at the time of registering for marriage, while in the 1760s, 70 percent of men and 44 percent of women were able to write their signature.[4] One mid eighteenth-century commentator, James Nelson, reflects a popular perception when he writes, in *An Essay on the Govern-*

ment of Children, "A Certain Author says, that there is not a Man in a thousand who reads well; if so, and Men assert a Superiority of Knowledge, it will be no unfair Conclusion to say, there is not a Woman in two thousand that does."[5] Similarly Wetenhall Wilkes indicates in *An Essay on the Pleasures and Advantages of Female Literature* (London 1741) that a gentleman at a coffeehouse "offer'd that not one Woman in Twenty, could write or dictate a Letter." Wilkes does not disagree with the alleged statistic, though he counters that women are deprived of an equal chance at learning.

Margaret Spufford has argued convincingly that the economic status of parents largely determined whether children would read and write.[6] Reading, for the most part transmitted by women to children, was more widely taught than writing among the artisan and laboring classes. But reading and writing were considered to be separate skills, and at mid-century, foundlings, for example, were taught only to read, not to write.[7] Though many wives of daylaborers taught reading, they may not themselves have known how to write. That is, in spite of their own lack of education, as ciphers of learning they were instrumental in preparing a generation of readers to enter the era of cheap print. The insistence on Bible reading and journal keeping as religious practices condoned by Quakers and Methodists may have spurred reading women to sharpen their skills and transfer them to reading and writing about the state of their souls. Early in the eighteenth century Susanna Wesley, John Wesley's mother, is explicit about the value she assigns to female literacy in a letter to her son: "That no girl be taught to work till she can read very well; and then that she be kept to her work with the same application, and for the same time, that she was held to in reading. This rule also is much to be observed; for the putting children to learn sewing before they can read perfectly is the very reason why so few women can read fit to be heard, and never to be well understood."[8] With the exception of her daughter Kezia, she says "all could read better in that time than the most of women can do as long as they live." In spite of her son's ambivalence toward women's preaching, Susanna Wesley gives priority to female education.

Quakers rather than Methodists constituted the largest sectarian group in England, drawing their membership largely from the middling sort, and at the turn into the eighteenth century their numbers (50,000 in 1691) equaled the next four largest Dissenting religious groups, Roman Catholics, Presbyterians, Independents, and Baptists.[9] Early in their history, Quakers took radical and subversive positions in relation to the monarchy and its strict regard for religious obeisance. Quakers refused to pay tithes for the support of the clergy, refused to submit to persons in authority, including representatives of the law or the state, and were imprisoned for refusing the Oaths of Allegiance and Supremacy. Further, their adherence to a belief in full equality encouraged equal deference to all people regardless of station. They professed religious convictions that encouraged the formation of a classless and antihierarchical society. The ideals of the Quakers rested heavily on the principle of individual revelation, of God's speaking directly to the "inner" person and infusing her or him with truth and light. With widespread dispersion of the King James Bible, personal interpretation of the Scriptures was not only possible, but was encouraged.[10]

Keeping an account of one's soul had the sanction of Quaker leaders. Particularly prone to contest state and civil authority, Friends such as Mary Mollineux and Mary Fell give accounts of imprisonment or stonings, but their writings also serve as instruments of passive resistance. Copies of the testimonies, journals, and tracts of the Quakers were widely distributed, and many were sold cheaply on the street. Yet paradoxically, the Quakers' own organization was hierarchical and patriarchal, its representations of the inner light often controlled by founder George Fox who exerted strong influence on the various writings of the Friends, even censoring many of the manuscripts that came his way.[11] Fox and other Quaker leaders urged the minute examination of the heart and an attitude of introspection as part of church doctrine, and he wrote journals himself. But he legislated that Quaker writings could be published only when they conformed to his prescribed notions of life experience and self-definition. Certainly the purpose of such widespread dispersal of conversion narratives among the newly and marginally literate was to proselytize. Women, then, who were seeking a "voice" were likely to tailor their identities and stories to the conventional expectations. Thus, the idea of spontaneity or of "truth" in the description of conversion is called into question, for certain patterns of perceiving and organizing one's experience were more approved than others.

Women were two or three times more likely than men to be Quakers or Dissenters, and it may have been their sheer numbers that placed pressure on conventional assumptions about women's place within religious sects.[12] "From the early days of the Separatist movement," asserts Michael Watts, "women usually outnumbered men in Dissenting congregations,

Episcopalian and Presbyterian pamphleteers had lamented the presence of women preachers in Separatist conventicles in the 1640s and women had figured prominently in the Quaker missionary movement, both in England and abroad. But for all this, women were not accorded equality with men."[13] There are instances of women's canvassing for signatures to petitions, of their petitions to Parliament and King, and of their prominence among the Levellers and Anabaptists; one historian finds that "of 360 Quakers in trouble for disrupting ministers during the period 1654 to 1659, 34 per cent were women; and of the fifty-nine Quaker ministers who arrived in America during the period 1656 to 1663, 45 per cent were women."[14] Women were authorized by conviction and by sect to challenge authority, interrupt ministers, travel, canvass, switch to a more devout husband, write and publish tracts, and sometimes to preach. John Lilburne, for example, argues against class and gender distinctions: "Every particular and individual man and woman that ever breathed in the world since [Adam and Eve] are and were by nature all equal and alike in power, dignity, authority, and majesty, none of them having [by nature] any authority . . . one over . . . another."[15]

Yet women are clearly positioned in contradiction in sectarian discourse. Though Fifth Monarchist John Rogers argued for women's fair treatment, according to his views they should still be prevented from preaching or sharing in governance of the sect.[16] William Winstanley, a Digger, also remained conservative in regard to women's equality in spiritual matters. Similarly, George Fox apparently wished to grant the separate women's meetings equality, but in effect, women did not fully participate in Quaker church government.[17] Though women shared imprisonment with their male counterparts for refusing the Oaths of Allegiance and Supremacy, Baptist women were excluded from full participation in the public activities of believers (from prayer and prophesying) and from holding church offices. The conversion narratives that sectarian women wrote may be read in some measure as instruments of resistance to the ways that those in authority perceived them.

For Quakers of both sexes, the moment of telling one's tale was also the moment of relinquishing the individual will—of giving over a sense of separation to the truth of the inner light which transcended time, place, and individual difference. They emphasized the importance of collective endeavor and mission, yet placed new authority in the individual's direction and regulation of her or himself. The number of actual autobiographical journals remained relatively small, but quite common were the collections of artifacts of an individual life that were often composed by a community of Friends and relatives. They aim to address a diffuse body of readers and describe the renouncing of an individual will. Included in these collections are testimonies, or conversion narratives, of usually less than a hundred pages. These first-person accounts or diaries, positioned within the religious ideology that each individual has direct access to experience, document the various authors' observations of God's actions in their lives. The purpose, of course, was to issue an urgent appeal to others to repent. They are schematic structures—a long period of searching for belief and meaning, often accompanied by profligacy, until the inner truth or light appears to them. What follows is a period of commitment and of witnessing to the power of God's message for all of humanity. For example, Joan Vokins's autobiographical account (published in 1691) opens with the testimony of acquaintances who corroborate that the self-accounting that follows is an identity publicly and collectively agreed upon.[18] External testimonies come from women friends, her husband, her eldest son, and a group of other Quakers in her community. The point of these multiple viewpoints is to emphasize a consistent soul, a sameness of character easily recognized and held in place for a reader. It is not a continuous narrative but a collection of letters and testimonies written from her sickbed in 1669. Without a conversion moment that she can make into an organizing event, she instead describes "taking up the daily Cross" (26) and her travels to New England and the West Indies. Like others, she envisions her commitment to the Friends as a turning away from "self" and toward community: "I cannot but abhor self, and breath, unto thee, that I and mine may for ever hold self in no reputation. . . . [B]ut self was very ready to hinder me, as the self-seeking Spirit is always those that are not aware of it" (47). In short, this Quaker journal moves toward a collaborative conceptualization of an individual identity, and the paradox of rapt attention to subjectivity combined with self-abnegation is reconciled in a practice of the soul's regulation.

Vokins's journal, like other Quaker journals, unfolds a model of a life well-lived, designed to convert others and to promote group identity. Quaker autobiographies often followed this predictable structure of describing their moral purpose, the period of conversion followed by becoming a Quaker, the wonderings about preaching, the resolution to speak and to minister, and the travels with Quaker companions to gain further converts. For both men and women, the Quaker testimonies frequently begin with descriptions of the narrator's early uncertainty and loneliness, which she or he takes to be unique. The temptations by the devil are frequently described as physical assaults on the body; and, spurred by Quaker doctrine, the testimonies use considerable imagery. Testifying believers find solace and companionship in the company of earthly friends, especially other Quaker women, as autobiography becomes a functional site of the emotional, a place to locate and represent it. Apparently Quaker doctrine allowed for public display of printed emotion and introspection. Wright places pressure on this idea to claim that Quakers were "pioneers in subjective autobiography."[19] In fact, Quaker journals were the primary ones published at the time, other diaries and journals being largely preserved as private documents.

Women who spoke out publicly began, then, to write publicly as well, and many ideas about gender and identity interplay in Quaker journals and other autobiographical writing. The Friends published nearly ninety confessions and journals from 1650 to 1725. Many early Quaker journals apparently derived from proclamation tracts that gave a warning, prophecy, or testimony of suffering experienced by believers,[20] but the practice of publishing the diaries of recently deceased people, diaries that were previously secret and sacrosanct, did not really begin in earnest until the early eighteenth century. One wonders about the economic benefits of the production of these publications. They may well have been published and sold to benefit the estate of the deceased, to pay for the burial, or to raise money for the sect in question. The authors frequently conclude with entries written on their deathbed, the diaries an indication of a lifelong struggle and an accounting in preparation for Judgment. But at first the diaries were published with the justification that they served as models of the virtuous life, that they reproduced the prevailing notions of religious women, and that they were records for the children of these women, who took full advantage of the religious justification for ending gender differentiation. In the case of Mrs. Housman, for example, Rev. Richard Pearsall makes such a claim: "Having perused the Diary which is here presented to publick View, we cannot but think, that as it exhibits a remarkable Example of the Christian Life, so it gives a fresh Testimony to the admirable Efficacy of the distinguishing Grace of God."[21] The extract of Mrs. Housman's diary that Pearsall includes demonstrates her methodical pattern of reviewing the week in her diary to identify blessings and sins. On 11 August 1711, for example, she reflects on herself through writing: "I enter'd my Chamber, and, I hope, with a Desire to enter into my Heart, that I might get some farther Acquaintance with myself, my State in general, and particularly what it hath been this Week and Day past; and methinks I can't forbear making some Remarks for my future Use" (40). The regular nature of self-review conflicts, however, with claims of naturalness Pearsall notes when he comments on her "unaffected, undisguised, and self-abasing Manner, and yet with that Degree of Pungency and Fervour" (v). These weekly bouts with the soul also become the occasion for dwelling on emotions and monitoring her knowledge, repentance, and obedience: "I think I realy felt my Heart burn within me. Such lively Impressions were made upon me, as cannot be express'd, nor conceived of, but by those that feel them. Surely it was that Joy, which a Stranger intermeddles not with" (84). The diary, then, is particularly useful in constructing an inner sentient self, a self inaccessible except when pondered in retreat, and unknown to itself except through regular writing but within the affectation of complete privacy.

The discovery of the "self" unaware of its public audience makes its artlessness seem more authentic. Thinking of the diary as secret transactions between herself and her God, Elizabeth Bury writes for many years in shorthand. In fact, speaking in the third person, she writes that she knew who she was only because she kept a diary; "were it not for her *Diary*, she should neither know what she *was* or what she *did*, or what she *had*." That is, her belief that she exists, that she possesses an identity, depends quite literally on its textual transcription. One of the first of the published diarists, Bury kept a diary that was intended to set out "a Pattern of welldoing before them."[22] Edited by her husband, it is a biography of nearly fifty pages until it becomes a verbatim diary that, he emphasizes, was written "without any Art or Affectation." He testifies that her manuscripts were never intended for public view, and he remarks on the enormously diverse nature of the topics included without prejudicing the reader against the work. Her diary, a place for "Wrestling with God," was crucial for monitoring every minute of her life: she "knew not how short her Day would be, and therefore she had no Time to loiter" (9). The inception of her diary and her moment of conversion seem to correspond: "When I was *Nine* or *Ten* Years old, I first began the *Work of Self-Examination*, and begg'd the All-searching God to try and discover me to myself: and I think, I may date my *Conversion* about that Time" (46). It was "the properest and most effectual Means to promote and carry on her spiritual and pious Designs; and at last determin'd upon this as one, *To keep a daily memorial of what she did;* which should be *A Witness betwixt GOD and her own Soul* (as she expresses it)" (9).

The sex of the soul preoccupies Bury as it does other Quaker women. Bury argues strongly that Christ is neither male nor female, and that *"Souls were not distinguished by Sexes"* (7), but she contradictorily accedes to a difference in women's ability to learn. She was angered "that so many *Learned* Men should be so uncharitable to her *sex*" as to place their philosophical disputes in language that is impermeable to women's limited understanding (7). Though her husband does not make this explicit, it would seem that Bury seems to assign this failure in the understanding of most women to custom, not nature. Thus Bury appears to waver about the inferiority of women's cognitive faculties. She counters Quaker practices of dominance over women, and the difference on which that denigration is based, by reconciling spiritual equality within an asexual Christ. In the funeral sermon she prepares for herself, she writes, "You must either think me extravagant in the Account, or you must conclude that in rational and religious Attainments, there is neither Male nor Female, but Christ is all and in all" (208). Certainly in the obscure sense in which Bury uses the word here, she is "extravagant"—that is, she strays beyond the bounds of moderation, exceeding the limits of the late seventeenth-century gender economy.

Elizabeth Harper's short extracts of longer journals also were published posthumously by a friend shortly after her death. In the case of Harper, a Methodist and wife of the shopkeeper Andrew Harper, the unnamed editor emphasizes the journal's unpremeditated quality: "I have published the following Extract from the artless Journal of a plain Woman, wrote merely for her own Use."[23] Attempting to make her claim of spontaneity and ordinariness credible, the editor says she "wrote down daily just what she felt, with all possible Artlessness and Simplicity" (iv). For Elizabeth Harper, as for other Methodists, the model for her life is another earthly being, a woman friend, rather than a scriptural example. For Harper, Mary Pearce "was a Spirit that sympathized with every one, both in their temporal and spiritual Trials. Indeed her own Life was a Life of Trials; which, she always said, was best for her, and no more than was needful to keep her from Pride, and to break her stubborn Will. But she bore all her Trials with Sweetness of Temper, and never mentioned them but to a near Friend. . . . May I tread in her Steps, and follow the Example of her Patience to the end" (44–45). Contemporary women, then, served as models for living, and the writing of their spiritual selves might make them at least as imitable as biblical characters.

Women wrote within the autocratic confines of their Dissenting sects, and the publication of their lives was often an act of devotion to husband or friend. Women's spiritual textual "selves" were guileless attempts to prepare their souls for an early death and judgment. These personal narratives police a community and contain dissent, but they also furnish women with voices that are often raised in opposition to prevailing gender norms and make possible more explicitly political documents that protest state restrictions on the sects.

☙ II

These spiritual records inspired notes of daily turmoil and struggle that take their constancy from the perception of friends and relatives rather than from a close look at the author's private thoughts. In addition to providing validation for private suffering, Quakerism also holds revolutionary power to give women first a public voice, and then a published identity and tradition, if a largely collective one. In fact recognition of women's mutual concerns brings gender into the foreground in these journals. Further, religious conviction gives women new authority to assert their independence from their husbands. George Fox suggested that a woman could leave her husband if he was insufficiently committed to the inner light, for God's will was to take precedence over an earthly master. Such a notion obviously was disruptive in the extreme to family life, and it did not find a sympathetic audience. Keith Thomas convincingly suggests that the Nonconformist sects during the Civil War appealed to women because of "spiritual equality, the depreciation of educational advantages, and that opportunity to preach or even to hold priestly office which they were otherwise denied . . . [as well as] self-expression, wider spheres of influence and an asceticism which could emancipate them from the ties of family life."[24] The contradictions in women's position within the church are many, however. Quaker women could serve as itinerant ministers or speak as prophets, but Quaker doctrine restricted women's preaching to women's meetings that were advisory to men's meetings, though even that freedom to speak in a segregated place was apparently denied to women in the early eighteenth century. Quakerism, then, provides tenuous grounds for subversion of patriarchal authority in language and in action, in preaching and in independent living.

Certainly women's own arguments for the right to preach also contributed obliquely to reinforcing the religious restrictions that were based on heterosexual difference. At the same historical juncture that brought Bunyan's *Grace Abounding* to publication, Margaret Fell, like many other Nonconformists, prepared tracts from her prison cell, including the best known, *Womens Speaking Justified, Proved and Allowed of by the Scriptures* (1666).[25] Second husband George Fox's view of her (the mother of eight children with Judge Fell) collapsed the distinction between political and domestic power into a maternal metaphor of matriarchal power and nurturance. She was envisioned as "a nursing mother . . . who feeds the hungry with good things, but the fat with judgement, who kiles and slayes the liveinge and raises the dead. Judgment is comited into thy hands . . . thou glorious daughter of Sion."[26] She had used her position as wife of Fell at Swarthmoor Hall to intervene with Cromwell and Parliament on behalf of Quakers, including Fox himself. Successful with Charles II, Fell obtained the release of all imprisoned Quakers, though the reprieve ended abruptly because of the Fifth Monarchy Plot. Serving as correspondent to traveling Quakers, she also traveled herself throughout England.

Women's preaching had been earlier defended on political and religious grounds by female participants in various Civil War sects. Fell follows these women in articulating a fuller argument for women's equality in public speech, one that George Fox had also voiced in *The Woman Learning in Silence* (1656) in which he had argued that Eve's fall did not condemn women to inferior and silent status. In Fell's treatise on behalf of women's preaching (albeit preaching only *to* women in the Women's Meetings), she contends that God joins man and woman in his image, and that sexual difference is created by men: "And God hath put no such difference between the Male and Female as men would make" (3). Though she repeatedly insists that difference is man-made, not God-ordained, Fell retreats from the radical implications of her ideas in order to reinstate a husband's authority over his wife in all areas except in matters of faith. But when Fell asks what authority guides a woman if she has no husband, she sows the seeds for further disruption of patriarchal authority; and, though Fell does not state them overtly, the implications of questioning traditional sexual hierarchies within religious discourse are disturbingly at stake within her text.

Fell's arguments raised political, religious, domestic, and sexual matters for debate and was potentially subversive of them. Fell's authority throughout is scriptural; that is, she newly imagines the creation story and the Pauline epistles as providing evidence for women's preaching.

Her justification is that God's gifts are granted to *all* of his children, not only men. She interprets Paul's injunction for silence in church as directed against the confusion of either sex's speaking, rather than against woman alone. In this hermeneutical argument against sexual difference, Fell transforms the church into the figure of a woman, so that condemning women's preaching is read as speaking against the church. Fell seeks authority in Christ's recorded words, as well as in reinterpreting traditional passages to identify women whom Christ ministered to and respected—Mary Magdalene, Joanna, and Mary the mother of James. More important, she describes these women as agents of Christ's message, establishing that divine messages can be channeled through the female body and voice. In addition, Fell makes distinctions among women, condemning some and praising others, thus avoiding a claim that women have special insights or superiority because of their sex. Rather, her argument is that because Christ was not limited by gender in seeking proselytes, we should follow his example: "Let this Word of the Lord, which was from the beginning, stop the mouths of all that oppose Womens Speaking in the Power of the Lord; for he hath put enmity between the Woman and the Serpent . . . and it is manifest, that those that speak against the Woman and her seeds Speaking, speak out of the enmity of the old Serpents Seed" (4). With a powerful rhetorical gesture, Fell acknowledges and then addresses men's fears of the devouring woman by envisioning a bestial Babylonian harlot, a dragon worshiper, who "hath made all Nations drunk with the Cup of her fornication," for she is "the woman that hath been speaking and usurping authority for many hundred years together" (10). She replaces this female monster with another woman, "the Bride, the Lambs Wife" who shines with clear light and represents the new inner truth, "*the Mother of us all*" who will cast out the harlot's brood. This woman testifies to the possibility of women's having a voice, consonant with motherhood, yet one that argues in behalf of their equality and autonomy in spiritual matters.

This equating of conversion with the destruction of a personified Babylon is commonplace in Quaker documents. What is remarkable is that Fell insists that turning to God means turning away from one sort of woman to another. She insists, then, on redefining the category of "woman": "For the Pope is the Head of the False Church, and the False Church is the Popes Wife: and so he and they that be of him, and come from him, are against Women speaking in the True Church, when both he and the false Church are called *Woman*, in *Revel.* 17" (17). Ultimately she finds precedents for granting women new privileges in God's coming through Mary, and her need to explain God's mission in choosing her as Christ's mother to her husband. Especially damning is her assertion that male preachers appropriate women's words in the Bible as texts for sermons, but remain unwilling to let present-day women preach. Thus Fell's revisionary acts are to authorize woman's public speech and her authority to make meanings for herself through rereading the scriptures. It was Fell's sense of apocalypse, her vision of a genderless church and of an androgynous divinity, that empowered her to testify to these possibilities for change. In other words, Fell refused to base church regulations on gender difference. Positioned at least partially within an ideology that allows her to imagine a world not dominated by heterosexual division and oppression, Fell can reinterpret religious doctrine with regard to gender even though the radical reforms that Fell and other Quaker women envisaged were held in check by their insistence that it was God's voice that spoke in transcendence and power rather than a collective and gendered voice protesting its subordination.

If such women found public vindication in preaching or in writing, others sometimes labeled them as lunatics or witches, their prophecy a sign of madness or of the devil at work. Such women insisted that God spoke through them, not that they spoke from an interior core of self. Such an overt and public vehicle of prophecy seemed to require that they were not "themselves," but agents of Christ. That is, their public identity belonged to them only in the loosest sense. Women's authority to preach was in fact sometimes compromised by their insistence that they were simply vessels for the divine: "I had now frequently to speak in meetings, and had satisfaction in so doing . . . [but] did not choose for myself, nor sought for openings . . . neither dared I to restrain openings, all which is unsavory. The Lord taught me to let it go just as it came."[27] Mrs. Elizabeth Andrews, a Quaker, describes the obligatory initial confusion and doubt so severely that madness seems imminent: "A great change, she found, had been wrought in her mind, tho' she knew not how it was effected," and she recounts her physical, as well as mental, sufferings in detail.[28] The madness is relieved when she begins to preach. Phyllis Mack has linked this sort of religious fanaticism to the figure of woman in order to argue that when women became public figures it was particularly as symbols beyond the social pale, as witches and visionaries.[29] But such arguments must be careful, I think, to recognize the way in which speaking in tongues or other enthusiastic activities were also passionately encouraged when Dissenting men preached publicly. There is, then, a relative genderlessness to the Dissenting vision.

What is especially remarkable for Dissenting women who wrote spiritual autobiographies, however, is less their emotional display than their record of turmoil over whether to speak publicly, often involving their conflict with scriptural, church, and domestic authority over public preaching. Many female spiritual autobiographers, more intent than Fell in maintaining a distinctive sexual identity, worried over the threat public speaking presented to it. Such a problem does not occur to men, but for women, the gap between their experience and the text that described it could only be negotiated by relinquishing their claim to being female. There is slippage between "soul" and "self" so that the assertion of the genderlessness of the soul makes possible a conviction that a female "self" is necessary and equal. Such women, too, had "no characters at all" in the sense that their selves seemed mere filters that allowed God to speak through them. But the women often disclaim any revolutionary intent, and they vindicate their writing because it will convert others. These personal narratives furnish women with "selves" that grant them power to imagine alternatives to prevailing gender hierarchies.

Many women reinterpret scriptural precedents to justify activities as they rewrote biblical history to recover a female tradition. In fact, Elizabeth Bathurst in *The Sayings of Women* (1683) compiled a list of examples of passages in which women speak about the manner in which they are witnesses to God's glory, including references to Sarah, Rebecca, Rachel, Leah, Miriam, Deborah, Hannah, Abigail, Esther, and others.[30] She argues, as did Margaret Fell and others before her, that Christ was of woman's seed, and that Christ unites male and female: "So I shall draw to a *Conclusion*, laying down this assertion, viz. That as Male and Female are made one in Christ Jesus, so Women receive an Office in the Truth as well as Men, and they have a Stewardship, and must give an account of their Stewardship to their Lord, as well as the Men. . . . Christ, who came of the Womans Seed . . . is the Healer of our Breaches, and Restorer of our Paths: And in him Male and Female are made all one, as saith the Apostle Gal. 3.28."[31] That is, women's ambivalence about preaching is much in evidence. The women frequently mention a youthful desire to be a minister which is dismissed because their sex restricts them to masking their ambition to speak through public disavowal.

In other testimonies and narratives women spiritual autobiographers give witness to their beliefs and focus their scattered views of "self" into a notion of a "woman" who can preach in such a way as to resist prevailing gender definitions. Jane Pearson anticipates the publication of her work after her death and justifies it because she believes it will serve as a precedent and reach those individuals who could not hear her preach. For Jane Hoskens, an upper servant, the representation of the painful uncertainty of considering whether or not she was called to the female ministry persists in her early adulthood. Throughout her short narrative, *The Life of that Faithful Servant of Christ Jane Hoskens* (published in 1837), she defends the importance of the equality of men and women.[32] She takes courage and inspiration for her conviction from a large outdoor meeting at Plymouth during which Thomas Wilson spoke on David's distributing bread, meat, and wine to women as well as men, "which Thomas repeated two or three times, from thence inferring the Lord's influencing females, as well as males, with Divine authority, to preach the Gospel to the nations"; after that she frequently speaks at meetings. Unlike those who claim their journals are private, Elizabeth Taylor Stirredge willingly makes her life available in *Strength in Weakness Manifest* (1711), as a witness to her beliefs.[33] Her diary, like that of other Quaker journalists, describes the construction of a private subjectivity of loneliness and repeated suffering, both because of Stirredge's Dissenting faith and because of her sense of inferior female status. Just as women were made akin to animals, killing a Quaker, she writes, is on a par with killing a louse (47). Thus she links persecution under patriarchy to persecution under the state. Further, the text is published as testimony to her having been granted "a Talent and Gift of the Ministry upon (which he is pleased to give unto both Male and Female, they being all one in Christ Jesus)" (preface). Thus, this distinction, this talent for preaching through and to biographical example, is *not* meant to separate her from others but to suggest an equalizing of spiritual possibilities across gender division. Women's preaching, then, is again given sanction through the unity of sexual difference in Christ.

Stirredge's struggle over whether to preach persists. After a typical introduction consisting of her friends' declarations of her piety, she assigns the belief in her own individuality to the devil: "But it was the Enemy's work to perswade me, there was none like unto me: And because I could not Pray in words, as others could, and likewise under afflictions, therefore the Lord had no regard unto me" (7–8). Like other spiritual women who believe themselves silenced as divine retribution for their sins, Stirredge found herself dumbstruck, unable to speak or to preach, and

paralyzed with questioning. This heresy of individualism also has economic consequences: it spurs her to deck herself in fine clothing and to
long for possessions. She also recounts the antagonism directed against
two women friends who dare to give testimony: "He grieved them, bidding them go Home about their Business, and wash their Dishes, and not
go about to preach. And said, that *Paul* did absolutely forbid Women to
preach; and sent them crying home" (57). In short, Stirredge's published
autobiographical writing, then, becomes an alternative means of giving
testimony, itself an act of resistance: "I will leave some Testimonies that
the Lord was pleased to lay upon in that Time of great Suffering *in Bristol*" (76). In other words, to speak and write publicly threatens the gendered division of labor, but it also grants women a textual space of
identity.

Like many other Quaker women, Elizabeth Ashbridge begins her account with her early recognition that she is bound by the limitations and
difficulties of being a woman within the faith. Influenced and educated
by her mother, she regrets that she "sometimes grieved at my not being a
boy, that I might have been one [a minister]." [34] In a brief but continuous
fifty-nine page narrative, women's preaching serves as an organizing feature in the tale: "At this meeting there was a woman spoke, at which I
was a little surprised; for though I had heard of women preaching, I had
never heard one before. I looked on her with pity for her ignorance, and
in contempt of her practice said to myself, 'I am sure you are a fool, for
if ever I should turn Quaker, which will never be, I would not be a
preacher'" (19), though the precise nature of her contempt remains unspoken. Ashbridge, more fully than most, tells a riveting story of long-
ings to steal, God's interruption of her preaching with thunder and a
loud voice, and temptations to suicide. In addition, Ashbridge recounts
her unsatisfying marriage to a stocking weaver. Her husband, wishing to
escape the embarrassment of having a Quaker wife, deserts her to become a soldier in Cuba. In the powerfully dramatic dialogue preceding
their separation, she describes a warning given to her husband by a
friend: "'There, did not I tell you your wife was a Quaker, and she will be
a preacher soon,' upon which my husband once, in a great rage, came up
to me, and shaking his hand over me, said, 'You had better be hanged on
that day'" (32). But in the concluding testimony from her second husband, we have a rare account of a woman's ministry: "As a minister, she
was deep in travail, clear in her openings, plain and pertinent in her expressions, and attended with that baptizing power, which is the evidence

of a living ministry" (58). Unwilling to succumb to prevailing definitions of woman, Ashbridge defied convention and patriarchal authority in speaking and writing publicly.

Margaret Lucas is explicit in her recognition that being born a woman precludes the possibility of university education and the right to preach. *An Account of the Convincement of Margaret Lucas* (1770), distributed posthumously in weekly numbers for four pennies, describes a double persecution and a double resistance.[35] First she relates a long period of moving toward the Quakers against the wishes of her uncle and aunt who abused her: "When any one came into the shop, [my aunt] told them, I was the newmade Quaker. . . . Each time she thus exposed me, she held me by the left arm, which was next to her; and when I used the plain language she pinched me very bad; and so often renewed her pinches, that it was very hard for me to bear them" (73). Her persecution is also gender-specific. As a child she hopes to enter the clergy but "often saying to myself, and others, if I had been a boy I would have been of their cloth (and brought up, as my brother was designed by my father to have been, at the University)" (10). She repeatedly describes her loneliness and sense of isolation, and she seeks models in Scripture including Zacheus, Joseph, and Jacob. Like Ashbridge, she specifically records her initial disgust toward women preaching: "The first time I ever heard a woman preach, from a prejudice imbibed from my companions, and, probably, an aversion in my own nature, I thought it very ridiculous; and the oftener I had opportunities to see it, the more I secretly despised it" (115). She presents herself as feeling great and protracted consternation over a period of years, fearing that she will be required to preach. Her ambivalence increases as she writes, "But like Naaman, the captain of Syria, [I] would fain be excused from this thing. I now began to believe that such exposures were something more than voluntary offerings, and was convinced, from many proofs, that my state had been as clearly spoken to by my own sex, as by the other" (117). Finally, she believes that her preaching is divinely ordained. God gives her a directive to speak, and instead she succumbs to a lethargy, sickness, and deep slumber: "Not many more meetings passed before I was tried again; when I fixed my body as firm as I could, but found it impossible to still my mind" (124). Convinced that she can no longer *voluntarily* resist, she gives her will over to God: "In a little time the trial came again; and, in that moment, the enemy of my soul suggested, that if I got up, I should not be able to stand; but, thanks to the Almighty, I was strengthened to try, and found him a liar. The expression of a few words produced a blessed change. There seemed now a new heaven and a new earth" (131). Her moment of speech, then, is presented as the second and most important climax, for, after her convincement, her release into speech becomes the activity toward which she is propelled.

In these texts as in others, Quaker women relate their quick and steady recognition of their persecution as Quakers. Their hesitation in taking up a public voice rests less on the fear of state persecution than on the ambivalence and even repulsion they initially feel at linking preaching to a female body. They indicate that the price of preaching may well be a private rather than a public one of separation from family and friends, and the loss of conventional sexual definition.

The *Memoirs of the Life of Catherine Phillips*, published near the end of the eighteenth century when the generic patterns of Quaker autobiographical writing were well entrenched in consciousness resolves the uncertainties of gender in a more linear narrative structured into chapters, anecdotes, dialogue, summary statements, analysis, and periodic self-assessment, unlike the earlier narratives.[36] In spite of having Quaker parents, Phillips describes an early period of distress in which she questions the religious principles of her parents and entertains the voice of the devil. A writer of poetry at an early age, she gives up the imaginative life after a call to the ministry because "it might have engaged my attention too much, or tended to make me popular" (21). In her travels to America as a minister with her friend Lucy Bradley, the first of many trips with a variety of companions, she glories in a sense of being a pioneer: "No women-ministers had visited part of this country before us, so that the people were probably excited by curiosity to attend some of the meetings we appointed" (85). She provides specific cautionary advice to single women who travel as itinerant ministers. She urges them "to guard their own minds, lest they admit of any pleasing imagination, and stamp it with the awful name of revelation; and so slide into a familiarity and freedom of conversation and behaviour, which might tend to engage the affections of young men" (111). In spite of her own extensive travels to dangerous areas, she still voices the belief that women are "the weaker vessels by nature" (158), and she accounts for the moments of female strength as anomalies, divinely produced.

These new opportunities for women's independence and travel also encourage female bonding within the sect. Crucial for women's gaining courage to speak is the sense of friendship and union with other women.

Jane Pearson's *Sketches of Piety*, a lively narrative extracted from her memoranda, describes the pleasure she found in her companion Mary Kirby of Norfolk.[37] She mentions an early sense of privation and loneliness, in spite of a happy marriage: "United to a choice husband, I swimmed as in an ocean of pleasure; but I witnessed, instead of peace on earth, a heart-piercing sword" (19) when the devil assaults her. She seeks precedent lives, but is convinced of the uniqueness of her situation, a tension only relieved after she gives testimony at a meeting at Greysouthern. That is, in speaking, she finds release and a sense of community. For Pearson, the change is specific and decisive: "And now I had great peace of mind, so that instead of my heart being a place for dragons, for owls, and for screech owls; for cormorants, and for bitterns; there began to be a melody in my heart, as it were the voice of the Son of God, whose countenance is comely; and the myrtle, box, and pine spring up in that heart that had been a breeding-place for nettles" (29). This autobiography, published in 1817, has begun to follow a more fixed and regularized form, and Pearson's text finds neat closure in the testimony of others and an account of her death.

By the later eighteenth century, then, diaries, journals, testimonies, and conversion narratives call into being a recognizable genre dominated by certain expected conventions, but the particular sect of the autobiographer becomes increasingly obscure as the conventions of Quakers, Methodists, Baptists, and Independents intertwine. Presbyterian Elizabeth West found *A Relation of the Fearful Estate of Francis Spira*, the work that had inspired the Baptist Bunyan, distressing in its apparent atheism: "I was once reading a book, called Francis Spira, which did hurt me more than all the books ever I saw; O that I had never seen it! for I thought, I would make the same end he made."[38] Instead, she turned to Bunyan's *Grace Abounding*. And it was Elizabeth West's journal, as well as Wesley's notes on Scripture, that inspired Mary Gilbert's journal (1769). In addition, woman can begin to look to other women for a recognizable published tradition as publication widely disseminates these texts. Spiritual selves inspire more spiritual selves, the construction of shared "private" emotions, as published writing and public preaching make a collective, if second-sphere, subjectivity available to women. For Gilbert, keeping a diary allowed her to move toward holding her mind constant and being able to locate the "wickedness" of her inward parts: "O my God! gather in my scattered Thoughts, and let my Mind be fixed entire on Thee!"[39] But she is quite explicit about her belief that she possesses a divided self:

"Saturday Jan 25 In the evening I retired, and entering into a strict Self-examination, I found I must own with the ROYAL PSALMIST, *My inward Parts are very Wickedness.*" She fears that her character is as barren as a fig tree, her soul cold and dead, and she meditates on the awesomeness of death. Every moment must count, and the diary will assure her vigilance: "O may I spend each Day and Moment in the Service of Him, who has so graciously preserved me to this Time!"[40] By the end of the century, a tradition of journal keeping begins to evolve in which autobiographical works (rather than Scripture or conversion experiences) inspire diary writing, so that a need for textual precedents and exemplary lives is both produced and reproduced.

III

Although women participated in all the radical sects in large numbers, some subtle differences between the sects manifest themselves regarding the status of women. According to Methodists, women were allowed to speak to an assembly of men and women—though with reservations and restrictions. Women were not encouraged to publish their lives, though in Wesley's journals, he seems to encounter and convert considerably more women than men. While lives of women were included in Wesley's *Arminian Magazine,* the lives of men outnumbered them 10 to 1. Most Methodist women's accounts were not written by themselves, but by husbands, sons, or friends. They are, in the main, stories of chaste and upright women who lead and record unremarkable lives, their stories less eventful than those of their male counterparts, and they are, unlike the journals of Quaker women journalists, largely untroubled, at least in public texts, with the desire to resist patriarchal church leaders on the question of women's preaching.

Susanna Annesley Wesley, mother of John and Charles, was the twenty-fourth child of her father's second marriage, her mother a Puritan, her father a clergyman with aristocratic connections who was ejected from the Church for his failure to subscribe to the Act of Uniformity.[41] Defending her right as a woman to encourage people to come to church, Susanna Wesley indicates her self-sacrifice for her children and her mission as mother to instruct her children in a "regular method of living" in a letter to her husband that John Wesley includes in his journal: "At last it came into my mind, Though I am not a man, nor a minister, yet if my heart were sincerely devoted to God, and I was inspired

with a true zeal for His glory, I might do somewhat more than I do."[42]
She records her excruciatingly methodical plan: "I resolved to begin with
my own children, in which I observe the following method: I take such a
proportion of time as I can spare every night to discourse with each child
apart. On Monday I talk with Molly; on Tuesday with Hetty; Wednesday
with Nancy; Thursday with Jacky; Friday with Patty; Saturday with
Charles; and with Emily and Suky together on Sunday" (3:33). In spite
of insisting on her girls' equal right to read, as noted earlier, Susanna
Wesley defines providing children's religious education as a female role—
a private function that conforms to traditional notions of female status
and reasserts gender difference.

Methodist women were encouraged to speak in the bands, where they
apparently seemed reticent, but not to speak in church. Not surprisingly,
there was segregation by sex and marital status in the bands that Wesley
organized for prayer and introspection. He notes in his journal for April
1759, "I likewise insisted on another strange regulation, that the men
and women should sit apart" (4:304). Wesley made very fine distinctions. The Bible (1 Cor. 14.35), he wrote, only forbade public preaching
when women were placed in positions of authority over men. Women
were not to speak in what was technically defined as the "church." In
other words, he told women that they could speak if they did not define
it as preaching, spoke only briefly with frequent interruption, and did not
preach from a text.

Wesley displayed considerable ambivalence about women preachers
in the Methodist movement, and he did not occupy a consistent position. Wesley distinguished the Methodist position from that of the
Quakers: "The difference between us and the Quakers in this respect is
manifest. They flatly deny the rule itself, although it stands clear in the
Bible. We allow the rule; only we believe it admits of some exceptions"
(2 December 1777; 6:290–91). One of the strongest proponents of
women's preaching, Mrs. Sarah Crosby, formed "The Female Brethren"
with friends, including Sarah Ryan and Mary Clark. In 1761 Wesley re-
sponded to her query about the subject, "You lay me under great difficulty. The Methodists do not allow of women preachers; neither do I
take upon me any such character." But he equivocated by allowing for
exceptions if women had what he termed an extraordinary call. He wrote,
"I advise you, as I did Grace Walton formerly, 1. Pray in private or public, as much as you can. 2. Even in public, you may properly enough
intermix *short exhortations* with prayer. But keep as far from what is called

preaching as you can: therefore never take a text; never speak in a continued discourse, without some break, above four or five minutes." Because they were successful, however, Wesley later gave his approval to Sarah Mallet's preaching: "We . . . have no objection to her being a preacher in our connexion, so long as she preaches the Methodist doctrines, and attends to our discipline."[43] Mary Bosanquet Fletcher wrote on 12 September 1810, "I was, as I have been told, in great danger of death from my tongue being tied, and much bleeding ensuing from having it cut. It was though I should be dumb. . . . How often have I abused thy goodness, and offended with my tongue."[44] A tradition of Methodist women preachers in Leeds, the birthplace of Sarah Crosby, continued with Mary Bosanquet, Elizabeth Ritchie, and Ann Cutler, who preached during a scarcity of ministers; but once there were sufficient male preachers, the antagonism against women ministering renewed itself in the early nineteenth century.

Women's spiritual autobiography is remarkable, then, for containing some of the first examples of women's taking themselves as subjects, and of their turning subjectivities into texts in spite of restrictions. These texts deserve to occupy an important place in the autobiographical canon emerging from the working and middle classes in the early modern period, the period that marks the beginning of women's public writing. Autobiographical texts encourage the organization and self-regulation of those classes in a technology of the spiritual self but simultaneously construct a lesser domain for woman. The formation of a tradition of such writing is historically important particularly as it begins to establish newly dominant experiental codes and categories for women. For Quaker women spiritual autobiographers, the emphasis falls upon their identity as *Quaker* more than upon their gender or class or sense of self. These and other spiritual autobiographies are largely shaped by male directives and patterns, but they depart from them when those paradigms cannot allow for the conflict produced by women's contradictory situation as silenced believers, urged to proselytize but muzzled by patriarchal restrictions on their sex within a persecuted sect. When women speak and write, their language derives from the codes of class, culture, and historical moment, their "voice" distinguishable from that of their male counterparts on subordination to husbands, in their forming close friendships with other women, their assuming the authority to reinterpret Biblical texts, and their resistance to the sexual division of labor regarding preaching. Further, the persecution under the state sometimes evoked women's protests to Parliament and in published political pamphlets. Thus these texts, instead of providing access to the universal feminine or its significance in language, may more usefully be seen as one location of a confrontation between the Dissenting ideology of equality under God and of sexual difference, a contradiction with which many of the women contend by separating a religious authorization to speak from all other forms of public discourse. Rather than representing an inherently female self, they define a predicament brought about by culturally produced gender distinctions in forms shaped and sanctioned by the state, husbands, and fellow believers who both supported and censured them.

Dissenting women autobiographers rarely reflect on their decision to write, except as they indicate that the function of self-writing is to ruminate regularly over their spiritual state or to convert others by example. This is, after all, to be expected, for few wrote with the expectation of publication during their lifetime, and the responsibility for posthumous publication could be shrugged off. They consistently confront the contradiction of being given voice through God, yet being denied the encouragement and opportunity to preach. These women are less interested in identifying a unique "self" than in collective endeavor, their sense of self deriving from divine inspiration. Religion gives them new independence yet severely restricts it as well. Within these spiritual autobiographies, the ideas of hierarchy based on sex and equality based on faith compete for dominance within the "voice" and self-inscription of women. Thus, they potentially expose the contradiction inherent in the term "sexual equality" in confining their speaking to authorized modes and, for Methodist women, in submitting to the ambiguities and even absurdities of Wesley's dicta on preaching. Assumptions about the oddity of women's preaching seem to persist throughout the century, and when sufficient male preachers became available as itinerants, religious women were again relegated to silence. That is, the sexual division of labor is reinstated, a subordinate realm of self-regulation is made available, and the advances that Quaker and Methodist women made are again tempered.

Gendered subjectivity at its public inception in autobiographical writing, then, finds ways to preserve the gaps between given ideologies as women persist in explaining their lives through God's will. Silenced within the church, women emerge publicly to publish. Autobiographical writing is a site of resistance as well as justification; heterosexual difference is reinscribed as much as it is resisted. There is, simultaneously, an acquiescence to existing patriarchal relations and the threat of newly expanded public spaces being opened to the previously silent private woman. And, later in the century, as a tradition of published spiritual autobiography becomes recognized, the narrative gaps close so that Quaker and Methodist lives have a repetitive and predictable quality, and their generic codes and structures are easily recognized. These "extravagant" women spiritual autobiographers, however, in an unorthodox genealogy, may have wandered astray to make apertures through public speech and writing for other women to violate gendered conventions. The scandalous memoirs written by women at midcentury serve as a later site of sexual transgression that offers more radical secular challenges to existing notions of female identity, and renewed potential for changing the female subject.

CHAPTER EIGHT

Heteroclites

The Scandalous Memoirs

*I wish to show that elegance is inferior to virtue, that the first object of a
laudable ambition is to obtain a character as a human being.*
—Mary Wollstonecraft, *Vindication of the Rights of Woman* (1792)

A woman's REPUTATION *is forfeited if she admits the other sex to privacy. . . . A man may do well enough without* FAME, *but how will the
woman go on when she has lost her* REPUTATION?
—Hester Thrale, *British Synonymy* (1794)

I

The middling common sense of Wesley's Methodism with its requirements of self-regulation and religious conversion held no appeal for the
scandalous memoirists who also wrote at midcentury. In her memoirs,
Laetitia Pilkington alludes to her refusal to conform to this discursive
model when she remarks, "I am a sad digressive writer—by which my
readers may plainly perceive I am no Methodist."[1] Pilkington's memoirs
(1748–54), like the memoirs of other women such as Teresa Constantia
Phillips (1748–49), Charlotte Charke (1755), Frances Anne, Viscoun-
tess Vane (1750–51), George Anne Bellamy (1785), Ann Sheldon
(1787), Elizabeth Gooch (1792), Margaret Leeson (1797), and others,
are intimately connected with canonical eighteenth-century literature.

Laetitia Pilkington, Cibber's protégée, corresponded with Samuel
Richardson and promulgated anecdotes about Jonathan Swift in her mem-
oirs. Richardson lamented Con Phillips's seduction by Lord Chesterfield
in his letters, and Fielding mentions her *Apology* in *Amelia* (1751).
Colley Cibber's daughter, Charlotte Charke, appeared in Fielding's plays.
Horace Walpole, Thomas Gray, and Lady Mary Wortley Montagu read

with interest Lady Vane's memoirs—inserted as the eighty-eighth chapter of Smollett's *Peregrine Pickle* (1751)—and their enormous popularity overshadowed the rest of the novel. John Cleland's *Fanny Hill* (1748) owed its inspiration as much to scandalous memoirs as to French erotica. But in spite of Wayne Shumaker's observation that "nonreligious confession seems to have begun in the eighteenth century with the lives-and-amours of Mrs. Pilkington, Connie Phillips, and the Lady Vane," the memoirs have received little serious attention in studies of the eighteenth century or books on autobiography. Shumaker gives credit to Charlotte Charke for "the earliest explicit justification in Engish for the writing of obscure lives." He continues, "The effect of these autobiographical romances coming on the heels of *Pamela* and *Clarissa,* may have been important to the development of a subjective emphasis"; but the implications of his observation remain unexplored.[2] What the scandalous memoirs have in common with Methodist writing is the production of a private emotional interiority as the "truth" of identity, but rather than reading them as precursors to the romantics, I will consider them as sites of converging and competing discourses that display ideologies of gendered character.

The scandalous memoirs relegated unlicensed sexuality to the lower classes. In this class coding of sexual desire, these dangerous women reveal a female sexuality out of control that signals the instability of lines of lineage and the uncertain transfer of property. Through sexual conduct and its textual representation, woman's sexuality and fertility thus escape the parameters of the bourgeois family, and the illegitimate production of heirs becomes increasingly likely. Largely excluded from traditional familial relations, the memorists refuse to recognize themselves as permanently attached and subjected to men. Destitute women, portraying themselves as victimized by cultural expectations of the female, take up the pen for the first time in the scandalous memoirs to earn money and publicly to defend their "character" against assault by their social betters. With these memoirs, aberrant sexual behavior and its control becomes identified as an important focus of gender conflict. These autobiographical writings function in the context of the energizing ideology of heterosexual difference to insist on the coherent, containable "character" of eighteenth-century woman: they respond to pressures toward a unified identity, and the memoirs work as moral lessons to encourage women to regulate themselves. At the same time, they disrupt conventional paradigms of that female character. Increasing numbers of women demand public published space, and women who transgress also publicize that transgression. In short, women's representation escapes its policing to threaten patriarchal relations as the scandalous memoirs negotiate the culture's clashes over character, class, and gender in published texts.

As we have seen, "character" and "identity" in the eighteenth century come to "mean" both a universal human nature and an individual principle, the ways in which we are the same and unlike others in our species. Identity implies permanence and sameness over time, a persistence throughout its narrative presence in spite of the changes that it tolerates or excites. "Character" in these mid eighteenth-century renderings is perceived as a public construction of a private interior reality, the essence of a person. A published interiority is, then, a code to the "real" character. But for women, subsumed within male definitions of character, defining a public character becomes especially difficult. Women must construct a public character when they are constructed as having no character at all.

II

The scandalous memoirs mark the point at which women widely produce as well as consume discourses about themselves and their experience. As women become the subject and object of their own scrutiny, they adopt stances, often situated in contradiction, in the ideology of gender. The scandalous memoirs, the first significant public form of self-writing that women take up, other than spiritual autobiography, are the narratives of experiences from which men are excluded. These works revive the Greek (male) form of public self-defense in the agora, but their content is a uniquely female situation—the Fall from chastity that transformed "character" and all other experience. Like the earliest autobiography—the ancient Greek encomium that was delivered to the public—these memoirs seek to mend the public and rhetorical image of the women's character though the revelation of the private.[3] Each text vindicates the apologist from blame, while, in contradiction, it attempts to escape the moral and social system that requires that very explanation.

Most scandalous memoirs find their genesis in an attack or accusation, and the texts function rhetorically to vindicate the apologist publicly from the charge. These texts are apologies in the classical sense of defense or justification within admission of guilt (a form made familiar in the nineteenth century by Cardinal Newman). The church played no small part in assigning guilt. Technically, a fornicating woman, even at the end of the eighteenth century, could be required to do public penance, "bareheaded, barefooted, and barelegged," and bound in a white sheet.[4] For fallen women to acknowledge their crime publicly and to provide minute particulars of it (often even while denying it) indicates a kind of implicit consent to their condemnation by the dominant powers. These works define and perpetuate sexist assumptions about women: they reproduce heterosexual difference. Thus, through the subject itself, the scandalous memoirs function culturally to maintain the gender division, confining women to categories of good or bad, virtuous or fallen, while the "masculine" is allowed a broader range and a superior sphere.

But the memoirs also counter the mandate to hide their shame, for the purpose of the narratives is actively persuasive; the memorist acts as a historian who compiles and relates the facts and encourages the reader to respond sympathetically as judge and jury. Thus, the scandalous memoirs also contradict authorized versions of "woman." In this sense, they are open to feminist as well as sexist constructions of character. These works implicitly contradict order and authority in their combination of a public defense of conduct with a stubborn resistance to reconciling the inconsistencies of character. To be an eighteenth-century woman speaking and writing is to appropriate cultural positions that may essentialize woman into the "natural" differences of, say, the medical discourses; but these texts also, by resisting pressures toward making character coherent, display multiple and contradictory ideologies of character and gender. From my point of view, this fundamental ambiguity raises the question of a text's intelligibility. The gender of the author may not dictate the terms of making texts intelligible, but it may "identify the issues at stake," as Michèle Barrett puts it. Barrett raises the crucial question in relation to gender: "So the image itself, or the play or whatever, might not necessarily be intrinsically sexist or feminist, it may depend on who is reading or receiving it and how they do so. The image itself may often be ambiguous, at least partially open to the different meanings we choose to construct upon it."[5] Thus women's autobiographical writing may be inserted into history, culture, and politics, and subject to various appropriations.

The radical dimension of these texts is also implied in their common designation as "scandalous." It is worth considering why these memoirs were deemed culturally unacceptable, and what semantic codes were required to make the female character produced within them seem offensive. A large part of the "scandal" of these memoirs, it would seem, is the very fact that they are public documents; woman's fall should be a matter of remorse privately confessed to one's God, and woman's "character" should only be revealed privately. Pope defined this private woman's sphere in the familiar lines of "Epistle to A Lady":

> But grant, in Public Men sometimes are shown,
> A Woman's seen in Private life alone:
> Our bolder Talents in full light display'd,
> Your virtues open fairest in the shade.
>
> (199–203)

But the memoirs require a reader and an audience, and they insist on a public forum—a new and remarkably different sphere for women's writing. Unlike fictional seduced maidens, these "real" women insist on the power of the published first-person narrative to vindicate their actions. In this sense, the scandalous memoirs give public language to a kind of gendered character and subjectivity that were previously unmentionable. For women to speak, Catherine Belsey has written, is "to threaten the system of differences which gives meaning to patriarchy." She continues, "The installation of woman as subjects is the production of a space in which to problematize the liberal-humanist alliance with patriarchy, to formulate a sexual politics, to begin the struggle for change."[6] Scandalous memoirists radically redefine the Fall, away from the notion of an irrevocable act that condemns women to solitude and retreat and toward an argument for contesting universalization of the female.

One reaction to women's insistence on a public sphere is evident in "The Heroines: or, Modern Memoirs," a poem published in the *London Magazine* that chastized Pilkington, Phillips, and Vane for boldly publishing their shame, unlike nymphs of old:

> by youthful passion sway'd,
> From virtue's paths incontinent had stray'd;
> When banish'd reason re-assum'd her place,
> The conscious wretch bewail'd her soul's disgrace;
> Fled from the world and pass'd her joyless years
> In decent solitude and pious tears:
> Veil'd in some convent made her peace with heav'n,
> And almost hop'd—by prudes to be forgiven.[7]

In this poem woman's private consciousness, her interior, is simplified and characterized as tantalizingly evil. For example, Bonnell Thornton posing as "Roxana Termagant" calls attention to the public infamy of the memoirists in *Have-at-you-all*: "I have also had the honour to be mistaken for some one of those Female Apologists, who have admitted us into the privacy of their most secret (I might say, most scandalous) intrigues."[8] Woman's subjectivity is constructed as private, secret, and evil. In other words, an individual woman's character is paradoxically impossible to know and yet, if known, it would be predictably consistent in its virtue or vice with other women's character.

The mid eighteenth-century public, then, read the scandalous memoirs as a canvas on which to construct their ideas of women, and the contradictions in the public's interpretations of them were widely varied, not unlike the responses to their fictional counterparts, *Pamela* and *Clarissa*. Readers sought recognizable shapes as they attempted to codify the traits and attributes described in the memoirs and the novels. In *The Tablet, or Picture of Real Life*, the anonymous author calls attention to two opposing camps, "particularly among the ladies, two different parties, *pamelists* and *antipamelists*," who argued "whether the young virgin was an example for ladies to follow . . . or . . . a hypocritical crafty girl . . . who understands the art of bringing a man to her lure."[9] Attitudes toward the subjects of the memoirs were similarly divided as to whether they were examples of virtue or vice. Calling Pilkington, Phillips, and Vane a "Set of Wretches, wishing to perpetuate their Infamy," Samuel Richardson places the blame on male shoulders for the corruption of young women, but he employs the tales to maintain women's subjection. At the same time, he encourages the reading of Lady Vane's scandalous memoirs and uses the occasion to divide women into good and bad, to set the female sex against itself. He writes to Sarah Chapone, "I send to your worthy son (I could not before) that Part of a bad Book which contains the very bad Story of a wicked woman. I could be glad to see it animadverted upon by so admirable a Pen. Ladies, as I have said, should antidote the Poison shed by the vile of their Sex."[10]

Female independence also threatens heterosexual difference. In another letter Richardson asks Chapone's opinion of Lady Vane "and her too-forgiving Lord" and then responds passionately to her query about why "it should be thought improper for a woman at *any* Age to be independent: I have enumerated upwards of Twenty Reasons to Miss Mulso, why Women, for their *own* Sakes, shou'd not wish to be so. Subordination, Madam, is not a Punishment but to perverse or arrogant Spirits." Richardson misses the point about the material conditions of production of the scandalous memoirs. He typically fails to note that most fallen women (unlike Clarissa) were not possessed of a fortune that would support their independence. In fact, scandalous memoirists typically wrote their stories while indigent and in distress. But Richardson utilizes the scandalous narratives to forge his argument against financially independent women who, in his view, are the most vulnerable to men's wiles: "The Little Histories I have of her [Mulso], of several Women who had failed in common Prudence and common Modesty, were given to elucidate this Point, and to shew that Women are safest when dependent." He continues, "The Designers of our Sex, make their first Enquiry after independent Women. . . . I cannot, but in a very few Cases, allow, that a Woman, tho' not perhaps indiscreet, is safest in her own Keeping, if she have a Fortune considerable enough to be a Temptation to the Hungry, the Indigent, the Presuming of our Sex."[11] This factually inaccurate fixation on financial independence suggests the extent to which Richardson found the scandalous memoirs a threatening, if elusive and contradictory, assertion of female autonomy and of an aggressive and distinctive female identity.

Many eighteenth-century readers, angered by the memoirists' moral defense of their sexual conduct, urge the women to admit their active participation in their own downfall, the way in which they, like men, are driven by passion rather than chance. An anonymous letter to Lady Vane acidly remarks on this failure: "I must own, it is at present the Fashion for Ladies of your Profession, to write the History of their Lives in order to induce the good-natured Part of the World to pity their Misfortunes; which, if you will believe these Apologists, always flow from some fatal Cause or other that they could not possibly avoid, and never from their own ill Conduct."[12] In *Amelia,* Henry Fielding also treats the scandalous texts as the location of the erotic and forbidden. Fielding draws the narrator's curtain down over Booth and Miss Matthew's imagined love nest in prison to "lock up . . . a Scene which we do not think proper to expose to the Eyes of the Public. If any over curious Readers should be disappointed on this Occasion, we will recommend such Readers to the Apologies with which certain gay Ladies have lately been pleased to oblige the World, where they will possibly find every thing recorded, that past at this Interval."[13] For Fielding, then, the scandalous memoir is codified into a universal and predictable representation of female transgression.

In another response that sets up opposing notions of female sexuality, eighteenth-century readers absolve the female apologists of passion, and nullify their sexual desire, as a means of excusing their unconventional behavior. In a pamphlet that appeared in response to Lady Vane's story, *An Apology for the Conduct of A Lady of Quality, Lately traduc'd under the Name of Lady Frail,* the author defends Lady Frail's "irreproachable Character." While she is held accountable for loving Mr. Vane, she is acquitted of excessive sexuality: "The misconduct of this *Lady* had been intirely owing to Ill-usage, on the Part of her Husband, and Indiscretion on her own; and did not proceed from any Impulse of Sensuality." Nevertheless, further intimate details of the affair "never before made publick" are included.[14] Paradoxically, the memoirs both illustrate woman's sexuality and assert her lack of sexual desire, to insist that lust is male; they both confirm and deny that every woman is at heart a rake. When Virginia Woolf read Laetitia Pilkington, she sensed this disparity, remarking that she was a "very extraordinary cross between Moll Flanders and Lady Ritchie, between a rolling and rollicking woman of the town and a lady of breeding and refinement,"[15] but, as we have seen, this combination of the lascivious and the chaste, of the lower class and the lady, produced a code in the troubling form of the scandalous memoirs.

In the mythology of eighteenth-century sexuality, as Patricia Meyer Spacks has pointed out, women must not acknowledge their own passion: "The characteristic tactic of women writing about themselves is to deny their own sexuality while perceiving the quality in other people."[16] These sexual feelings that make up the gendered subjectivity I am delineating here are not inherent but rather are desires situated in particular historical circumstances. Thus, at this point in the definition of female textual identity, the reading of scandalous memoirs for both men and women would seem to give access to the innermost recesses of women's sexuality, but in writing scandalous memoirs, women articulate feelings that were previously unwritten. These feelings allow women to make female interiority an object of consumption and a commodity for exchange as they possess themselves. Once a "fallen woman" speaks a textual "self," she becomes a subject—the perceiver instead of the perceived. In contrast with seeming to be a generic abstraction, she is an "individual" who participates in the particular and the universal through loneliness, anger, and passion. Though some scandalous memoirists capitalize on their woe, in others self-pity coexists with the celebration of sexuality. At this moment of loosening restrictions on the representations of desire, women's autobiographical writing produces a new individuated yet universal female subjectivity that has public value. Female subjectivity is for sale.

The memoirs also function in part to satisfy an emergent fascination with aspects of sexual life in the eighteenth century. The voyeuristic reader, urged to adopt a position of moral reproof, is simultaneously compelled toward sexual excitement that makes men potent through domination. Many versions and translations of French confessional erotica made their way into England throughout the century, and most focus on women's imagined private subjectivities.[17] The English New Atalantis (1709) had much in common with the French chroniques scandaleuses, and, as John Richetti has pointed out, "the scandal novel or 'chronicle' of Mrs. Manley and Mrs. Haywood was a successful popular form, a tested commercial pattern" of vicarious pleasure in the public scandals of the aristocrats perpetrated by their less fortunate victims.[18] Of course, Memoirs of a Woman of Pleasure (Fanny Hill) was published in 1748. Nonfictional narratives of trials for adultery that focus on "the object of the scorn, pity, and derision of [a woman's] relations, her former associates, and the public" were published throughout the century. Like the memoirs, the trial volumes advertise themselves as moral tracts designed to prevent others from committing the crime of adultery. The preface to the second volume of A New Collection of Trials for Adultery, 1780–1802 suggests that "to publish to the world these illicit Amours may, therefore, be found the most effectual Means at present of preserving Religion and Morality . . . and should the Evil complained of still increase, we shall still continue to expose it . . . and render Vice ashamed of its own Deformity."[19] These accounts, accompanied by suggestive engravings, reprint a series of depositions filled with sexually explicit details of the adulterous act. As such, they condemn specific women through the "characters" that the narratives produce. With the proliferation of newspaper and periodical accounts of details previously considered private, a woman with a public reputation had in turn to publish contradictory evidence if she was to alter the version of her public character already in circulation.[20]

John Richetti characterizes the fictional scandalous memoirs as myths of persecuted innocence which portray "the destruction of female innocence by a representative of an aristocratic world of male corruption." Setting out a conflict between moral innocence and erotic fantasy, the seduced-maiden narratives of Haywood and Manley simultaneously represent sacred religious values that center in woman and secular values that center in man. Richetti sees these texts as romantic tales of resignation and self-abnegation that appeal to a largely female readership.[21] These novels are often collapsed into the same category with the autobiographical texts as displaying familiar characters and urging the reader to pity yet feel superior to the fallen woman. But perhaps more than in the novels, the heroines of the autobiographical memoirs defy the boundaries of archetypes and stock characters from earlier genres. They often refuse to demonstrate any remorse or to reform; they take on male libertinism, frequently defining themselves as other than typical "woman." Many narratives bristle with energy and passion rather than anguished submission to female strictures. If some scandalous memoirists cite passages from *Jane Shore* and characterize themselves as victims, they also exhibit ways that the pattern of the seduced maiden is insufficient to contain many of these women's lives.

The scandal then, in the works of these eighteenth-century memoirists who recount their fall from *man's* grace, derives as much from the power of producing an economically independent female public character that deviates from the known as from the power of the salacious content. What also leads these tests to exceed definitions of "woman" is the persistence of Pilkington, Charke, and other secular autobiographers in assigning responsibility for their fate to "man," not God, so that the memoirs may be read as a corpus of antimasculinist literature in their frequent attempts to blame men and circumstance, "not so much to *justify* or *apologize* for [a woman's] own Conduct, as to fix the Saddle on the right Horse."[22] Frail blames her husband's impotence, Robinson her father's desertion, Leeson her brother's tyranny, Phillips her husband's polygamy. If Lady Vane writes "I have been unhappy because I loved and was a woman," Charlotte Charke announces "I THEN WAS WHAT I HAD MADE MYSELF," and Elizabeth Gooch claims, "I have a soul that will never bend under the yokes of tyranny and oppression."

III

These familiar gendered characters of the lascivious whore or the seduced maiden are among the models available for thinking about women's interiority and allowing readers to harness their individual lives into conventional forms. But as I have demonstrated, the memoirs also threaten to expose the contradictions in limiting text and character to these paradigms. In fact we can discover in the scandalous memoirs an-

other model for the definition of female character, one that both over-
laps and takes a different course from that of the seduced maiden or the
whore. This production of female identity finds its source in the imitation of spiritual typologies, but it also testifies to the absence of the female "self" from theological and philosophical formulations of identity
in the period.

For example, the male fortunate fall of the prodigal son—the compelling spiritual and familial myth of separation and reunion, of independence accepted and rewarded—seems largely unappealing to the eighteenth-century woman. The fall, the moment of spiritual identity crisis
for male figures that assumes an originary essence, leads to metamor-
phosis from one assumed "character" to another. The prodigal son par-
able portrays a crisis of filial rebellion that reaches resolution in the son's
ability to turn a tyrannical father into a caring one who respects his son's
newfound right to an independent character. For the prodigal son, the
separation from family and the fall into sin enables him to achieve independence, as well as return to the father's fold.[23] In contrast, the female
autobiographers in their writing subvert the idea of permanent regret or
change after the fall. Because women are largely excluded from this spiritual myth of separation and reunion, of independence accepted and rewarded, some female memoirists celebrate their fall from chastity and familial favor in assaulting those who would deny them the "character"
they assert. As Richardson warns, asserting female independence brings
turmoil rather than reconciliation. These writing women translate the
female fall into public notoriety; the fall from chastity and familial favor
becomes the pattern of a public declaration of identity.

The parallels between the fall into knowledge of sin and the fall from
chastity are familiar to eighteenth-century readers, and both kinds of
falls spur woman's release into language and discourse. According to the
serpent in the garden, Eve's eating from the tree of knowledge unfetters
both speech and reason. Such a temptation to possess divine power and
autonomy is especially compelling in Milton's *Paradise Lost*, where man
is woman's author and authority. Eve reminds Adam of her subservience:
"My Author and Disposer, what thou bidd'st / Unargu'd I obey; so God
ordains, / God is thy Law, thou mine: to know no more / Is woman's
happiest knowledge and her praise" (IV. 635–38). Sexuality is frequently associated with women's writing in satiric attacks written at the
same time. Women who write are portrayed as lustful monsters who
scratch their scribbling itch in such antifeminist satires as *The Great Birth*

of Man (1686), *The Folly of Love* (1691), *Sylvia's Revenge* (1688), and *The Poetess* (1688). In this sense, then, women's sexual histories fulfill conventional formulations of women's characters in the eighteenth century. These formulations make it difficult for a female memoirist to claim individuation and difference, for they are read as the universal failings of the whole sex.

But Charke, Phillips, Pilkington, Robinson, and others speak within a secular gendered interiority that revises the fall of spiritual conversion narrative. Though it is structured around a literal fall from chastity, the memoirists' moment of transformation is usually also a fall away from social acceptance and culturally sanctioned discourse. The female autobiographers capture this moment of crisis as a particular occasion for articulating a "character." In traditional spiritual autobiography, crisis brings transformation, a time when the individual becomes inevitably and incontrovertibly different from what she or he was. The crisis requires a permanent change in identity which, for the female apologists, is an attempt to convert the *reader* to a belief in a version of their character as innocent. In a lengthy plea for her virtue to the reader, Mary Robinson writes in the late eighteenth century, "GOD . . . will know how innocent I was of the smallest conjugal infidelity. . . . These pages are the page of truth, unadorned by romance, . . . and I know that I have been sufficiently the victim of events, too well, to become the tacit acquiescer where I have been grossly misrepresented. Alas! of all created beings I have been the most severely subjugated by circumstances more than by inclination." [24] Laetitia Pilkington gives lip service to providential harmony and order at the conclusion of her narrative, but she suggests that whatever structure the deity has designed is overwhelmed by the competing constructions of her life and character. Both defiance and manipulation of religious convention thus produce the female character.

IV

Autobiographical texts such as those by Charke, Pilkington, and Phillips devise new tropes for women's lives, while simultaneously reproducing the cultural languages and familiar patterns of human chronology available to them. These and other eighteenth-century women writers insert the possibility of making themselves their own object into the current discourses on character and, in doing so, subvert and contest male life patterns and female stereotypes. Because no existing model fully or consistently satisfies them—not seduced maiden, remorseful convert, lusty lass, or prodigal son—these women and their texts are both victims and revisionists of received ideas about female character. The scandalous memoirs implicitly consent to domination according to gender and class to confirm male superiority. But they also contradict that authority by redefining the fall and the status of women, by exploiting a public forum to insist on the power of the printed word, and by resisting the textual production of a consistent and unified female identity that rests safely within middling common sense.

I want to look more closely here at a number of these autobiographical texts to mark the many ways that they unveil the impossible ideological contradictions of eighteenth-century female character. Charke, Pilkington, Phillips, and Vane excite the reader with the erotic and even violent consequences of producing public female character. For example, in her Apology (1748), Phillips indicates the difficulty of the task of countering the versions of her character that are circulating: "The Minions of publick Fame are generally dress'd out with accumulated Virtues, to which they have no manner of Pretension. On the other Side, let the Cry begin against any Person (especially a Woman and a fine one too) she shall instantly be loaded with Crimes that her very Thoughts are a Stranger to, and utterly abhor." [25] Seduced at the age of ten by Thomas Grimes (Lord Chesterfield), she writes to defend her innocence to the public, even including extracts from legal pleas and answers in Chancery. The Apology testifies against the aristocracy and its inevitable patriarchal biases: "Once in a thousand Years, a Woman should be found who has the Courage to take up Arms against her Oppressors, and prove that even a Lord may be—a Villain" (3:40). The Apology recounts lurid details of the seduction, which resembles Clarissa's with its woman panderer, entrapment, drugging, and exchange of letters; later, she is beaten, stripped, and branded with a red-hot poker because she is unwilling to sleep with her bigamous husband, Henry Muilman, a prominent Dutch merchant. The question Phillips raises is, which sex is to be blamed in the gender war: "It was to be taken for granted, I must be the worst of all Women, or the Tables would turn, and you must appear the vilest of all men" (1:iii).

The scandalous memoirists often attempt to regain control over the fragments of gossip that destroy their reputations. Teresa Constantia Phillips personally oversaw the advertising and production of her autobiographical narrative. [26] Angered that the London Gazette, the London Eve-

ning Post, and the *General Daily Advertiser* had refused to advertise her book because of Mr. Muilman's influence, she distributed it from her own house. When publishers were unwilling to include an announcement that she was being threatened with Newgate, she included the details in the second number of the *Apology.* [27] Print becomes the courtroom and the reader the jury as Phillips notes with some pride that she has been her own best promoter, her public notoriety paradoxically bringing economic gain with it: "I have, on that Account, already reaped considerable Benefit" (1.iii). In short, Phillips openly acknowledges the way in which she was able to make her unfortunate life into property to be sold.

Biographical passages in the *Apology* describe Phillips as an innocent persecuted maiden whose true story warns young girls of a similar fate, but the spirited and lively autobiographical letters interspersed among these passages contradict the suffering-maiden model. The male narrator congratulates her because she does not resort to the usual female responses. Both male and female narrators argue that her "character" exceeds her gender: "She is formed with a Disposition very opposite to this *Female Supineness.* Her Misfortunes have shewn her the Necessity of becoming superior to them, and every new Oppression she meets with, adds fresh Vigor to her Fortitude: . . . for she has a Soul too masculine, to become an Opponent fit to answer his Lordship in the *Billingsgate Stile*" (3:33). In the letters mingled with the biography, Phillips acknowledges the futility of her effort to argue her case convincingly, for a woman can never recover from her fall: "No, my Lord, these are the Disadvantages we labour under from being born Women; and they are such, that, for my own Part, were Beauty as lasting as our Date of Life, to change my Sex I would be contented to be as deform'd and ugly as *Aesop*" (3:13). Her lived experience cannot be contained within the definition of "woman." She writes to an unknown gentleman, "My Fingers are crampt, and my Mind no more at Ease than it was; nor will it be, 'till I have the Pleasure of seeing you; for in this Particular, I am no Woman" (2:117). The *Apology* reveals the gaps and contradictions in the category of "woman" when Phillips courageously attempts to defend herself from male oppressors.

The lively popular version of the memoirs of Lady Vane that appears in Smollett's *Peregrine Pickle,* filled with sexual encounters, also makes plain the oppositions in female subject positions. In these memoirs, Vane's "essential" gendered character brings about her misfortune. She calls herself an innocent, but paradoxically feels she must account for woman's supposedly natural envy and pride. She is without remorse for sleeping with Mr. S. but refuses to separate from her husband "as her character was still unblemished."[28] Wondering how her own individuated character can fit the category of woman, Vane is divided between self-defense and self-alienation in condemning her whole sex. She writes, "I found as many trifling characters among the men, as ever I observed in my own sex" (519). Her husband's character, she writes, is weak and womanlike. In fact, she concludes by completely turning the tables to aim the lines from Pope's "Epistle to A Lady" ("Tis true, no meaning puzzles more than wit") against her reprobate husband who, she says, has no human character at all (538). For both Phillips and Vane, conventional male character serves as a resource and an enabling contrast that produces an unconventional female identity. The resulting tensions, typical of the scandalous memoirs, highlight the fluidity of gender relations.

Writing memoirs may set the autobiographer against "herself" as well as against other cultural norms. The female apologists assent to this splitting, which makes recognizing one's own "character" or "self" difficult. Laetitia Pilkington invents a dialogue between these divided parts and criticizes her own style and content. Speaking to herself she writes, "Madam, your story has nothing in it either new or entertaining; the occurences are common, trivial, and such as happen every day; your vanity is intolerable, your style borrowed from Milton, Shakespeare, and Swift, whom you pretend to describe, though you never knew him; you tell us a story of his beef being over-roasted, and another of a mangy dog—fine themes truly!"[29] Charlotte Charke goes further than Pilkington in distancing herself from the "self" or "character" she hails in the text. Calling herself a "nonpareil," a great curiosity, she begins with "The Author to herself" rather than the author to the traditional patron. "I . . . shall, for the Novelty-sake venture for once to call you, FRIEND; a Name I own, I never *as yet have known you by.*"[30] Her individuation produces a divided self and segregates her from any potential alliances with other women, fallen or otherwise.

Both Charke and Pilkington display their "inner" character as an index to their "real self"; but both puzzle over the contradictions made manifest in trying to explain the disparity between their unconventional actions and their conviction of worth. Pilkington constantly indicates that she writes, in part, to controvert her husband's public accusations and to revise the public's version of her personal history: "Though I led the life of a recluse, I had every day some new story invented of me" (166). The world lies about her disobedience to her parents and about her elopement, and she writes to correct those unauthorized versions of her public character (210–14). She repeatedly appeals to the reader as the judge and jury to believe the fact that she is *not* the "Irish whore" of her public reputation. But she also describes her triumph over titillating situations, including the teasing seductive talk of the male subscribers to her poetry.

At times Pilkington, like Phillips, presents herself as passive, persecuted, and helpless as she falls into seduced-maiden tropes. Her early history calls for a pitying reader who will believe that her unfortunate marriage was meant to assuage her parents, not to rebel against them. "As solitary in London as the pelican in the wilderness" (210), she recalls the biblical Martha as well as the classical Niobe and her tears. At another point, resorting to the language of sentimental tragedy, she plays Jane Shore to a lover's Lord Hastings (250) to lament "one fatal folly" and claims that her alleged infidelity occurred because an admirer trapped her in a room: "but Lovers of Learning will, I am sure, pardon me, as I solemnly declare it was the attractive Charms of a new Book, which the Gentleman would not lend me, but consented to stay till I read it through, that was the Motive of my detaining him" (100). Pilkington then enacts the cultural expectation that reading leads to female downfall.

Yet, commenting within the memoirs on the public's response to the earlier volumes, Pilkington also revels in the power of the published word, "more especially as my word is passed to the public; and my word I have ever held sacred." She usurps the language of spiritual autobiography, claiming that she is the Word, but she rejects the identity between body and language implied, and she instead emphasizes the peculiarity of her identity: "I am, in short, an heteroclite, or irregular verb, which can never be declined or conjugated" (35). She is both verb and noun: "But, alas! poor I have been for many years a *noun substantive*, obliged to stand alone, which, praise to the eternal goodness! I have done, notwithstanding the various efforts of my enemies to destroy me, many of whom I have lived to triumph over, though they encompassed me on every side like so many bulls of Basan" (307). The salient facts of Pilkington's life can be extracted, but the text is achronological and disjunctive. In the narrative, written a decade before Sterne's *Tristram Shandy*, the trivial is always disrupting the linear description of the past. Pilkington peppers

the narrative with liberal quantities of her own poetry; her mind publicly
roams from gossip to dreams, from anecdotes about Swift to opinions on
conjugal bliss.

Though she has obviously read Shakespeare, Milton, and Pope, her
female muses are Madame Dacier and Katherine Philips, "the matchless
Orinda." Her poetry insists on woman's right to distinguish herself from
men, and from other women, by representing private and individual feelings as "the inmost recesses of my soul" (242). Unquestionably Pilkington
includes the poetry to pad the blank pages; but the poems also become a
vehicle for the felt experience of her loneliness—poems on memory, solitude, sorrow, and adversity, and a prayer for tranquility. The original
poems she incorporates become another convincing argument against ac-
cepting public versions of her character, male typologies for a female
identity, or generalized assumptions about women's interiority.

One of her longest poems, "The STATUES or, the Trial of Constancy:
A Tale for the LADIES," answers Mr. Pilkington and Swift, and accuses
men of the inconstancy they level against women (69). *Man* is tested,
and *man* fails, offering the lovely maid a chance to deliver an anti-
masculine diatribe. Within the poem, the maiden's attack paralyzes the
pursuing prince, and turns him into a statue:

> She spoke. Amazed the list'ning monarch stood,
> And icy horror froze his ebbing blood;
> Thick shades of death upon his eyelids creep,
> And closed them fast in everlasting sleep;
> No sense of life, no motions he retains,
> But, fixed, a dreadful monument remains;
> A statue now, and, if revived once more,
> Would prove, no doubt, as perjured as before.
>
> (11. 67–74)

If Pilkington bemoans her fate because of her husband's supposed
tricks, she also celebrates the power of the public word against her ac-
cusers, the force of her vital female character against a lifeless male convention. In short, when the character displayed in all three volumes is
weighed, the memoirs seem less self-pitying and plaintive, less passive,
than recent readings suggest. If reading, writing, and learning bring about
her downfall, these activities take on agency for her release from conventional female character. They enable her financial gain, the expression of
emotion, a means of self-defense from those who would despise her, a

mask of self-scrutiny behind which to reconceive authority, and, finally, a contestatory public version of gendered character through the publication of a private one.

But whenever Pilkington's character begins to resemble an autonomous and coherent whole, she fractures it by adopting the mask of anonymity or of Mrs. Meade (a pseudonym she assumed soon after leaving Dublin). She frees herself to redefine Mrs. Pilkington's public character: "for by that [Mrs. Meade] I always went in London; so that the numerous stories of Mrs Pilkington's being in taverns, bagnios, etc, which my husband says he can prove (*Mem.* he lies) never appertained to me; but to his own Cousin Nancy Pilkington, whose father lives in Pill Lane—and who is herself as common a prostitute as ever traversed the Hundreds of Drury" (228). Or she plays at switching gender so that she will be treated less deferentially. She recounts an incident with Swift: "'I wish, sir,' said I, 'you would put the question to the company, and accordingly to their votes, let my sex be determined.' 'I will,' said he. 'Pilkington, what say you?' 'A man, sir.' They all took his word; and, in spite of petticoats, I was made a man of after dinner: I was obliged to put a tobacco-pipe in my mouth" (411). Pilkington explores a variety of identities that mock traditional gender distinctions, and affects to care very little about the world's opinion.

Pilkington defends herself by writing her text but she is also quite literally befriended by Colley Cibber, the poet laureate after 1730, actor and manager at Drury Lane, author of his own *Apology* published in 1740, and, oddly, father of Charlotte Charke, who wrote her own autobiographical narrative as a plea to be restored to his favor. Like Laetitia Pilkington's, Charke's *Narrative* (1755) describes a disguised, fragmented, and isolated character that defies universal typologies. A heteroclite like Pilkington, Charke also invents multiple and serial subjectivities that play among the available possibilities for gendered character in the period.

An actress and author of three novels and three plays, Charke, like her father, exhibits a contrived eccentricity. Charke's work begins in the spiritual autobiographical mode. If her earthly father Cibber allows her to return to his bosom, she will enact the role of the prodigal daughter. I am not, she declares, as sinful as the prodigal son, yet my father cannot forgive me (121). Because Cibber ignores the first installment of her memoirs, a reconciliation to her earthly father is thwarted and the reader, not God, will judge her: "The Reader may remember, in the First Number of my Narrative I made a publick Confession of my Faults, and, pleased with the fond Imagination of being restored to my Father's Favour, flattered myself, ere this Treatise could be ended, to ease the Hearts of every Humane Breast, with an Account of a Reconciliation" (117). The happy ending Cibber demanded of *Clarissa* was denied to his own daughter. Her secularized prototype is to be found in the sentimental reconciliation exemplified by Thorowgood's forgiveness of Barnwell (a role she frequently played) in Lillo's play *The London Merchant:* "If my Pardon, or my Love be of Moment to your Peace, look up secure of both" (121). Her history, like a criminal's, ought "to be properly examin'd, before it is condemn'd," and she acknowledges that she has done "a Thousand unaccountable Things" (11–12).

Charke also toys with the dramatic fiction of seduction and betrayal. Announcing that she was the tenth child of a woman of forty-five, "an unwelcome Guest" and an "impertinent intruder" (15–16), she describes how her rebellious marriage to Mr. Richard Charke, a violinist, sours when he turns unfaithful. She blames her father's tyranny on the malice of her eldest sister who played Goneril to her Cordelia. Certainly the material conditions of Charlotte Charke's life were, to judge from all reports, incontrovertibly tragic. According to Mr. Samuel Whyte, an eighteenth-century witness, she presented a pitiful figure near her death, "a tall, meagre, ragged figure, with a blue apron, indicating what might else have been doubted, the feminine gender; a perfect model for the copper Captain's tattered landlady." Only "a mutilated pair of bellows" served as a substitute "for a writing desk, on which lay displayed her hopes and treasures, the manuscript of her novel." She presented a sorry vision of a woman writing, with a broken teacup for an inkstand and "the pen worn to a stump; she had but one!"[31] But the extremity of her poverty remains outside her personal narrative.

In the *Narrative* the suffering innocent oppressed by male tyranny gives way to a comically aggressive character: "There is none in the World MORE FIT THAN MYSELF TO BE LAUGH'D AT" (86). Her favorite character type, she writes, is a low comic, the one she anticipates that her daughter will take up. A low-comic woman, she postulates, can undergo more transformations throughout her acting life: "For when they have out-lived the Bloom and Beauty of a Lady *Townly* or a *Monimia*, they may make very pleasing Figures in a Mrs. *Day* or a Widow *Lackit*" (244). She alternates between humor and pathos, encouraging the reader to construct her writing as comedy or tragedy. The title page of the second edition cites a passage in *The What d'ye Call it: "This* Tragic Story, *or this* Comic Jest, / May *make you* laugh, *or* cry—As *you like best."* She transforms desperate moments into comic drama, perhaps imitating her father's technique of deflecting anticipated pity or scorn. She mocks herself as a quack doctor and as an oil woman and grocer; she makes her riding over a three-year-old child a comic situation. When she fell ill, and a "hungry cur" stole her last three pounds of pork, she describes the landlord knocking at the door for his rent, she and her child staring at each other over the empty table interrupted by a deus ex machina, an old gentlewoman who provides money. Similarly she turns the tyranny of her father and her brother Theophilus into comic absurdity. When Theophilus's daughter was forbidden to act in a play with Charlotte, she turns the slight on the perpetrators: "'Tis plain the rancourous Hate to me had spread itself to so monstrous a Degree, that they rather chose to make themselves, I may say in this Case RIDICULOUSLY CRUEL, than not load me with an additional Weight of Misery" (173). Charke fills the typological void left by renouncing scriptural, epic, or allegorical models for her character—not with the tragic female figure of Jane Shore, but with comic male figures like Captain Plume in *The Recruiting Officer,* Macheath in *The Beggar's Opera,* Lord Foppington in *The Careless Husband,* and Bevil junior in *The Conscious Lovers.*

Cross-dressing in life as well as in the imagination allows her to escape gender restrictions. Learning traditional male activities such as shooting and hunting, being a hog merchant, pastry cook, farmer, and puppeteer, Charke describes adopting the identity of a Mr. Brown, dressing in men's clothes, and taking a female companion. Several times she must reveal herself to unsuspecting heiresses who propose marriage. Becoming the gardener after her family dismissed one, she writes, "I was entirely lost in a Forgetfulness of my real Self; and went each Day with that orderly Care to my separate Employments, that is generally the recommendatory Virtue for the FIRST MONTH ONLY of a new-hired Servant" (42). Though she worries about what her self really is, for "I was as changeable as Proteus" (203), she is convinced that she possesses something called "self." Charke, like other scandalous memoirists, remains uncertain about the way to assign gender to her subjectivity. Her regular resort to comedy indicates the centrality of conventional genre in her production of a female identity, but at every turn of the narrative those conventions are tipped or skewed by her protean "changeability," her subversive undercutting of gender distinctions.

Charke, playing with the fixity of name as assigning identity, by her own account lived as Mr. Brown with a wife and daughter. But Charke was not alone in her radical adoption and inversion of secular male patterns to invest female "character" with meaning in the mid eighteenth century and to tease the reader with the erotic possibilities of gender shifts. She remarks in her *Narrative* that her daily world was filled with cross-dressed imposters. Susannah Centlivre lived for many years dressed as a man, and a woman named Sally Paul, according to the *Monthly Review* (1760), was brought before the magistrate for being married to a woman. Mary Hamilton, also known as "George," came to trial in 1746 for transvestism and marriage to another woman. The Hamilton case probably inspired Fielding's *The Female Husband*, a fictional history depicting Mary Hamilton's invented sexual exploits in masquerade and her threat to sexual difference.[32]

The Female Soldier; or, the Surprising Life and Adventures of Hannah Snell . . . Who took upon herself the Name of James Gray; and, being deserted by her Husband, put on Mens Apparel, and travelled to Coventry in quest of him, where she enlisted in Col. Guise's Regiment of Foot. . . . (1750) recounts Hannah Snell's adventures when she dressed as her brother-in-law, James Gray. Born in 1723 in Worcester, she served in 1745 as soldier and sailor during the Siege of Pondicherry while searching for the husband who had deserted her and her daughter. Snell's book is addressed to female readers who are invited to admire Snell's disguise and moral strength, and to male readers who are encouraged to unleash their prurient imaginations concerning a woman's life on a ship filled with men. A comrade testifies to Snell's Amazonian courage when she is wounded in the groin: "This Wound being so extreme painful, it almost drove her to the Precipice of Despair; she often thought of discovering herself, that by that Means she might be freed from the unspeakable Pain she endured, by having the Ball taken out by one of the Surgeons." On another occasion, forced to bare her breasts during whipping, she camouflaged her breasts with a handkerchief tied around her neck.[33] Snell's account describes one woman's aggressive response to male perfidy. She maintains her female virtue while usurping male prerogatives to travel, swear, and fight.

In describing their characters, these women represent themselves as something they are not: men. Female identity is here aggressively asserted, but in such a way as to undercut the ideology of the gendered subject that eighteenth-century theorists of character were attempting so desperately to preserve. The sexually ambiguous man/woman certainly supplies individuation, but only by obliterating entirely the category of sameness, the consistency of the species of "woman."

The public narrative of women's lives continues to serve as a location where the contradictions of gender and character surface throughout the eighteenth century. A later spate of texts including Ann Sheldon's *Memoirs* (1787), Elizabeth Gooch's *Life* (1792), George Anne Bellamy's *Apology* (1785), Elizabeth Steele's *Memoirs of Sophia Baddeley* (1787), and Margaret Leeson's *Memoirs* (1797) further confront the problems of writing "woman's" character and experience. Some of these memoirists, adopting male typologies, find the conventional cultural paradigms of "woman" sufficient and satisfying, but others draw attention to the inadequacy of the erotic, the pathetic, and the spiritual. Like the earlier autobiographies, these narratives display the tensions among various discourses on woman—the sexual, the religious privatization of self-inspection, and the production of a language that defines a gendered inner life. They speak of the coercion of the notions of "male" and "female" which pressure women to make their public characters unified and intelligible to eighteenth-century readers. In that process, the scandalous memoirists often essentialize the male sex, especially men of privilege, as the patriarchal oppressors who act against women. These narratives, then, are complicit in the very gender and class systems they would seek to disrupt.

Scandalous memoirs present an ideological field of gendered subjectivity where some women employ the private and the subjective to individuate themselves and to insist that they cannot be treated as unfeeling abstractions or members of a universal category, woman. They possess themselves of an interiority to assist in the construction of a private "self" and are unwilling to relinquish it to lover or husband, but they also underscore the challenges to that female identity taking place on every side. Unlike earlier women writers considered here, such as the spiritual autobiographers or Mary Astell, these women fail to draw upon their *mutual* interests in ending exploitation and oppression to focus instead on individual satisfaction. Writing themselves into a heteroclite individualism that makes them regard themselves as anomalies, each autobiographical narrator isolates herself from collective concerns. Consequently, each woman's difficulties may be read as her private individual failing, without relation to economic or political conditions in an eighteenth-century Britain that severely restricted female opportunity and required female virtue in order to accord women the privileges of class.

These scandalous memoirists, in responding to the way their "characters" were constructed in the public domain, indicate that the production of women's private subjectivities evoked disturbing discoveries that
sometimes violated public assumptions. Positioned between excessive sexuality and lack of desire, between virtue and vice, eighteenth-century
"woman" is defined as all of a kind, yet characterless. These public narratives of private character divide women from "themselves" and threaten
the coded character of "woman" current in the culture. No simple code
contains the contradictions; no existing paradigm of gender reproduction
suffices to mold the memoirists' writing so that each distinctive detail is
expressive of a unified and essential personality. The texts both refuse
and adopt the substantial unified identity that the socioeconomic and
political system requires in order to reproduce itself.

Eighteenth-century women autobiographers recuperate and sabotage
the (male) culture's signifying practices about gender and identity through
their texts. They usurp the discourse that defines them while they invent
disguises to mask their dissension from it. In speaking and writing publicly for the first time, the scandalous memoirists push toward defining a
new typology for the "female"; they disrupt hegemonic hierarchies of
value while inevitably confirming them. Women's published autobiographical writing, then, becomes a paradigmatic instance of struggles
over the meaning of female "character" at a historical moment of erosion
of the old and rigidification of new gender boundaries.

CHAPTER NINE

Managing Women

Thrale's "Family Book" and *Thraliana*

*We have got a sort of literary Curiosity amongst us; the foul Copy of
Pope's Homer, with all his old Intended Verses, Sketches, emendations &
c. strange that a Man shd keep such Things!—stranger still that a Woman
should write such a Book as this; put down every Occurrence of her Life,
every Emotion of her Heart, & call it a Thraliana forsooth—but then I
mean to destroy it.*

—Hester Thrale, *Thraliana* (1780)

Doctor Johnson always said there was a sex in words.

—Hester Thrale, *British Synonymy* (1794)

I

By the latter half of the eighteenth century, a private subject who engaged in constant textual self-scrutiny throughout her or his life is a commonplace. James Boswell, Fanny Burney, and Hester Thrale all wrote
multiple serial volumes that seemingly account for each and every activity and desire. Mrs. Thrale agreed that Boswell's method to live no
more than he could record was "a good way," but she countered that it
did not fit a mother's life, for it "is scarce long enough to talk, & to write,
and to live to rejoyce in what one has written—at least I feel that I have
begun too late,"[1] as she, too, unceasingly attempted to textualize her
"reality." Unlike Boswell's accounts of the male social institutions of
clubs and coffeehouses, Thrale's diaries principally focus on the world of
children, home, and relationships. Boswell begins his journals on the occasion of traveling to London and seeking employment in the Guards,
while one of Thrale's private diaries is inspired by Thrale's daughter's

birth and another is motivated by her husband's gift of blank volumes that ironically are later to be structured by her successive marriages.

One of the commonplaces of feminist criticism is the frequent claim that diaries and journals are intrinsically female, and that women's experience particularly lends itself to the unstructured narrative for its expression. Among such critics are those who argue, for example, that "women's autobiographies tend to be much less clearly organized, much less synthetic" than men's, and those who contend that women's style develops from the "concept of dailiness as a structuring principle of women's lives."[2] Estelle Jelinek seems to agree in suggesting that "irregularity rather than orderliness informs the self-portraits by women"; women's autobiographies, she claims, are fragmented, interrupted, formless, and even anecdotal and disruptive when basically linear.[3] Similarly, at the end of the eighteenth century, at least some commentators relegate the authority to trifle to women, and women's secondary sphere of influence is justified as natural: "The female attends to those minute particulars, often unperceived, and generally carelessly considered as unworthy of an elevated mind, . . . for surrounding objects her perceptions are vivid; but she cannot, with the prescient eye of philosophy, distinctly trace objects at a remote period. Her intellectual arithmetic can calculate as far as days and months, but extends not to years."[4] Such reasoning in the contemporary moment and in the eighteenth century fails to account, on the one hand, for the large number of diaries and journals written by men; and, on the other hand, for many women's autobiographies (such as conversion narratives) that display narrative closure—a beginning, middle, and end, and an epiphany that produces the textual effect of a full and transcendent self.

What then are the political uses of calling into place such an inherently female identity and its expression in a particular form, in the eighteenth century or the twentieth, from D'Israeli's essays to contemporary feminism? The issues at stake in marking female difference shift depending upon its deployment, and *difference* may have various and conflicting political applications at particular historical moments. In mid and late eighteenth-century England, the emergence of female difference allows for the production of a distinctly female voice, one that claims the uniqueness of its "experience," the possession of the property of a female "self," and the formation of a female collectivity; but it is also employed, as in the case of D'Israeli, in the service of maintaining gender hierarchies. The emergence of female difference paradoxically authorizes women's voices for speaking their own inferiority. But female difference also means at midcentury an assertion of sexual difference in every bone, muscle, and vein, an idealization of motherhood, and an increased privatization as women moved from doing productive paid work to attending principally to their children.

As we have seen, diaries and journals proliferated in the seventeenth and eighteenth centuries in England with the expansion of literacy, and both sexes reflect the difficulty, if not impossibility, of representing character. Gendered subjectivity might escape established paradigms in its private versions where it did not have to be contracted and condensed into recognizable ideologies of genre in order to attract subscribers and patrons, or conform to publicly sanctioned versions of moral and social authority for the "self." Thus, serial writing with its structure of daily entry and repetition, by encouraging a rereading of the previous day and its revision in succeeding entries, makes the elision of contradictions in experience and its representation a revisionary task. In short, private first-person narrative is a particularly apt ideological grid for recording a subject held in perpetual conflict with itself, requiring regular revision and self-regulation.

Though diaries are not exclusively female, not always a site of difference, certain women at particular times used diary to bear witness to the plurality of their gendered positions and to register opposition to circulating notions of "self." Eighteenth-century woman was given coherence, especially in the latter half of the century, as middle-class "wife" and "mother." Urged to have "character," a public phenomenon, yet increasingly relegated to the domestic sphere, eighteenth-century women often use diaries to construct a private space that experiments with alternative ways of achieving a gendered "self." In an important way, the diaries present a "self" that is impossible for the writer who reads her own text to absorb. This sense of illegibility also holds true for twentieth-century critics, as we have seen. In writing principally to themselves, eighteenth-century women produce a "free" space of interiority beyond the boundaries of a gendered hierarchy in the unwomanly, the unspoken, and the undervalued. These private daily records reflect and reproduce multiple gendered positions in text and in culture, as the women read, reread, and revise their private formulations. By making themselves their own object, they subvert and contest modes of conceiving "self" beyond the paradigms made available for them.

For Hester Thrale, private—even secret—writing becomes an end in

itself as she describes her various positionings as wife, mother, intellectual, writer, tradeswoman, and election campaigner, as well as hostess
and confidante to Samuel Johnson. The narrative experiments and the
commonplace content she adopts do not fit predictable textual strategies
or tropes such as the fallen woman, the rebellious child, the spiritual heroine, the familial myth of separation and reunion, or independence accepted and rewarded. Thrale regularly rewrote the subjectivity that was
too diffuse to confine to one version, often repeating the same incident,
with variations, in sequential accounts to represent her own identity as
defying easy categorization. Thrale's autobiographical writings set her
firmly within the ideologies of gender, genre, and class; yet like women's
spiritual autobiographies and the scandalous memoirs, they also make
available an oppositional space.

Thrale's major publications, in contrast with her private writing, include anecdotes of Samuel Johnson (1786), as well as letters they exchanged (1788), *Observations and Reflections made in the Course of a Journey through France, Italy, and Germany* (1789), *British Synonymy* (1794),
and *Retrospection* (1801) as she moves from the personal to a comprehensive historical study. But throughout her life she simultaneously kept voluminous private journals and notes that were not published in her lifetime. With the exception of one late autobiographical fragment written
to Sir James Fellowes, Mrs. Thrale's notebooks and diaries do not follow
a narrative line or come to closure. They lack a crisis that, in retrospect,
is described as the moment when one's real "self" begins or the critical
moment when the meaning of experience unfolds. In addition to compiling books of Johnson's sayings, she simultaneously recorded the remarks
of famous contemporaries and collected two books of Queeney's achievements—the "blue Cover Book" and the "little red Book"—as well as a
"Family Book" of her children's births, deaths, illnesses, and achievements. Further, she kept a "New Common-Place Book" and various
small diaries; later, as Mrs. Piozzi, she prepared a five-volume literary
autobiography for her adopted son, John Salusbury.[5] From 1776 until
1809 she regularly made entries in a multivolumed diary of anecdotes,
personal history, and noteworthy stories. These various notebooks afforded a safe secret place to accumulate the commonplaces of her life, a
record of her subjectivity, and the thoughts and events that gave "meaning" to her existence. Of special interest here are *Thraliana*, among the
very first English ana, and the "Family Book," the original and unusual
document that records the details of her children's early lives. All this

material offers a textual ground for the contest over the privatizing of "woman," the production of a consciousness formed at the behest of men, and the questioning of the generic limitations inherent in such autobiographical activities.

In addition, within these texts Hester Thrale rehearses with conviction the conventional expectations of women. The female tradition of private writing, the verbatim transcription of wise sayings from Johnson and other "great men," and the burgeoning publication of medical and educational works directed at mothers make up some of the diverse and discrepant discourses that Thrale adopts to define her own experience. Thrale constructs her private life in the context of the more public discourses that parallel her diary keeping, and reading them in conjunction with *Thraliana* and the "Family Book," two of her private writings, sets the notion of "self-expression" in a cultural rather than a purely individual frame to assign meaning to that consciousness.[6] In their privatizing of the public, and publicizing of the private, Thrale's many autobiographical writings raise important questions about gender and genre.

II

Among the discourses that manage eighteenth-century women are those generated by the medical profession, and I want to examine several in the context of Thrale's "Family Book" and *Thraliana*. Female difference in the body is called firmly into place from the 1730s, when William Cheselden published the first drawing of a female skeleton.[7] An ideal of motherhood made the uterus, which had been the site of sickness, into the site of maternal health and the location of unquestioned sexual difference. In the emergent economy of the female body, representations of the pelvis (which contains the uterus) become decidedly bigger, the skull (which contains the female brain), much smaller.[8] But sexual difference is inscribed in every aspect of the female body. For the first time, at midcentury, a large body of child-rearing books directed at a newly literate and largely middle-class female audience were published and widely disseminated. These books, many of which Hester Thrale read, named women for the first time as "managers" of their children and of the domestic space—in spite of a competing series of medical texts that defined women as prone to hysteria and irritability because of their reproductive organs and related diseases that influence character and identity. In *A Guide for Self Preservation, and Parental Affection; or Plain*

Directions for Enabling People to Keep Themselves and their children Free from several Common Disorders [1793?], Thomas Beddoes clarifies the gender distinctions of an efficiently run family: "The father must be sober and industrious; and the mother learn to manage well."[9] These texts serve to demarcate a cadre of bourgeois mothers who are to withdraw from the public and to remain estranged from its power. The "family" as it is constituted by medicine, politics, and law provides for a notion of "mother" as the (male) doctor's agent in the home, his active partisan, as medicine and education begin to take over the functions of "management" that the church, conversion narrative, and confessional had served and before psychiatry and the other human sciences had been conceptualized. Such interventions through medicine and education evolve in moments of cultural disarray to provide new modes of behavior and child rearing. In a time when only half of the infants born survived, Hester Thrale relies on the medical manuals such as William Buchan's much reprinted *Domestic Medicine; or the Family Physician* (1769) to allow her to function as the household authority on matters of health: "Another day when somebody among the Serv:ts was sick, I bid Harry fetch me Buchan's domestick Med'cine to consult, or rather says I—calling him back—fetch me *Tissot* 'tis the better Book—*Tis so* replied Harry archly."[10] In aiming such texts quite specifically at mothers, as well as defining the proper measures necessary to raise gender- and class-identified children, the authors perpetuate these categories within the family.

In the now familiar passages, Blackstone interprets eighteenth-century law to read that the married woman's existence is suspended so that the wife's being is assimilated into the man's.[11] Women's subordinate status under the law is justified by the claim that she is favored by its protection. Specifically, women are excused from providing for their children because they act under serious disadvantage: "The mother finds a thousand obstacles in her way;—shame, remorse, the constraint of her sex, and the rigor of laws;—that stifle her inclinations to perform this duty: and besides, she generally wants ability" (1:447). Married women and mothers, then, according to the law, are defined as being *inclined* to take responsibility for their children but, in a circular logic, judged incapable because of the laws that constrain them and because of the categorical inadequacies of their sex, apparently ascribed to a deficiency in their natural ability.

In short, as pediatric medicine begins to codify itself in midcentury, male doctors usurp the functions previously performed by midwives, denigrate women's work, blame women for all manner of illness and deformity, and idealize motherhood within the same breath; and it is this multiple positioning in particular that Thrale both echoes and challenges in her accounts of her family. These prescriptive texts include, in addition, William Cadogan's *An Essay upon Nursing and the Management of Children* (1748); T. Mantell's *Short Directions for the Management of Infants* (1780), William Moss's *An Essay on the Management and Nursing of Children in the Earlier Periods of Infancy* (1781), and Michael Underwood's *A Treatise on the Diseases of Children, with General Directions for the Management of Infants from the Birth* (1793). These works, and others like them, were usually written by men to women, though they were occasionally published under a female pseudonym. Women were taught the received wisdom about children's education and medical care in "plain words." In this way, women were granted ostensible authority and responsibility for the physical care of their children, assisting the physicians but without sufficient knowledge to effect change in the practice of medicine or in the way women were regarded by the medical profession. They qualified, but insufficiently.

Though child care would seem to be transferred to mothers directly because of the plethora of books on management addressed to them, it shifts instead to male doctors who then dispense and publish advice to mothers who do their bidding. In *An Essay upon Nursing and the Management of Children*, William Cadogan, M.D., approves that the governors of the foundling hospital will direct the care of the children and put it in the realm of scientific "Observation and Experience."[12] Women had long cared for children as mothers, nurses, and midwives, and yet at midcentury child management assumes sufficient importance for it to be directed, though not enacted, by men. Cadogan writes, "It is with great Pleasure I see at last the Preservation of Children become the Care of Men of Sense" for nursing has been "too long fatally left to the Management of Women, who cannot be supposed to have proper Knowledge to fit them for such a Task, notwithstanding they look upon it to be their own Province."[13] Yet in a kind of Swiftian reversal at the end of the essay, he asserts that his knowledge and authority derive from his being a father, rather than from his medical credentials.

Similarly, William Buchan, head of the foundling hospital at Ackworth in Yorkshire and author of *Advice to Mothers* (1803), as well as the *Domestic Medicine* already mentioned, seems to give over all power to mothers. He writes, "The more I reflect on the situation of a mother, the more I am struck with the extent of her powers, and the inestimable value of her services. In the language of love, women are called angels; but this is a weak and silly compliment; they approach nearer to our ideas of the Deity: they not only create, but sustain their creation, and hold its future destiny in their hands."[14] As Hugh Downman, M.D., puts it in "Infancy. A Poem" (1774),

> Come Virgin, teach
> How on the management of these first Years
> Depends the future Man; the Theme not mean,
> Not useless, if thy Aid be not refus'd."[15]

John Hill also idealizes the mother and makes her omnipotent: "Ask him to what it is owing that he is straiter, ruddier, and more healthful than other Men? he will tell you he owes it all to his Mother."[16] Yet this deification has awesome consequences. Buchan holds mothers to blame: "In all cases of dwarfishness and deformity, ninety-nine out of a hundred are owing to the folly, misconduct or neglect of mothers."[17] In associating convulsions, idiocy, and deformity with women, especially midwives, he seems to argue that there is something inherently deficient in "woman" rather than recognizing the way that insufficient access to certain realms of knowledge may lead women to errors. Similarly, Michael Underwood blames even upper bourgeois mothers for their children's deformed bodies and characters: "The laudable affection of the fondest mother frequently becomes a source of manifold injury to her tender offspring: And this is not only the case among the lower class of people, or in situations where medical assistance is procured with difficulty, but even in the metropolis itself, and in the higher ranks of the community, where many prejudices very hurtful to the ease and health of children still prevail."[18] And for John Hill, like the other doctors mentioned, the mother is quite literally responsible for the shape of her child's body which, like character, is assumed to be acquired rather than inherited: "For one Girl who is born crooked, five Hundred are made so by bad Management; and the Case is just the same with the disposition of Children as their Persons; there may be a few naturally forward, morose, indolent, and obstinate; but for one of these there are a thousand made so by bad Conduct."[19] In *An Essay on the Government of Children*, James Nelson also advises mothers to rely on the doctor, for "when Diseases happen, which cannot be obviated, nor even foreseen, it is not the reading a single Volume that will qualify Parents to undertake the Cure of them: no; they must apply to those who make it their Study and their Profession; to those whose Judgement, whose Integrity, and whose Diligence they can confide in." [20] In fact, he warns, parents must be on guard against two particular evils: "the Neglect of calling for Help in time; the other, that amazing Attachment to Nurses, and what they call good old Women" (143). Thus, the doctors compete in convincing women of their ignorance, of their utter dependence on the advice that only the doctors can provide.

By newly construing pediatric medicine as a proper "science," medical discourses construct child care as a regime of truth to which women are allowed only limited access. This explicit public assumption that middle-class women should be chiefly responsible for the health and welfare of their children fosters individualism and consolidates opinion on the proper manner for raising middle-class gendered subjects. It also helps maintain new work patterns in which the family is increasingly separated from the work site and privatized, and its labor (especially the labor of women and servants) is made invisible. These medical discourses mobilize a middle class that is preoccupied with its health, and the body becomes a locus of its management through class- and gender-specific ideologies of education and maintenance. At the same time, the hierarchy of male over female labor is enforced. Texts such as the "Family Book" and *Thraliana*, then, confirm prevailing assumptions about women as they fashion private female subjects who, in reflecting on themselves, do not recognize or acknowledge the ways their individual subjectivity intermingles with the ideological production in the culture at large designed to keep them in place.

One text among many that locates strong gender differentiation in the body and associates character and identity traits with the physical, is *On the Management and Education of Children*, written by John Hill in 1754, under the pseudonym of Juliana-Susannah Seymour, ostensibly as a series of letters of advice to a niece. Interestingly, Hill presents his reader with a fiction of a widowed niece left to mother her children alone, and he takes a female voice, if an oddly avuncular one. In the character of a woman throughout, he emphasizes the importance of writing in plain sense, plain words, and the language "of ordinary conversation" as he outlines what it means to be a good mother and wife, "the two great Characters which our Sex have to support, and more than the Welfare of our own Sex depend upon them." [21] He claims a connection between the future of the nation and the matters he addresses, and he repeatedly emphasizes the importance of a mother's task: "I look upon the Behaviour of a Wife, and the Education of Children, to be the two greatest Points in the Conduct of Society; and yet, I think, there is Reason to say, none are so much neglected, or so little understood" (2).

Hill's advice is quite specifically directed toward the education and management of a class- and gender-identified child for whom the mother is totally responsible. Boys are to be encouraged to engage in vigorous exercise, including playing with balls, throwing iron bullets, and regular swimming in cold water. Hill urges tender mothers not to fret about possible broken bones, and to adopt a laissez-faire attitude, allowing the boys to roam freely with their servant. Girls, on the other hand, are to be treated with care and protection: "I would not have the little Girls be kept altogether without the same Benefits; but they being intended for a different Kind of Life, and the Advantages at which they are to aim being of another Kind, I think a great deal of Difference is to be observed in this Part of their Management" (77). The girls, of course, must be kept virtuous, passive, and subservient. In fact, Hill writes, "I should think it would be more to the Satisfaction of a Mother to hear that her Favourite behaved like a Woman, than that she was the smartest little Creature in the World" (113). Boys run, girls walk; boys swim in the pond, girls wash in their chamber. Much attention is directed toward the protection of girls' pale and delicate complexions, and natural and symmetrical shape. For Hill, *woman*, by definition, is synonymous with heterosexual attraction and its rituals: "You see Youths aiming to be Men by acting up to what they see in Men: You see Girls full of the Idea of Woman from the Expectation of Courtship. The Address, come from whom it will, is sure to be well received, because it is the Stamp and Character of Woman" (191). Hill's discussion of gender distinctions is finally an ambivalent and somewhat contradictory one, however, for he wavers regarding the extent to which sexual difference is inherent, and the extent to which it should be an educational goal: "Human Constitutions, my Dear, are still human Constitutions, to whatever Sex they belong; and, therefore, whatever I have recommended to you as essential to the preserving those of your Sons in Health and Vigour, will do the same with respect to your Daughters: the Effect will be the same in both; only that the less will do with the more delicate: therefore, the Thing in general ought to be the same, only the Degree different" (82). Similarly, James Nelson recommends that sexual difference should be insisted on from the first through a politics of gendered spaces. In separating the sexes from infancy, he aims to suppress their sexuality: "I cannot but recommend, what I doubt very few will comply with, that Boys and Girls, even when Infants, have not only separate Beds, but, wherever it is practicable, always lie in separate Rooms: nor should they ever be exposed to one another, . . . and we cannot begin too soon to shut up every Avenue to Vice" (183). Commerce between the sexes, even among children, is imagined to lead to sexual activity.

As for class distinctions, the laborer's child, Hill writes, is disciplined and healthy, while the children of the people of quality are undernourished and overindulged. Bourgeois mothers in the city, then, should imitate the regimen of the rural laborer's family, rising and retiring early to avoid the damp night air, eating lightly from the garden and avoiding sweets. Thus, what the poor must do from necessity, Hill recommends as the preferred method for the middle class. Hill writes, "The Mistakes of the People of Fortune you see are of two Kinds: they either starve their Children by the Advice of their Doctors, or pamper them to their Destruction by following their own. I would have you practice a Method between both" (43). Similarly, James Nelson, drawing his evidence from London, divides the nation into those five classes that should be educated in distinctly different ways, which he outlines in detail; the five classes consist of the nobility, the gentry, the "genteel Trades and good Businesses" ("all those particularly which require large Capital"), the common trades, and the peasantry (273). As the bourgeois class learns to recognize itself, the advice is quite explicitly addressed to middle-class mothers, who should raise middle-class children, though James Nelson also emphasizes the importance of an education to class when he writes, "There ought to be made a considerable Difference between the Children of inferior People, and those of Rank, with regard to their Tuition" (33). Women of this middle class, unlike the other female objects of his directive, are specifically positioned as middle managers of the domestic economy, "to understand the Management of a House, be acquainted with the various Seasons of Provisions, the Price of Markets, Skill in Carving, Demeanour at Table, and, in a Word, the whole Oeconomy of a Family" (328). Such women are to understand the vital function that children play in this economy, and to educate children to inhabit willingly their class position. But class distinctions extend as well to the physical care of children. These medical texts, then, insert a growing medical apparatus within the privatized space of the family to make gender distinctions seem natural and the "mother" in the family responsible for its transmission and replication, especially among the middle ranks.

Within these texts there are implications of consequences for the nation—that is, that mothers are uniquely qualified to perform a service for the country in helping to form its destiny. Even Queen Charlotte is addressed as "the happy mother of a numerous, healthy, and beautiful Offspring" in George Armstrong's *An Account of the Diseases Most Incident to Children*.[22] Though the specific consequences of mother care are not fully displayed in any of these treatises, there are allusions to its "political importance," its significance for changing morals, and its necessity in producing children as the wealth of the country. William Buchan insists on mothers' importance "to make men healthy or valetudinary, useful in life, or the pests of society."[23] He confirms that nature destined and designed mothers to conduct early education, and Michael Underwood is even more specific in identifying children with the nation's economy. In the emergent industrialized society, middle-class English children must be salvaged in a national imperative to make them healthier than the "naturally" healthy laborer's child or the more distant "savage." According to Underwood, "The destruction of infants is eventually the destruction of adults, of population, wealth, and every thing that can prove useful to society, or add to the strength and grandeur of a kingdom."[24]

☙ III

Hester Thrale, even in her private writing, clearly situates herself within these emergent directives that categorize women as the wives and mothers who manage a nation of middle-class subjects whose rank is determined by their capital, not by their birth. By attending to class as well as gender, we can complicate the notion of women's oppression in the eighteenth century as women are recruited to these various subject positions. For Thrale, that means she enjoyed the privileged position of upper bourgeoise though her husband thought of her as "a passive, tho' well born & educated Girl; who should be contented to dwell in the Borough, which other Women had refused to do" (*Thraliana*, 307). Married in 1763, Hester Lynch Salusbury brought an ancient family and £10,000 to a wealthy but unconnected Henry Thrale, a brewer ten years her senior with a country home at Streatham. Thrale offers a most explicit example of the kind of urban mother being addressed by these medical discourses. Emphasizing the commonplace, Thrale becomes a diligent historian of the private in the "Family Book" as she attempts to give validity to her position as procreator, nurturer, and indefatigable worker.

The "Family Book," first published in 1976, is extraordinary and original, and the editor Mary Hyde writes of it, "Since the undertaking was so unusual, one wonders how the idea came to Mrs. Thrale" ("Family," vii). Hyde accounts for it through Johnson's influence, Queeney's precocity, and Mrs. Thrale's inexplicable predilection for diary keeping. Thrale's journals are less expressive of her self or of a female voice than an intersection of discourses about "woman," especially "mother" and "wife," that are effective in reproducing class and gender divisions. Thrale's "Family Book" shows the ways that education through the mother is a process that instills culture, makes it intelligible, and imbues the children with class ideology—a crucial task that is both idealized and denigrated within the discourses of the period. Thrale regulates herself and her children within recognizable categories of identity, but she also finds her way in a new genre to record a "mother's" private subjectivity as well as contribute to an emergent genre, the "ana," as she forwards new hierarchies that value woman's domestic and reproductive labor. To the extent that she possesses a whole and unified identity, Thrale defines herself as mother and daughter, as producer, educator, and sustainer of children.

In the "Family Book," Thrale establishes herself as a guardian of the domestic who fosters the development of an individual character in each child. Positioned as "a Centre of Unity" in her parents' unhappy marriage, she thought of children as cementing the connection, and she welcomed each of her pregnancies. From 1764 to 1778 Thrale bore twelve children who lived from ten hours (Penelope, born 15 September 1772) to ninety-two years (Queeney, the firstborn). In fact, Hester Lynch Thrale began her "Family Book," first named the "Children's Book," by recording this first daughter's birth: "Hester Maria Thrale [Queeney] born on the 17: Septr. 1764 at her Father's House, Southwark" (21). In this "Register of my Children's Powers of Mind and Body beginning with the first down to the last" ("Family," 254), she measures her life in pregnancies, children's birthdays, illnesses, deaths, and the visits of Samuel Johnson. The culture expects her to marry well, serve her husband, obey her mother, and remain in relative isolation. In the "Family Book," Thrale frequently indicates that she understands and accepts her economic function as a breeder—she is to produce an heir, preferably a male heir, and she is to educate him and keep him alive. She also wishes to keep her own estate within her family ("Family," 190), and thus she indulges in long fantasies of believing her life must be exchanged for a live son: "Why if I *should* die! what does it signify? Let me *but* leave a Son, I shall die happy enough" ("Family," 201).

Taking up her woman's role as the principal one responsible for educating and doctoring the children, Hester Thrale documents each child's regular progress (or disturbing lack of it) in the "Family Book," as well as her predictions for the children's progress through life based on her readings of their character and physical stamina. She teaches Queeney astronomy, geography, multiplication, and religion at age two: "She has this day repeated her Catechism quite thro', her Latin Grammar to the end of the 5 Declensions, a Fable in Phaedrus, an Epigram in Martial, the Revolutions Diameters & Distance of the Planets. . . . With regard to her Person it is accounted exquisitely pretty; her Hair is sandy, her Eyes of a very dark blue, & their Lustre particularly fine; her Complexion delicate, and her Carriage uncommonly genteel" ("Family," 29–30). Thrale tells us that, while pregnant or recovering from childbirth, she constantly tutors the children and records their mutual achievement. On occasion her despair at investing energy in educating children who may soon die breaks through; she finds teaching her seventh child, Sophia Thrale, an unbearable duty: "I have really listened to Babies Learning till I am half stupified—& all my pains have answered so poorly—I have no heart to battle with Sophy . . . but I will not make her Life miserable as I suppose it will be short. . . . [A]t Present I can not begin battling with Babies—I have already spent my whole Youth at it & lost my Reward [a male heir] at last" ("Family," 163).

The "Family Book" also carefully chronicles her medical efforts and judgments in an age when a child could quite literally have a fever in the morning and die in the afternoon. It is a space to record their sufferings in excruciating detail—Lucy's ear that seeps a perpetual infection, Ralph's smallpox, Queeney's worms, and Henry's death. Just before Henry's death after a few hours of infection, she writes that "a universal Shriek called us all together to Harry's Bedside, where he struggled a Moment—thrusting his Finger down his Throat to excite Vomiting, & then—turning to Nurse said very distinctly—don't Scream so—I *know* I must die" ("Family," 152). In fact, when Hester Thrale failed as doctor to Henry, her sole male heir, she takes her failed identity from Pope's "Epistle to A Lady" as the line "Childless with all her Children—wants an heir" runs through her head ("Family," 162). Her constant quarrels with doctors, family, and friends over the proper medication contest male authority. When the children, each in succession, catch measles, she tends to them herself: "I sent for no Drs. nor 'Pothecaries, but kept diluting all I could with cooling Liquors varied so as to avoid Disgust" ("Family," 74), but with Lucy (who dies at age four), she appeals to a stream of advisers: "/I/ applied to [Dr.] Pinkstan who ordered the Sarsaparilla Tea & bid me do nothing else. Lucy however [was] fading away very fast, though every body in the house persisted She was well, I took her to Herbert Lawrence, who said it was the original humour repelled by Pinkstan, which was fastening on her Brain but that he would try to restore it" ("Family," 83). The physical state of the children and the question of medical care consume her attention as she attempts to locate effective treatment and ultimately take responsibility for medical decisions. In fact, her disagreement with friend Baretti over the treatment for Queeney's persistent worms eventually caused an altercation never to be resolved.

When we read the legal, medical, and educational treatises on mothering in conjunction with the "Family Book" we find new explanations for gendered subjectivity in the eighteenth century. Hester Thrale used the prevailing modes to define herself as the prototypical bourgeois mother in the "Family Book," yet she counters by asserting her authority against doctors and by granting practical "mothering" a systematic textual representation. In other words, Thrale sets out the justification for the impossible task of "mothering" in which the various systems of representation intersect and collide. She recognizes, but does not elide, the contradictions of her gendered subjectivity that make the production of a linear tale with a consistent and authoritative point of view quite remote. Quick to dismiss the philosophical complexities of the controversy over identity still lingering in the late eighteenth century, she nevertheless embodies them. Her narrative insists on women's possessing inherently different characteristics from men, but she believes that "character" is something of one's own choosing: "People have a strange Power of making their Own Characters;—Commended in Youth or even in Childhood perhaps, for some particular Quality—they drive the Thing forward by that delight which every one naturally takes in talking of himself—Yes I was always mischievous; or I was always a good natured Fool" and thus, she concludes, people should be careful about assigning traits to children in their presence (Thraliana, 357). She repeatedly indicates her belief that women have special powers over men in inspiring private confidences and making them submit, though the exact nature of that sexual power remains unexamined.

The questions of gender and genre are powerfully at issue in both the "Family Book" and *Thraliana*. By insisting on her difference from men, Thrale unwittingly colludes in reproducing her inferior status, but in part *Thraliana* also mediates the various splittings required of her:

> All my Friends reproach me with neglecting to write down such Things as drop from him [Johnson] almost perpetually. . . . [B]ut ever since that Time I have been the Mother of Children, and little do these wise Men know or feel, that the Crying of a young Child, or the Perverseness of an elder, or the Danger however trifling of any one—will soon drive out of a female Parent's head a Conversation concerning Wit, Science or Sentiment, however She may appear to be impressed with it at the moment: besides that to a *Mere de famille* doing something is more necessary & suitable than even hearing something; and if one is to listen al Even and write all Morning what one has heard; where will be the Time for tutoring, caressing, or what is still more useful, for having one's Children about one: I therefore charge all my Neglect to my young ones Account, and feel myself at this moment very miserable that I have at last, after being married fourteen Years and bringing eleven Children, leisure to write a *Thraliana* forsooth:—though the second Volume *does* begin with Mr. Johnson. (*Thraliana*, 158)

Clearly the text highlights the perturbing incongruity between the duties of a mother and a writing woman, and writing *Thraliana* in part resolves Thrale's distress. Less explicit than the "Family Book" in dealing with the character of woman as wife and mother, *Thraliana* pits her identity against Samuel Johnson and her two successive husbands Henry Thrale and Gabriel Piozzi. Hester Thrale's father had forecast difficulties for her first marriage, and his words were prophetic. She soon finds herself nursing the veneral disease that Mr. Thrale apparently acquired from his mistress: "No peace saith my God for the wicked! no quiet Gestation for me! on Sunday Night the 3d. of Sept. Mr. Thrale told me he had an Ailment, & shewed me a Testicle swelled to an immense Size" ("Family," 165). After Mr. Thrale proposes sending for a doctor who specializes in venereal complaints, she recognizes, to her relief, that the disease is not cancer, and she becomes grateful that it is only the pox: "I now began to understand where I was, and to perceive that my poor Father's Prophecy was verified who said If you marry that Scoundrel he will catch the Pox, /&/ for your Amusement set you to make his Pultices. This is now literally made out; & I am preparing Pultices as he said, and Fo-

menting this elegant Ailment every Night & Morning for an Hour together on my Knees, & receiving for my Reward such Impatient Expressions as disagreable Confinement happens to dictate" ("Family," 166).
Thrale finds herself pleased that the disease is not life threatening, for
she fears for the economic survival of the family. Yet she feels contempt
for a husband who caught a venereal infection and expects her, though
pregnant, to minister cheerfully to him. "I have always sacrificed my own
Choice to that of others, so I must sacrifice it again," she writes in another context (Thraliana, 544). Oddly, this moment of contradiction
marked the beginning of her most sustained diary keeping, for in gratitude for her nursing, Mr. Thrale gave her the six bound volumes with
Thraliana imprinted on the cover. The gift suggests her husband's silent
collusion in enabling Hester Thrale to construct a secret anecdotal "self,"
for Mr. Thrale's behavior seems to authorize her production of an interiority in a private place.

Though Mr. Thrale provided the volumes for the journals, it was
Samuel Johnson who urged her to keep diaries, in part as an antidote to
depression. In spite of Johnson's heavy demands on her time during his
regular visits, she counted him at times as her closest friend. Johnson
seeks intellectual companionship but he also sets her in contradiction by
advising her to maintain the traditional seductive female attributes in
order to attract her husband. Her mother (who lived with her until her
death) insisted that Hester Thrale should remain at home to nurse her
babies; Johnson told her in counterpoint that she should learn the brew-
ing trade and move into the public world: "You divide your Time between your Mamma & your Babies, & wonder you do not by that means
become agreable to your Husband" (Thraliana, 309). She did not, however, go into public until six years later, for to take his advice, she
thought, would destroy her mother. Thrale idealizes her mother at one
level, though she is frequently angered by her dominance. She believes
that filial loyalty is natural, and that civilization erodes such feelings. In
fact, Thrale argues against Johnson's belief that maternal instinct does
not exist: "In Italy 'tis otherwise: more filial piety; less spurning at the
common Ties of Nature . . . Johnson always maintained that no such
Attachment naturally subsisted and used to chide me for fancying that I
loved my Mother" (Thraliana, 739–40).

In some regards, Thrale thinks of herself as an independent powerful
woman, as "any Man's equal" (Thraliana, 531). Woman's power, however, derives in large part from the sexuality that renders a man vulner-

able, though she and Johnson bicker about the exact ages when such power prevails: "And yet says Johnson a Woman has *such* power between the Ages of twenty five and forty five, that She may tye a Man to a post and whip him if She will" (*Thraliana*, 386). But she nevertheless figures her written private consciousness in relationship to the men in her life. Her writing is authorized by Thrale and Johnson; she marks the greatest event of her life as the selling of the Thrale brewery; she judges her marriage to Piozzi as the happiest day of her life; and *Thraliana* ends on the day Piozzi dies: "Every thing most dreaded *has* ensued,—all is over; & my second Husbands Death is the last Thing recorded in my first husband's Present! Cruel Death!" (*Thraliana*, 1099).

Thrale's private diaries evidence considerable ambivalence about her evaluation of the merit of *Thraliana* and the "Family Book." At her most confident, she places them in the literary and intellectual female tradition that Swift's "Stella" and Sterne's "Eliza" followed, women whose fame came from their association with a major literary figure as Thrale's was to come from her friendship with Johnson. She writes, "I do not think my bons Mots like Stella's the best among those of my Friends, but I think Stella's very paltry ones; and much wonder at the moderate degree of Excellence with which Dr Swift was contented to make a Bustle with my Namesake Miss *Hester* Johnson."[25] But she also recognizes and records the perils of women's intellectual display, through Johnson's report: "He used to mention Harry Fielding's behaviour to her [Sarah] as a melancholy instance of narrowness; while She only read English Books, and made English Verses it seems, he fondled her Fancy, & encourag'd her Genius, but as soon [as] he perceived She once read Virgil, Farewell to Fondness, the Author's Jealousy was become stronger than the Brother's Affection" (*Thraliana*, 79).

At other times Hester Thrale remarks that her brand of diary keeping is an unprecedented oddity: "that a Woman should write such a Book as this; put down every Occurrence of her Life, every Emotion of her Heart, & call it a *Thraliana* forsooth—but then I mean to destroy it" (which, of course, she did not do) (*Thraliana*, 464). Ambivalent about her self-assigned task, she questions the uses of secrecy and its association with women, though finally she agrees with Dr. Collier who cautions her "against any Tendency towards secrecy or Clandestine Conduct; never said he be mysterious about Trifles; it is the first advance towards Evil, particularly in the Female Sex" (12). Occasionally she dismisses what she writes as mere trash, nonsense, or trifles—a view she cannot reconcile with her devotion to the task: "But when the last [volume] comes as near to ending as this now does—my fingers will shake lest I should be near ending as well as my Book. [M]y heart tells me that he [Henry Thrale, her husband] said something when he presented me with the Volumes, as if—I don't know as if: but this I know, that fifteen Years have elapsed since I first made the *Thraliana* my Confident, my solitary Comfort, and Depositary of every Thought as it arose" (799). She characterizes the volumes as "poor foolish wild—confused" (839), the keeping of anas "a silly desire" (467). Several times she indicates that they are "a good Repository" for her "Nonsense." Failing to find satisfying precedents for her manner of writing, she lacks confidence in her achievement.

Included in *Thraliana* is also Thrale's somewhat more sustained autobiographical fragment written when, morbidly obsessed with the fantasy that she might die while giving birth to Henrietta Sophia, she determines to set down a record of herself, "a little Epitome of whence I came, who I am & c. before I go hence and am no more seen" (*Thraliana*, 274). In the portion of a formal "character" in the Theophrastan mode included in the fragment, she is severely critical of her own studied grace, irascible temper, avariciousness, and poor poetry. But the fragment of the intended "life of my self" does not attempt narrative closure or the formulation of a fixed or finished identity. Memories of the random incidents of her childhood lack thematic unity—her seeing the eclipse of the sun through smoked glasses, contracting smallpox and being pushed out to the home of a mantua maker, being pinched and having her hair pulled by Lord North at fifteen, reading Milton to Lord Godolphin, learning dancing, Sukey Hill's dying of consumption. The early parts of the autobiographical fragment describe crisis and resolution, economic despair, and recovery. The imitations, translations, bad verse, and letters to the newspaper in *Thraliana* become Hester Thrale's cryptic substitute for a typology that would encompass and vindicate her life. She uses the volumes to polish her prose-writing skills, as well as to record authoritative comments uttered in her hearing. And when she occasionally ventures her own opinion about the topics on which authorities have spoken, it is usually to agree with them rather than to subject their views to analysis.

In *Thraliana* Hester Thrale includes personal revelations (especially about Samuel Johnson), reports of social gatherings and visits, a series of stories on an arbitrary topic, translations and imitations and original compositions, tidbits of information—whatever occurs or is told to her that she thinks is worth remarking and remembering. The journals are a mnemonic device as well: "I now wish I had pursued Mr Murphy's Advice of marking down all Passages from different Books which strike by their Resemblance to each other . . . , for one forgets again in the hurry & Tumult of Life's Cares or Pleasures almost every thing that one does not commit to paper" (*Thraliana*, 24). *Thraliana*, like the "Family Book," attempts various genres without settling on any one, and gives a version of female experience that is informal, repetitive, and rough-hewn. But Thrale is only occasionally troubled by the eclectic nature of the volumes that put the high moments of Johnson's conversation in contiguity with tidbits about her black-and-white speckled hen, comparative ratings of friends, or determinations of a tree's longevity.

Thrale does write a very finished autobiographical piece with dialogue, crises, and linear progression in what is apparently her final, though still private, revision of her life story in the brief autobiographical manuscript that she wrote for Sir James Fellowes in December 1815.[26] She records both her victimization and her pluck. Hester Thrale begins the account with her birth: "After two or Three dead Things, *I* was born alive" (2), and she punctuates the manuscript with delicious details such as her uncle's calling her "Fiddle," the actor Quin's teaching her Satan's speech to the sun in *Paradise Lost*, and David Garrick's making her "sit in his Lap feeding [her] with Cakes" (7). In the narrative she is the pampered child whose accomplishments were much touted to a series of suitors, but she becomes the last resort for Henry Thrale. Her conviction is that she was "too often, and too long confined" (13) when pregnant. She wishes to ride horses in spite of its being considered too masculine an activity for ladies. Mr. Thrale's refusal to allow her to "stink of the Kitchen" drove her instead to her books and children. She both confirms and questions gendered expectations.

The obligatory moment of change comes at the point of Mr. Thrale's entrance into politics as a candidate for Parliament for the Borough of Southwark in 1765, because this move required her entry into the public realm: "Foxhounds were sold, and a Seat in Parliament was suggested by our new Inmate as more suitable to his Dignity, more desirable in every Respect. I grew Useful now, almost necessary; wrote the Advertisements, looked to the Treats, & People to whom I was till then unknown, admired how happy Mr. Thrale must be in such a *Wonder of a Wife*" (16). The pleasure of the public life is short-lived, for Henry Thrale's lack of business acumen at the brewery leads to serious loss and debt. The narrative concludes with hope, however, as Thrale presents an allegory

through a female character named Imagination who first searches unsuc-
cessfully for happiness in love and ambition, and finally turns to health,
temperance, contemplation, and piety in order to achieve it. Thrale's
self-narrative to Fellowes concludes, then, with an emblematic flight of
fancy, the "magical" resolution to otherwise unresolvable contradictions.

In this brief but highly polished autobiographical description, Thrale
defines her identity in large part in relation to men and fortune. Her father, Samuel Johnson, and Mr. Thrale rather than her mother or other
females figure importantly here. A woman's value, she intimates, varies
with her fortune, and when Henry Thrale went into debt, "my Heart
prepared to shut itself quite up, convinced there existed not a human
Creature who cared one Atom for poor H. L. P., now She had no longer
Money to be robbed of" (17). Rather than providing a summary character of her "self" at the end, as Pilkington and Charke had before her, she
moves to the fictional level in imagining a unified female character
whose contradictions are resolved in a fantasy. Such a woman takes pleasure in moderation and private pieties, her urges to usurp masculine
privilege safely quelled. This manuscript, privately circulated to a male
reader, ends with a fable that molds her struggle into forms that hold the
matrices of subjectivities together convincingly.

But this is the exception. Elsewhere in Thrale's journals the only
unity and structure come from her imagining that the journals are a "person" to whom something precious is entrusted—a repository, in the obscure sense of the word as "confidante." She confides to Sophia Streat-
feild that she expects that only God—imagined as a sympathetic and
even vaguely female presence—will read it. She attempts to protect the
Thraliana from prying eyes, and hopes to keep its existence a secret (323,
460). Similarly, her "Family Book" becomes a place to relieve an over-
burdened consciousness: "I have nobody to tell my Uneasinesses to, no
Mother, no Female Friend—no nothing: so I must eat up my own Heart
& be quiet" ("Family," 198). *Thraliana*, like the "Family Book," is a mass
of unpolished serial entries, and only in envisioning its entries as a consistent and unchanging auditor can Thrale hold the various parts together. Thus, in repeatedly emphasizing the unified human quality of
Thraliana, she constructs it as a person whom she discredits as trivial yet
values highly as a friend. This idealized reader, whose gender alternates,
is often figured as someone who can absorb the contradictions of a woman's lived experience that Thrale cannot. Thrale's journals and diaries
construct a woman gazing on lived experience and radically reassign its

"meanings," an individual consciousness that reads and writes being the only organizing principle.

As a writing woman, Thrale replicates her second-sphere status and reflects the prevailing definitions of the female. Her diaries do not so much "express" the essential female voice as they reinscribe the hetero-sexual division that the culture required to reproduce itself. By contain-ing the imagined alternatives within the private sphere, Thrale sets up a cycle of self reading self, of woman reading woman, of complicity in re-straining female transgression. She offers us a paradigmatic instance of the failure of a new paradigm—a woman's account of her family life—to prevail in the public domain. In short, she succeeds in reproducing a bourgeois gendered subject, a woman who manages and is managed.

But the "Family Book" and *Thraliana* also contest cultural assump-tions about women's identity. Located in asymmetrical positions as a privileged upper bourgeoise but also a characterless and contradictory "woman," Thrale's tangle of subjectivities at one level embraces oppres-sion as it repels it at another. Though she writes privately, Thrale thinks of her work within the female journal-writing tradition; she opens a space, albeit a private one, for a collective female subjectivity in writing the new genres of the "Family Book" and *Thraliana*. In addition, Thrale's writing offers an alternative organization to the dominant values. Both the "Family Book" and *Thraliana* put the "important" next to the "unim-portant" without assigning relative value, thus suggesting that each in-sertion is equal to the next.[27] In fact, we may argue that the texts place bits and pieces together as if they held equal power and rank in order to interrogate the usual assignment of value to them. For Thrale, and per-haps for other eighteenth-century women, diaries and journals are a commonplace to hold together the commonplaces of female experiences, even those judged trivial by the cultural hegemony, and to grant them parity with those given higher value by the culture. If some of the bits and pieces seem significant to the larger culture (such as Johnson's witty sayings), their removal to private text to be placed alongside the newly valued daily lived experience holds the disarming potential to force their reevaluation, though her resistance stops short of explicitly criticizing that which constrains her. The "Family Book" and *Thraliana* lay bare for inspection the relations of domination within the family and within fe-male subjectivity, in part by changing the terms of determining what is worth remembering and knowing. These texts are locations of power

within the private, within the family, where there is struggle over the
authority to define the possibilities of transgressing medical, legal, and
educational codes of the female.

ॐ IV

When Isaac D'Israeli chides women about their public and political
power at the end of the century, he might be imagined as speaking directly to the case of Boswell and Thrale in their contest for textual authority over Samuel Johnson's minute particulars. "The female character
is a cruel sovereign who admits of no toleration in her empire," writes
D'Israeli. "He who has discovered the art of giving importance to trifles,
and rendering important things trifling, is certain of her admiration. . . .
Why has the female character, in all ages, and through all the diversities
of human manners, been most severely treated, by men of the finest dis-
cernment? Because it is a kind of revenge; men of great talents must
never expect to receive their celebrity from women; for they must first
become frivolous; that is, great men must submit to become women."[28]
In short, the sexual division of labor in autobiographical writing demands that men, if they are to rise above the frivolous, maintain a masculine command over their public character by controlling its representation. According to D'Israeli, women deserve their misogynist treatment
at the hands of male biographers. If women dare to reverse the terms of
the equation to write personal biographies of men, they jettison the established boundaries of sexual difference, and they stand accused of feminizing and trivializing their subject. At the end of the eighteenth century, as autobiography becomes conceptualized as a narrative that requires
making the accumulated details cohere in the recognizable ideological
codes of class- and gender-identified character, to be a "woman" is to
relinquish authority even over one's own limited and stationary sphere.
Women who theorize, who delineate and codify human behavior into a
"science" from a consistent point of view, trespass into territory that is
out of sexual bounds. The production of public textual identity rests in
large part in the masculine domain. This culturally produced difference—like the prohibitions against women's preaching, the linkages between woman's identity and her sexuality, and the restrictions that confine the middle-class mother to private realms—consolidate the female
tradition and delegate it to a second-sphere significance.

But in autobiography as well as biography, some women's texts resist subordination within this politics of sexual difference based on dominance. Women's autobiographical writings mark their differences from men, but not *de novo* through a language that derives from an essentialized female body or one that evolves from an expressive center. Rather, women's self-reflective texts rewrite the discourses of "woman" and thus expose incoherencies in their positionings, as well as make it possible to imagine their collective interests, in spite of their isolation and individuation. Women's autobiographies reveal, finally, the ways in which ideologies of gender, genre, and class enable certain kinds of subjectivities to be spoken, but also at certain moments make other kinds of subjectivities unthinkable or unsayable. To return to Thrale's words in the epigraph, the struggle *is* over whether there is a sex in words, but more important, over what forces will name and manage gendered subjectivity and its representation in texts.

Notes

INTRODUCTION

1. Michel Foucault, *The History of Sexuality, Vol. 1: An Introduction*, trans. Robert Hurley (New York: Vintage Books, 1980), p. 58. See also *Technologies of the Self: A Seminar with Michel Foucault*, ed. Luther H. Martin, Huck Gutman, and Patrick H. Hutton (Amherst: Univ. of Massachusetts Press, 1988).

2. Michel Foucault, "On the Genealogy of Ethics: An Overview of Work in Progress," in *Beyond Structuralism and Hermeneutics* (Chicago: University of Chicago Press, 1982), pp. 247, 229–52. See also *The History of Sexuality*, Vol. 2: *The Use of Pleasure* and *The History of Sexuality*, Vol. 3: *The Care of the Self* (New York: Pantheon, 1985, 1987).

3. Feminist readings of Foucault are only beginning to emerge, among them *Feminism and Foucault: Reflections on Resistance*, ed. Irene Diamond and Lee Quinby (Boston: Northeastern Univ. Press, 1988); Isaac D. Balbus, "Disciplining Women: Michel Foucault and the Power of Feminist Discourse," in *Feminism as Critique: On the Politics of Gender*, ed. Seyla Benhabib and Drucilla Cornell (Minneapolis: Univ. of Minnesota Press, 1987), pp. 110–27; and Mary Lydon, "Foucault and Feminism: A Romance of Many Dimensions," *Humanities in Society* 5 (1982), 245–53. For new historicism's intersections with feminism, see Nancy Armstrong, "Introduction: Literature as Women's History," *Genre* 19 (Winter 1987), 347–69; Marguerite Waller, "Academic Tootsie: The Denial of Difference and the Difference it Makes," *Diacritics* 17 (1987), pp. 2–21; and Ellen Pollak, "Feminism and the New Historicism: A Tale of Difference or the Same Old Story?" *The Eighteenth Century: Theory and Interpretation* 29 (Fall 1988), 281–86.

CHAPTER I
The Ideology of Genre

1. When Southey used the word, he was characterizing the work of Portuguese poet Francisco Vieura as "auto-biography" in *Quarterly Review* 1 (1809), 283. The review of D'Israeli is in *The Monthly Review*, 2d series, 29 (1797), 375, presumably written by William Taylor of Norwich. D'Israeli (1766–1848) wrote

A *Defence of Poetry*, the popular *Curiosities of Literature* (1791), and A *Dissertation on Anecdotes* (1793). See especially Isaac D'Israeli, "Some Observations on Diaries, Self-Biography, and Self-Characters," *Miscellanies; or, Literary Recreations* (London, 1796), pp. 95–110. See also Coleridge's mention of Wordsworth's "divine Self-biography" in *The Notebooks of Samuel Taylor Coleridge*, ed. Kathleen Coburn, 2 vols. (New York: Pantheon Books, 1957), 1, no. 1801, cited in Jerome Hamilton Buckley, *The Turning Key: Autobiography and the Subjective Impulse since 1800* (Cambridge: Harvard Univ. Press, 1984), pp. 169–70 n. 36.

2. [W. P. Scargill], *The Autobiography of A Dissenting Minister* (London, 1834), p. 111. Scargill's audience is Dissenters, his avowed purpose instructive. See also *The Autobiography of an Irish Traveller*, 3 vols. (London, 1835) and *The Autobiography of a Private Soldier Showing the Danger of Rashly Enlisting* (1838). James Olney, in his introduction to *Autobiography: Essays Theoretical and Critical* (Princeton: Princeton Univ. Press, 1980), pp. 3–27, calls attention to these texts.

3. The title continues: *With Compendious Sequels Carrying on the Course of Events to the Death of each Writer*, 34 vols. (London, 1826–33). Subsequent references to this collection, by volume number, are given parenthetically in the text. The volumes included the lives of Colley Cibber, David Hume, William Lilly, Voltaire, Marmontel, Robert Drury, George Whitefield, James Ferguson, Mary Robinson, Charlotte Charke, Lord Herbert of Cherbury, Kotzebue, William Gifford, Thomas Ellwood, Lewis Holbey, James Hardy Vaux, Gibbon, Cellini, James Lackington, Princess Frederica Sophia Wilhelmina, Goldoni, Vidocq, and Madame du Barri, among others. Though three women's narratives are included, no women are mentioned in the general introduction as providing studies of human character.

4. Jeffrey Mehlman, *The Structural Study of Autobiography: Proust, Leiris, Sartre, Lévi-Strauss* (Ithaca: Cornell Univ. Press, 1974); Elizabeth W. Bruss, *Autobiographical Acts: The Changing Situation of a Literary Genre* (Baltimore: Johns Hopkins Univ. Press, 1976); and Paul Jay, *Being in the Text: Self-Representation from Wordsworth to Roland Barthes* (Ithaca: Cornell Univ. Press, 1984).

5. Philippe Lejeune, *Le Pacte autobiographique* (Paris: Seuil, 1975), p. 14. For a similar definition see, for example, Jean Starobinski's phrase "a biography of a person written by himself" in "The Style of Autobiography," trans. Seymour Chatman, in *Autobiography: Essays Theoretical and Critical*, ed. James Olney (Princeton: Princeton Univ. Press, 1980), p. 73. See also Paul Delany, *British Autobiography in the Seventeenth Century* (London: Routledge and Kegan Paul, 1969); and William Spengemann, *The Forms of Autobiography: Episodes in the History of a Literary Genre* (New Haven: Yale Univ. Press, 1980).

6. Donald A. Stauffer, *The Art of Biography in Eighteenth Century England* (Princeton: Princeton Univ. Press, 1941); William Matthews, *British Diaries: An Annotated Bibliography of British Diaries Written between 1442 and 1942* (Berkeley and Los Angeles: Univ. of California Press, 1950); and Matthews, *British Autobiographies: An Annotated Bibliography of British Autobiographies Published or Written Before 1951* (Berkeley and Los Angeles: Univ. of California Press, 1955). Georges Gusdorf, "Conditions and Limits of Autobiography," trans. James

Olney, in *Autobiography: Essays Theoretical and Critical*, pp. 28–48, cites Rousseau's *Confessions* as the only eighteenth-century autobiography meriting our attention. William Spengemann in *The Forms of Autobiography* jumps from *Grace Abounding* to Franklin, Rousseau, and Wordsworth. William L. Howarth in "Some Principles of Autobiography" (also in the Olney anthology, pp. 84–114) takes Bunyan and Gibbon as his representative texts. Karl Weintraub, in *The Value of the Individual Self and Circumstance in Autobiography* (Chicago: Univ. of Chicago Press, 1978), considers Bunyan, Franklin, and Richard Baxter (1615–91), whose *Reliquiae Baxterianae* was published in 1696, though he does mention Vico. And when Avrom Fleishman seeks cultural representatives in autobiography, he cites Cellini for the Renaissance, Rousseau for the early romantic period, and Nabokov for the present. There is no representative drawn from the period 1660–1760. Such an approach to canon largely excludes diaries, journals, and women's autobiographical writing.

7. John N. Morris, *Versions of the Self: Studies in English Autobiography from John Bunyan to John Stuart Mill* (New York: Basic Books, 1966), p. 7.

8. Morris, *Versions of the Self*, p. 96.

9. Wayne Shumaker, *English Autobiography: Its Emergence, Materials, and Form* English Studies 8 (Berkeley and Los Angeles: Univ. of California Press, 1954).

10. Shumaker, *English Autobiography*, p. 6.

11. Buckley, *The Turning Key*, p. 52. In Buckley's formulation, "The ideal autobiography presents a retrospective of some length on the writer's life and character . . . a voyage of self-discovery, a life-journey confused by frequent misdirections, and even crises of identity but reaching at last a sense of perspective and integration" (pp. 39–40).

12. Roy Pascal, *Design and Truth in Autobiography* (Cambridge: Harvard Univ. Press, 1960), p. 9. Subsequent references to page numbers in *Design and Truth* are given parenthetically in the text.

13. Patricia Meyer Spacks, *Imagining A Self: Autobiography and Novel in Eighteenth-Century England* (Cambridge: Harvard Univ. Press, 1976). References to page numbers are given parenthetically in the text. See also John O. Lyons, *The Invention of the Self: The Hinge of Consciousness in the Eighteenth Century* (Carbondale: Southern Illinois Univ. Press, 1978); and Karl Weintraub, *The Value of the Individual: Self and Circumstance in Autobiography* (Chicago: Univ. of Chicago Press, 1978).

14. William Spengemann, *The Forms of Autobiography: Episodes in the History of a Literary Genre* (New Haven: Yale Univ. Press, 1980).

15. Spengemann, *The Forms of Autobiography*, p. 76.

16. Robert Elbaz, "Autobiography, Ideology, and Genre Theory," *Orbis Litterarum* 38 (1983), 187–204, 199.

17. Elbaz, "Autobiography," p. 199.

18. A term coined by Stephen Greenblatt in "The Forms of Power and the Power of Forms in the Renaissance," *Genre* 15 (1982), 1–4, it is discussed in more detail by Jonathan Goldberg in "The Politics of Renaissance Literature: A Review Essay," *ELH* 49 (1982), 514–42; Jonathan Dollimore, "Introduction: Shakespeare, Cultural Materialism, and the New Historicism," in *Political Shake-*

speare: New Essays in Cultural Materialism, ed. Jonathan Dollimore and Alan Sinfield (Ithaca: Cornell Univ. Press, 1985); and Jean Howard, "The New Historicism in Renaissance Studies," and Louis Montrose, "Renaissance Literary Studies and the Subject of History," both in *English Literary Renaissance* 16 (1986) pp. 13–43, 5–12. See also Greenblatt's important *Renaissance Self-Fashioning from More to Shakespeare* (Chicago: Univ. of Chicago Press, 1980) where he focuses on the relation of the individual to systems of power, "the cultural system of meanings that creates specific individuals by governing the passage from abstract potential to concrete historical embodiment" (p. 304). For counter-arguments see, for example, Edward Pechter, "The New Historicism and its Discontents: Politicizing Renaissance Drama," *PMLA* 102 (1987), 392–409; and A. Leigh DeNeef, "Of Dialogues and Historicisms," *South Atlantic Quarterly* 86.4 (Fall 1987), 497–518. Catherine Belsey's *The Subject of Tragedy: Identity and Difference in Renaissance Drama* (London: Methuen, 1985) offers an important feminist and cultural materialist approach.

19. See William Dowling, "Teaching Eighteenth-Century Literature in the Pocockian Moment (Or, Flimnap on the Tightrope, Kramnick to the Rescue)," *College English* 49 (September 1987), 523–32.

20. Michel Foucault, "Nietzsche, Genealogy, History," in *The Foucault Reader,* ed. Paul Rabinow (New York: Pantheon, 1984), p. 82.

21. Fredric Jameson, *The Political Unconscious: Narrative as a Socially Symbolic Act* (Ithaca: Cornell Univ. Press, 1981), p. 82.

22. Hayden White, *The Content of the Form: Narrative Discourse and Historical Representation* (Baltimore: Johns Hopkins Univ. Press, 1987), p. 57. See also White's *Tropics of Discourse: Essays in Cultural Criticism* (Baltimore: Johns Hopkins Univ. Press, 1978); and Dominick LaCapra, "Rethinking Intellectual History and Reading Texts," in *Modern European Intellectual History: Reappraisals and New Perspectives,* ed. Dominick LaCapra and Steven L. Kaplan (Ithaca: Cornell Univ. Press, 1982), pp. 47–85.

23. John E. Toews, "Intellectual History After the Linguistic Turn: The Autonomy of Meaning and the Irreducibility of Experience," *American Historical Review* 92.4 (October 1987), 879, 881–82.

24. Toews, "Intellectual History," p. 882.

25. For new historical and cultural materialist work in the eighteenth century, see, for example, *The New Eighteenth Century: Theory/Politics/English Literature,* ed. Felicity Nussbaum and Laura Brown (New York: Methuen, 1987); Laura Brown, *Alexander Pope,* Rereading Literature series, gen. ed. Terry Eagleton (Oxford: Blackwell, 1986); John Bender, *Imagining the Penitentiary: Fiction and the Architecture of Mind in Eighteenth-Century England* (Chicago: Univ. of Chicago Press, 1987); Nancy Armstrong, *Desire and Domestic Fiction: A Political History of the Novel* (New York: Oxford Univ. Press, 1987); and William Epstein, *Recognizing Biography* (Philadelphia: Univ. of Pennsylvania Press, 1987).

26. In Walter Cohen's very useful essay, "Political Criticism·of Shakespeare," in *Shakespeare Reproduced: The Text in History and Ideology,* ed. Jean E. Howard and Marion F. O'Connor (New York: Methuen, 1987), pp. 18–46, he writes that the stream of new historicism called cultural materialism is more explicit

than American versions in "its [political] commitment to the transformation of a social order which exploits people on the grounds of race, gender, and class" (p. viii).

27. Foucault, "Nietzsche, Genealogy, History," p. 81.

28. Foucault, "Nietzsche, Genealogy," p. 81.

29. William Labov, in *Language in the Inner City* (Philadelphia: Univ. of Pennsylvania Press, 1972), argues that plot in "natural" or constructed narrative is based on causation. Labov assumes that language transparently imitates reality and that it can be transcribed, but that narrative, by definition, also requires assigning meaning to those events: "This is what we term the *evaluation* of the narrative: the means used by the narrator to indicate the point of the narrative, its raison d'être, why it was told and what the narrator was getting at" (p. 366). For a critique of Labov, see Jonathan Culler, *The Pursuit of Signs: Semiotics, Literature, and Deconstruction* (Ithaca: Cornell Univ. Press, 1981), pp. 184–87.

30. See especially Hayden White, "The Value of Narrativity in the Representation of Reality," in *The Content of the Form*, pp. 1–25. Subsequent references to page numbers are given parenthetically in the text. Wallace Martin, *Recent Theories of Narrative* (Ithaca: Cornell Univ. Press, 1986) provides a survey of recent approaches.

31. Pat Rogers, *Literature and Popular Culture in Eighteenth-Century England* (Sussex: Harvester Press, 1985; New York: Barnes and Noble, 1985), p. 178. Rogers indicates that "the chapbooks [of *Moll Flanders*] are hasty, formulaic, with no sense of tempo or climax, and no relation beyond plot outline to the original text . . . [and] such abridgements of the classics belong to the main corpus of chapbook texts: unlike the longer adapted versions, they have virtually no relation of a literary kind to the parent work" (p. 196).

32. According to Elizabeth Eisenstein, "Printing forced legal definition of what belonged in the public domain. A literary 'common' became subject to 'enclosure movements,' and possessive individualism began to characterize the attitude of writers to their work" (*The Printing Revolution in Early Modern Europe* [Cambridge: Cambridge Univ. Press, 1983], p. 84). See also Raymond Williams, *The Long Revolution* (London: Chatto & Windus, 1961), and Richard Altick, *The English Common Reader: A Social History of the Mass Reading Public, 1800–1900* (Chicago: Univ. of Chicago Press, 1957). Oddly, the technology that made possible "exactly repeatable pictorial statements" such as self-portraits also encouraged individuation, to make "the emergence of a new sense of individualism . . . a by-product of the new forms of standardization" (Eisenstein, *The Printing Revolution*, p. 56). Selling books in a numbered series was apparently quite profitable for the publisher, in part because advertisements were geared to inducing subscribers to sign up for the entire projected series of a given title. See R. M. Wiles, *Serial Publication in England before 1750* (London: Cambridge Univ. Press, 1957).

33. James Olney, *Metaphors of Self: The Meaning of Autobiography* (Princeton: Princeton Univ. Press, 1972), pp. 155 n. 1, 177.

34. Luella M. Wright, *The Literary Life of the Early Friends, 1650–1725*, (1923; reprint, New York: Columbia Univ. Press, 1966), p. 160. Wright re-

marks, "The insertion of numerous papers previously published—epistles, legal documents, and court trials repeated verbatim—sadly interferes with unity in autobiographical writing" (p. 192).

35. In a recent study of Baxter, N. H. Keeble writes, "The arrangement of *Reliquiae Baxterianae* is bewildering. There are two parts to Book I and a part iii; pagination is continuous throughout Book I, but each part has separate numeration of sections; the second pagination is continuous throughout part iii, but the number of sections begins afresh on p. 177, where a new heading seems to denote a fourth part, which is not, however, recognized by the page headline" (*Richard Baxter, Puritan Man of Letters* [Oxford: Clarendon Press, 1982], p. xi.).

36. Nehemiah Curnock, *The Journal of the Reverend John Wesley, A.M.* (1909; reprint, London: Epworth Press, 1938), 1:36–70.

37. Robert Latham and William Matthews, *The Diary of Samuel Pepys* (Berkeley and Los Angeles: Univ. of California Press, 1970), vol. 1, 1660, esp. xli–lxvii.

38. I am using *diary* here to mean the daily recording of thoughts, feelings, and activities of the writer, entered frequently and regularly; *journal* is used interchangeably, though often diaries are considered to be the less elaborate form. See Valerie Raoul, *The French Fictional Journal: Fictional Narcissism and Narcissistic Fiction* (Toronto: Univ. of Toronto Press, 1980); and Janet Gurkin Altman, *Epistolarity: Approaches to a Form* (Columbus: Ohio Univ. Press, 1982). Arthur Ponsonby's *English Diaries: A Review of English Diaries from the Sixteenth to the Twentieth Century with an Introduction on Diary Writing* (London: Methuen, 1923) offers a descriptive history. Other scholarly discussions include the introduction to *The Diary of Samuel Pepys* cited above; Robert Fothergill, *Private Chronicles: A Study of English Diaries* (London: Oxford Univ. Press, 1974); Alain Girard, *Le Journal intime* (Paris: Presses universitaires de France, 1963); Beatrice Didier, *Le Journal intime* (Paris: Presses universitaires de France, 1976); Peter Boerner, *Tagebuch* (Stuttgart: J. B. Metzler, 1969); and Lorna Martens, *The Diary Novel* (Cambridge: Cambridge Univ. Press, 1985).

39. Donald A. Stauffer, *The Art of English Biography before 1700* (Cambridge: Harvard Univ. Press, 1930), p. 55.

40. William Matthews, *British Diaries*, p. ix.

41. Walter Ong has written, "The personal diary is a very late literary form, in effect unknown until the seventeenth century" (*Orality and Literacy: The Technologizing of the Word* [London: Methuen, 1982] p. 102). Similarly, Arthur Ponsonby indicates his belief that diary writing did not arise until the sixteenth century, and did not flourish until the seventeenth century (*English Diaries: A Review of English Diaries from the Sixteenth to the Twentieth Century with an Introduction on Diary Writing* [London: Methuen, 1923], p. 38). Most scholars have ignored the non-Western tradition of the diary. Earl Miner, however, has pointed to a "continuous tradition of the literary diary" in Japanese from 935 until the present, including a particularly strong flourishing from 935 to 1350 (*Japanese Poetic Diaries* [Berkeley and Los Angeles: Univ. of California Press, 1969], p. vii). William Matthews, *British Diaries*, lists 2,500 diaries written in the United Kingdom between 1442 and 1943.

42. H. Porter Abbott, *Diary Fiction: Writing as Action* (Ithaca: Cornell Univ. Press, 1984), pp. 18, 85–94.

43. Thomas Warton, *Idler* 33 (2 December 1758), *The Idler and the Adventurer*, ed. W. J. Bate, John M. Bullitt, and L. F. Powell, The Yale Edition of the Works of Samuel Johnson (New Haven and London: Yale Univ. Press, 1963), II. 102–103.

44. Review of the *Memoirs of the Life and Writings of Percival Stockdale Written by himself*, in *Quarterly Review* 1 (May 1809), 386.

45. Review of *Memoirs of the Life of Peter Daniel Huet*, in *Quarterly Review* 4 (August 1810), 104.

46. Isaac D'Israeli, "Some Observations on Diaries, Self-Biography, and Self-Characters," in *Miscellanies; or, Literary Recreations* (London: T. Cadell and W. Davies, 1796). References to page numbers are given parenthetically in the text.

47. George Whitefield, "Journal of a Voyage from London to Savannah in Georgia" in *Autobiography. A Collection of the Most Instructive and Amusing Lives Ever Published, Written by the Parties Themselves.* 34 vols. (London, 1826–33). Vol. 4, preface.

CHAPTER 2

The Politics of Subjectivity

1. Paul Fussell, *The Rhetorical World of Augustan Humanism: Ethics and Imagery from Swift to Burke* (Oxford: Clarendon Press, 1965), p. 121.

2. Samuel Johnson, *Rambler* 151, 27 August 1751, in *The Rambler*, ed. W. J. Bate and Albrecht B. Strauss, The Yale Edition of the Works of Samuel Johnson (New Haven: Yale Univ. Press, 1969), 5:42.

3. Émile Benveniste, *Problems in General Linguistics*, trans. Mary Elizabeth Meek (Coral Gables, Fla.: Univ. of Miami Press, 1971), p. 226. Benveniste claims, however, the status of "objective testimony" for the subject speaking about himself. For theories of the semiotic subject, see Rosalind Coward and John Ellis, *Language and Materialism: Developments in Semiology and the Theory of the Subject* (London: Routledge and Kegan Paul, 1977).

4. Benveniste, *Problems in General Linguistics*, p. 224.

5. Jacques Lacan, *The Language of the Self: The Function of Language in Psychoanalysis*, trans. Anthony Wilden (Baltimore: Johns Hopkins Univ. Press, 1968). Julian Henriques, Wendy Hollway, Cathy Urwin, Couze Venn, and Valerie Walkerdine provide a provocative analysis of the self's historicity in *Changing the Subject: Psychology, Social Regulation, and Subjectivity* (New York: Methuen, 1984). See also Paul Smith, *Discerning the Subject*, Theory and History of Literature Series 55 (Minneapolis: Univ. of Minnesota Press, 1988).

6. Mieke Bal, "The Rhetoric of Subjectivity," *Poetics Today* 5.2 (1984), 343. See also Catherine Belsey's important study, *The Subject of Tragedy: Identity and Difference in Renaissance Drama* (London: Methuen, 1985): "Subjectivity is discursively produced and is constrained by the range of subject-positions defined by the discourses in which the concrete individual participates. Utterance—and action—outside the range of meanings in circulation in a society is psychotic. In this sense existing discourses determine not only what can be said and understood, but the nature of subjectivity itself, what it is possible to be" (p. 5).

7. For a discussion of ideology, see Raymond Williams, *Marxism and Literature* (Oxford: Oxford Univ. Press, 1977), esp. pp. 55–71.

8. Louis Althusser, "Ideology and Ideological State Apparatuses (Notes toward an Investigation)," in *Lenin and Philosophy and other Essays* (New York: Monthly Review Press, 1971), pp. 127–87.

9. Althusser, "Ideology," p. 162.

10. Antonio Gramsci, *Selections from the Prison Notebooks*, ed. and trans. Quintin Hoare and Geoffrey Nowell Smith (New York: International Publishers, 1971), p. 161. For discussions of the complexities of post-Althusserian Marxism, see especially *Rethinking Ideology: A Marxist Debate*, ed. Sakari Hanninen and Leena Paldan (New York and Bagnolet, France: International General, 1983); and Terry E. Boswell, Edgar V. Kiser, and Kathryn A. Baker, "Recent Developments in Marxist Theories of Ideology," *The Insurgent Sociologist* 13 (Summer 1986), 5–22.

11. Boswell, Kiser, and Baker, "Recent Developments," p. 20. The formulation of affirmations and sanctions and their effectivity derives from Göran Therborn, *The Ideology of Power and the Power of Ideology* (London: New Left Books, 1980). Ernesto Laclau and Chantal Mouffe, *Hegemony and Socialist Strategy* (London: Verso, 1985), also address the question of how to articulate together a "relative autonomy of ideology and the determination in the last instance by the economy" within a historical materialism that regards ideology as productive of the real. See also Chantal Mouffe, "Hegemony and Ideology in Gramsci," in *Gramsci and Marxist Theory*, ed. Chantal Mouffe (London: Routledge and Kegan Paul, 1979).

12. Michel Pêcheux, *Language, Semantics, and Ideology: Stating the Obvious*, trans. Narbans Nagpal (London: Macmillan, 1982), p. 112.

13. Pêcheux, "Language, Semantics," p. 159.

14. Diane Macdonell, *Theories of Discourse: An Introduction* (Oxford: Blackwell, 1986). V. N. Volosinov, in *Marxism and the Philosophy of Language*, trans. L. K. Matejka and I. R. Titunick (New York: Seminar, 1930), earlier emphasized the social construction of language in regarding discourses as historically and culturally produced. See also Pierre Machérey, *A Theory of Literary Production*, trans. Geoffrey Wall (London: Routledge and Kegan Paul, 1978).

15. Joseph Priestley, *Disquisitions relating to Matter and Spirit* (London, 1777; Arno Press: New York, 1975), p. 4 and preface. I am also much indebted to Christopher Fox's important essay, "Locke and the Scriblerians: the Discussion of Identity in Early Eighteenth-Century England," *Eighteenth-Century Studies* 16 (1982), 1–25, and his *Locke and the Scriblerians: Identity and Consciousness in Early Eighteenth-Century Britain* (Berkeley and Los Angeles: Univ. of California Press, 1988) which Christopher Fox kindly allowed me to see before its publication.

16. [Zachary Mayne], *Two Dissertations Concerning Sense and the Imagination with an Essay on Consciousness* (London, 1728), p. 143 and preface.

17. Catherine Cockburn [Trotter], "A Defense of Mr. Locke's *Essay of Human Understanding*" (1702), in *The Works of Catherine Cockburn, Theological, Dramatic, and Poetical. Several of them now first printed, Revised and Published, with an Account of the Life of the Author*, ed. Thomas Birch, 2 vols. (London, 1751), 1:72.

18. Joseph Butler, "Of Personal Identity," in *The Works of Joseph Butler, D.C.L.*, ed. The Right Hon. W. E. Gladstone, 2 vols. (Oxford: Clarendon Press, 1896), 1:393.

19. Vincent Perronet, *A Second Vindication of Mr. Locke, Wherein his Sentiments relating to Personal Identity Are clear'd up from some Mistakes of the Rev. Dr. Butler, in his Dissertation on that Subject* (London, 1738), p. 2.

20. John Locke, *An Essay concerning Human Understanding*, ed. P. H. Nidditch (Oxford: Clarendon Press, 1975), bk. 2, chap. 27, sec. 9. Subsequent references to this edition are given parenthetically in the text by book, chapter, and section. See also John W. Yolton, *Perceptual Acquaintance from Descartes to Reid* (Minneapolis: Univ. of Minnesota Press, 1984); and *Thinking Matter: Materialism in Eighteenth-Century Britain* (Minneapolis: Univ. of Minnesota Press, 1983).

21. Anthony Collins, *Answer to Dr. Clarke's Third Defence of his Letter to Mr. Dodwell*, 2nd ed. pp. 44, 56, and c., cited by Joseph Butler in "Of Personal Identity" in *Works*, ed. W. E. Gladstone (Oxford: Clarendon, 1896), 1:392.

22. The Collins-Clarke controversy appears in Samuel Clarke, *Works* (London, 1738), 3:870.

23. David Hume, *A Treatise of Human Nature* (1748), ed. L. A. Selby-Bigge and rev. P. H. Nidditch, 2d ed. (Oxford: Clarendon Press, 1983), bk. 1, pt. 4, sec. 7.

24. David Hume, *Enquiries Concerning Human Understanding and Concerning the Principles of Morals* (1748), reprinted from the posthumous edition of 1777 and edited with an introduction by L. A. Selby-Bigge and rev. P. H. Nidditch (Oxford: Clarendon Press, 1975), sec. 8, pt. 1.

25. *An Essay on Personal Identity, in Two Parts* (London, 1769), p. 85. Subsequent references to page numbers in this edition are given parenthetically in the text.

26. Perronet, *A Second Vindication*, p. 9.

27. Philip Doddridge, D. D., *A Course of Lectures on the Principal Subjects in Pneumetology, Ethics, and Divinity* (London, 1763), p. 26.

28. Butler, "Of Personal Identity," p. 393.

29. Samuel Johnson, *Idler* 84, 24 November 1759, in *The Idler and The Adventurer*, ed. W. J. Bate, John M. Bullitt, and L. F. Powell, The Yale Edition of the Works of Samuel Johnson (New Haven: Yale Univ. Press, 1963), 2:263.

30. Adam Smith, *An Inquiry into the Nature and Uses of the Wealth of Nations* (London, 1776), 1:ii.

31. Smith, *Wealth of Nations* 1:ii.

32. Bernard Mandeville, *The Fable of the Bees: or Private Vices Publick Benefits* (London, 1714), introd.

33. Mandeville, *Fable of the Bees*, p. 63.

34. E. P. Thompson, "Eighteenth-Century English Society: Class Struggle without Class?" *Social History* 3 (May 1978), 148. See also Thompson, *The Making of the English Working Class* (New York: Random House, 1963); R. S. Neale, *Class in English History 1680–1850* (Totowa, N.J.: Barnes and Noble, 1981); Gareth Stedman Jones, *The Languages of Class: Studies in English Working Class History, 1832–1982* (Cambridge: Cambridge Univ. Press, 1983); Erik Olin

Wright, *Classes* (London: Verso, 1985); and Donald Morton and Mas'ud Zavara-deh, "The Nostalgia for Law and Order and the Policing of Knowledge: Politics of Contemporary Literary Theory," *Syracuse Scholar*, supplementary issue (Spring 1987), 25–71. For a feminist corrective, see Leonore Davidoff and Catherine Hall, *Family Fortunes: Men and Women of the English Middle Class, 1780–1850* (Chicago: University of Chicago Press, 1987).

35. James Nelson, *An Essay on the Government of Children, Under Three Heads: viz. Health, Manners and Education*, 2d ed. (London, 1756), p. 317.

36. Nelson, "An Essay," p. 328.

37. *Sketches in Bedlam: or Characteristic Traits of Insanity As displayed in the Cases of One Hundred and Forty Patients of Both Sexes, Now, or Recently, confined in New Bethlem* (London, 1823). See also Klaus Doerner, *Madness and the Bour-geoisie: A Social History of Insanity and Psychiatry*, trans. Joachim Negroschel and Jean Steinburg (Oxford: Blackwell, 1981).

38. R. Freeman, *Gentleman's Magazine* 8 (July 1738), 247. Subsequent refer-ences to page numbers are given parenthetically in the text.

39. Especially relevant to working-class identity is Robert Malcolmson, *Life and Labour in England, 1700–1780* (New York: St. Martin's Press, 1981), pp. 93, 101.

40. See Elizabeth Eisenstein, *The Printing Revolution in Early Modern Europe* (London: Cambridge Univ. Press, 1983). Lawrence Stone, *The Family, Sex, and Marriage, 1500–1800* (New York: Harper and Row, 1977), calls attention to new architectural structures— such as the ha-ha, the corridor, and the dumbwaiter— that signal greater privacy demands in the later eighteenth century.

41. For a recent treatment of class destabilization and the novel, see Michael McKeon, *The Origins of the English Novel, 1600–1740* (Baltimore: Johns Hopkins Univ. Press, 1987).

42. Cockburn [Trotter], 19 February 1704–5, "Letter to Mr. Burnet," *Works* 2:190.

43. Hester Lynch Thrale Piozzi, "Identity and Sameness," in *British Synonymy* (London, 1794), 1:295.

CHAPTER 3
Dissenting Subjects: Bunyan's *Grace Abounding*

1. Among those who have considered the Puritan paradigm in detail are Henri Talon, *John Bunyan: The Man and His Works*, trans. Barbara Wall (Lon-don: Rockliff Publishing, 1951), pp. 49ff.; Perry Miller, *The New England Mind: The Seventeenth Century* (Cambridge: Harvard Univ. Press, 1954); Margaret Bot-trall, *Every Man a Phoenix: Studies in Seventeenth-Century Autobiography* (London: John Murray, 1938); Dean Ebner, *Autobiography in Seventeenth-Century England: Theology and the Self* (The Hague: Mouton, 1971); Paul Delany, *British Autobiog-raphy in the Seventeenth Century* (London: Routledge and Kegan Paul, 1969); and Owen C. Watkins, *The Puritan Experience: Studies in Spiritual Autobiography* (New York: Schocken Books, 1972).

2. Isaac Watts, *Philosophical Essays on Various Subjects* (London, 1733), pp. 289, 306.

3. Catherine Cockburn [Trotter], "A Vindication of Mr. Locke's Christian Principles, from the injurious Imputation of Dr. Holdsworth," *The Works of Catherine Cockburn, Theological, Dramatic, and Poetical. Several of them now first printed, Revised and Published, with an Account of the Life of the Author,* ed. Thomas Birch, 2 vols. (London, 1751), 1:283. From another standpoint on the same issue, Catherine Cockburn Trotter defends Locke's religious commitments to reconcile his understanding of identity with the church's teaching about the resurrection of the body.

4. Joseph Priestley, "Observations on Personal Identity with respect to the future state of Man," *Disquisitions Relating to Matter and Spirit* (London, 1777), sec. 13. Subsequent references, by page number, are given parenthetically in the text.

5. Thomas Morrell, *Notes and Annotations on Locke on Human Understanding. Written by Order of the Queen* (London, 1794), p. 64.

6. Samuel Drew, *An Essay on the Identity and General Resurrection of the Human Body: in which the Evidences in Favour of these Important Subjects are Considered, in Relation both to Philosophy and Scripture* (London, 1809), pp. 136, 148.

7. William Penn, *No Cross, No Crown, A Discourse Shewing the Nature and Discipline of the Holy Cross of Christ and that the Denyal of Self, and Daily Bearing of Christs Cross, is the alone Way to the Best and Kingdom of God* (London, 1669), pp. 34–35.

8. Samuel Clark, *Self Examination Explained and Recommended. In Two Discourses* (London, 1761), p. 1. Subsequent references to page numbers are given parenthetically in the text.

9. Laurence Sterne, "On Self-Knowledge," Sermon 4 in *The Sermons of Mr. Yorick* (London, 1760), 1:27–80. Subsequent references, to page numbers in vol. 1, are given parenthetically in the text.

10. Laurence Sterne, "Self-Examination," Sermon 14 in *The Sermons of Mr. Yorick* 1:207.

11. For recent studies of *Grace Abounding*, see Elizabeth W. Bruss, *Autobiographical Acts: The Changing Situation of a Literary Genre* (Baltimore: Johns Hopkins Univ. Press, 1976), pp. 33–60; William Spengemann, *The Forms of Autobiography: Episodes in the History of a Literary Genre* (New Haven: Yale Univ. Press, 1980), pp. 44–51; and Robert Bell, "Metamorphoses of Spiritual Autobiography," *ELH* 44 (1977), 108–26. Peter J. Carlton, in "Bunyan, Language, Convention, Authority," *ELH,* 51 (Spring 1984), 17–32, calls attention to confession's power to make an inspired message seem authoritative and legitimate. Anne Olivia Hawkins, in "The Double Conversion in *Grace Abounding,*" *Philological Quarterly* 61 (1982), 259–76, finds parallels in *Grace Abounding* to the title, structure, and content of the Pauline epistles. Wolfgang Iser considers *Pilgrim's Progress,* though not *Grace Abounding,* in *The Implied Reader: Patterns of Communication in Prose Fiction from Bunyan to Beckett* (Baltimore: Johns Hopkins Univ. Press, 1974), p. 12.

12. Frank Mott Harrison, "Notes on the Early Editions of 'Grace Abound-

ing,'" *The Baptist Quarterly* 11 (1943), 160–64 (Harrison provides details on the various editions); Joan Webber, *The Eloquent 'I'; Style and Self in Seventeenth-Century Prose* (Madison: Univ. of Wisconsin Press, 1968), p. 23.

13. Anne Williams Dutton, *A Brief Account of the Gracious Dealings of God, with a Poor, Sinful Creature,* 3 pts. (London, 1743). For references to the eighteenth-century readers of *Grace Abounding,* see Richard Lee Greaves and James F. Forrest, *John Bunyan: A Reference Guide* (Boston: G. K. Hall, 1982).

14. For a description of a nationalized version of spiritual identity and the requirements of early American congregations, see Patricia Caldwell, *The Puritan Conversion Narrative: The Beginnings of American Expression,* Cambridge Studies in American Literature and Culture, ed. Albert Gelpi (Cambridge: Cambridge Univ. Press, 1983).

15. As N. H. Keeble has written in *Richard Baxter, Puritan Man of Letters* (Oxford, Clarendon Press, 1982), Baxter asks in his "self-review," "How have I progressed (or regressed) from day to day? rather than What am I like as a human being?" (p. 139).

16. Adam Martindale, *Written by Himself,* ed. Richard Parkinson, Chetham Society Remains, vol. 4 (Manchester, 1845); James Fraser, "Memoirs of the Rev. James Fraser of Brae, Minister of the Gospel at Culross. Written by Himself," in *Select Biographies* 2:87; Elizabeth Cairns, *Memoirs of the Life of Elizabeth Cairns 1762* (London, 1857). See also George Starr, *Defoe and Spiritual Autobiography* (Princeton: Princeton Univ. Press, 1965), pp. 36ff.

17. John Bunyan, *Grace Abounding to the Chief of Sinners, and, the Pilgrim's Progress from this World to that Which is to Come,* ed. Roger Sharrock (London: Oxford Univ. Press, 1966), p. 66. Subsequent references to page numbers in this edition are given parenthetically in the text.

18. Roger Sharrock, *John Bunyan* (London: Hutchinson's Univ. Library, 1954), pp. 57–58.

19. Harrison, "Early Editions," pp. 160–64. The fullest account of the revisions is available in the notes to Roger Sharrock's earlier edition of the text (1962). Roger Malcolmson has noted in *Life and Labour in England, 1700–1780* (New York: St. Martin's Press, 1981) that activities for the laboring classes such as patronizing public houses, dancing, and bell ringing "celebrated those ideals that transcended self; they reinforced the individual's consciousness of his group identity, his sense of belonging" (p. 101).

20. Karl Weintraub, *The Value of the Individual: Self and Circumstance in Autobiography* (Chicago: Univ. of Chicago Press, 1978), p. 234, notices the repetition without exploring its functions. In his introduction to *Grace Abounding,* Roger Sharrock remarks on this anomaly (pp. xi–xliii). No one, however, has observed that Bunyan's great temptation period after his conversion, sometime in 1650, coincided with the birth of his first child Mary, baptized 20 July 1650, a child who was born blind. This providential sign must have contributed substantially to Bunyan's temptation, which, we are told, he resisted "for the space of a year" before he convinced himself he had rejected Christ. In addition, he tempted God to know his desire to stop his wife's false labor. To some extent, of course, he

reiterates the temptations to demonstrate that he, the chief of sinners, is also the most grievously tried by God.

21. Bunyan was publicly accused of associating with the Ranters, or Antinomians, in 1672, 1680, 1690, and again in 1769. See, for example, [Edward Fowler], *Dirt Wip't Off: or a Manifest Discovery of the Gross Ignorance, Erroneousness and Most Unchristian and Wicked Spirit of One John Bunyan* (London, 1672).

22. John Morris, *Versions of the Self: Studies in English Autobiography from John Bunyan to John Stuart Mill* (New York: Basic Books, 1966), p. 139. Morris writes of William Cowper, "It seems likely to me that, in his assertion of his uniqueness, the sufferer may sometimes be proclaiming at the same time the integrity of his self that refuses to submit finally to the sanctions of a religion that in its inclusiveness promises—or, as it appears to the self, threatens—salvation at the price of identity" (p. 139). See also L. D. Lerner, "Puritanism and the Spiritual Autobiography," *Hibbert Journal* 55 (1956–57), 381.

23. William James represents the extreme position in arguing that Bunyan's attention to the aural, visual, and kinetic reveals his psychoses. James fails to note, however, that a broad appeal to the sensory systems was common to Dissenting preachers: "He was a typical case of the psychopathic temperament, sensitive of conscience to a diseased degree, beset by doubts, fears, and insistent ideas, and a victim of verbal automatisms, both motor and sensory." James continues, "There were usually texts of Scripture which, sometimes damnatory and sometimes favorable, would come in a half-hallucinatory form as if they were voices, and fasten on his mind and buffet it between them like a shuttlecock" ("The Divided Self, and the Process of its Unification," in *Varieties of Religious Experience: A Study of Human Nature*, Gifford lectures, [Edinburgh: Random House, 1901–2], p. 154).

24. Leopold Damrosch explains Bunyan's political struggles in psychological terms: "Many Puritans seem to have sought humiliation which they might well have avoided, glorying in a separateness that to outsiders seemed merely willful." Bunyan, Damrosch argues, "mythicizes his own psychology . . . It is thus important to recognize not only that Bunyan was neurotic but also that he knew it." See *God's Plot and Man's Stories: Studies in the Fictional Imagination from Milton to Fielding* (Chicago: Univ. of Chicago Press, 1985), pp. 124, 131–32. John Morris interprets *Grace Abounding* as an individual's personal conflict with God, and he labels it "an account of a man's struggle with his neurotic constitution" (*Versions of the Self*, p. 92).

25. Roger Sharrock, *John Bunyan* (London: Hutchinson's Univ. Library, 1954), p. 18.

26. Michael R. Watts, *The Dissenters from the Reformation to the French Revolution* (Oxford: Clarendon Press, 1978), p. 234. *Grace Abounding* was published by George Larkin, a London bookseller who "suffered much in the cause of free expression, being once jailed for 'having a hand in printing and compiling dangerous books.'" according to William York Tindall in *John Bunyan, Mechanick Preacher* (New York: Columbia Univ. Press, 1934), p. 107. Note, however, that the 1660 settlement silenced the women who had founded churches.

27. Watts, *Dissenters*, p. 261.

28. See Talon, *John Bunyan*, esp. pp. 40–64.

29. Sharrock, *John Bunyan*, p. xxx.

30. Christopher Hill, *The World Turned Upside Down: Radical Ideas during the English Revolution* (London: Temple Smith, 1972), pp. 328–36.

31. Roger Sharrock, "The Origin of 'A Relation of the Imprisonment of Mr. John Bunyan,'" *RES*, n.s., 10 (1959), 256.

32. Sharrock, "The Origin of 'A Relation of the Imprisonment,'" p. 251. "A Relation of the Imprisonment of Mr. John Bunyan" is included in the modern edition of *Grace Abounding*, ed. Roger Sharrock, pp. 107–35. The account first appeared anonymously in *Gentleman's Magazine* 35 (April 1765), 168–71.

33. For nineteenth-century texts that mention Bunyan's class affiliations, see Greaves and Forrest, *John Bunyan*.

34. See especially Jack Lindsay's *Maker of Myths* (1939; reprint, Port Washington, N.Y.: Kennikat Press, 1969), pp. 70–73.

35. E. P. Thompson, "Eighteenth-Century English Society: Class Struggle Without Class?" *Social History* 3 (May 1978), 143. For a discussion of *Pilgrim's Progress* as a text important to the working class, see Thompson's *The Making of the English Working Class* (New York: Pantheon Books, 1964).

36. Christopher Hill, "John Bunyan and the English Revolution," *Marxist Perspectives* 2 (1979), 13–14.

37. In his review essay "Labor and Leisure in Eighteenth-Century England," *Eighteenth-Century Life* 8, n.s., 3 (May 1983), 99–107, Isaac Kramnick writes of the emergence of the "middling sort," containing "perhaps as many as a million of the seven million English—between the patrician elite and the laboring poor. These were men of movable property, professionals, tradesmen, and shopkeepers who broadened the base of the economic market" (p. 105). See *The Birth of a Consumer Society: The Commercialization of Eighteenth-Century England*, ed. Neil McKendrick, John Brewer, and J. H. Plumb (Bloomington: Indiana Univ. Press, 1982).

38. Margaret Spufford, "First Steps in Literacy: The Reading and Writing Experiences of the Humblest Seventeenth-century Spiritual Autobiographers," *Social History* 4 (1979), 418, 428, 407.

39. Göran Therborn, in *The Ideology of Power and the Power of Ideology* (London: Verso, 1980), outlines his theory of the formation of subjects through subjection and qualification.

CHAPTER 4

Methodized Subjects: John Wesley's Journals

1. Michael R. Watts, *The Dissenters from the Reformation to the French Revolution* (Oxford: Clarendon Press, 1978), p. 360. From the vast literature of Methodism I focus here on the narratives of experience and the formulation of individual and collective identity. See also Norman Sykes, *Church and State in the Eighteenth Century* (Cambridge: Cambridge Univ. Press, 1934).

2. Whitefield's *Journals*, p. 48, cited in Watts, *The Dissenters*, p. 397.

3. Erik Routley, *English Religious Dissent* (Cambridge: Cambridge Univ. Press, 1960), p. 157.

4. Watts, *The Dissenters*, p. 342.

5. John Haime, *Arminian Magazine* (April 1780), 211. The narrative was serialized from April to June 1780.

6. Luella M. Wright, *The Literary Life of the Early Friends, 1650–1725* (1923; reprint, New York: Columbia Univ. Press, 1966).

7. John N. Morris, *Versions of the Self* (New York: Basic Books, 1966), p. 125.

8. David Hempton, in *Methodism and Politics in British Society, 1750–1850* (Stanford: Stanford Univ. Press, 1984), links Methodism and the Enlightenment in Wesley's "concern for religious toleration, his hatred of persecution and violence, his desire that all men should be saved . . . his strenuous advocacy of slavery abolition, and his doctrines of perfection and assurance which should be seen as the theological equivalents of Enlightenment optimism" (p. 22).

9. Hempton, *Methodism and Politics*, pp. 29, 43–44. John Rule, in *The Experience of Labour in Eighteenth-Century Industry* (New York: St. Martin's Press, 1981), connects Methodism with manufacturing communities: "The amazing rapidity with which Wesley on Methodism was taken to, and spread among, miners was the most striking cultural change they underwent in the eighteenth century" (p. 208). Geoffrey Homes in *The Whig Ascendancy* (London, 1980) argues that Wesley's radical movement required the political stability of the single-party government and relative harmony between King and Parliament at midcentury.

10. Frederick Dreyer, "A 'Religious Society under Heaven': John Wesley and the Identity of Methodism," *Journal of British Studies* 25 (January 1986), 62–83.

11. Watts, *The Dissenters*, p. 78; Harold Perkin, *The Origins of Modern English Society, 1780–1880* (London: Routledge and Kegan Paul, 1969). See also *The Journal of George Fox*, rev. ed., ed. John L. Nickalls (Cambridge: Cambridge Univ. Press, 1952).

12. E. P. Thompson, *The Making of the English Working Class* (New York: Random House, 1963), p. 141. Subsequent page references are given parenthetically in the text. See also Paul K. Alkon, "Changing the Calendar," *Eighteenth-Century Life* 7 (January 1982), 1–18.

13. Alan D. Gilbert, *Religion and Society in Industrial England: Church, Chapel, and Social Change, 1740–1914* (London: Longmans, 1976), p. 89.

14. John Wesley, *The Journal of the Rev. John Wesley, A.M.*, ed. Nehemiah Curnock (1909; reprint, Epworth Press, 1938), 4:542. Subsequent references to volume and page numbers are given parenthetically in the text.

15. See E. P. Thompson, "Time, Work-Discipline, and Industrial Capitalism," *Past and Present* 38 (1967), 69.

16. *An Extract of the Life of the late Rev. Mr. David Brainerd*, in *The Works of the Rev. John Wesley* (Bristol, 1771–74), 12:313.

17. Alexander Mather, *Arminian Magazine* 3 (April 1780), 204.

18. Thomas à Kempis, *The Christian's Pattern; or, A Treatise on the Imitation of Christ. Written in Latin by Thomas à Kempis. Abridged and published in English by*

John Wesley, A.M. (London: Wesleyan Conference Office, n.d.), p. 5. This tiny pocketbook is in the possession of the Beinecke Rare Books Library at Yale University.

19. See especially the introduction to *The Journal* 1:1–78.

20. John Wesley, *Sermons on Several Occasions*, 2 vols. (New York: Daniel Hitts, 1810), 1:iv.

21. Samuel Clark, *Self Examination Explained and Recommended. In Two Discourses* (London, 1761).

22. Clark, *Self Examination*, p. 28.

23. William Penn, *No Cross, No Crown. A Discourse Shewing the Nature and Discipline of the Holy Cross of Christ, and that the Denyal of Self, and daily bearing of Christ's Cross, is the alone Way to the Rest and Kingdom of God.*

24. [Benjamin Fawcett], *Preaching Christ, and Not Self. A Sermon preached at Tuckers-Street-Meeting, Bristol, at the Ordination of the Rev. Mr. Thomas Janes. May 26th, 1774* (Shrewsbury, 1774).

25. David Sommervail, *The Preaching of Self exploded, and the preaching of Christ explained and enforced. Delivered at Paisley, March 12, 1776.* (Glasgow, 1776), pp. 7–8.

26. Isabel Rivers, "'Strangers and Pilgrims': Sources and Patterns of Methodist Narrative," in *Augustan Worlds: Essays in Honor of A. T. Humphreys*, ed. J. C. Hilson, M. M. B. Jones, and J. R. Watson (Leicester: Leicester Univ. Press, 1978), p. 194. See also Isabel Rivers, "John Wesley and the Language of Scripture, Reason and Experience," *Prose Studies* 4 (1981), 252–87.

27. Thomas Jackson, ed., *Lives of the Early Methodist Preachers. Chiefly Written by Themselves*, 3 vols. (London, 1838), p. vi. The collection appeared in four editions before 1871.

28. "An Extract of the Life and Death of Mr. Thomas Haliburton," in *The Works* 10:257, 284.

29. "The Life of Mr. Gregory Lopez written Originally in Spanish" (1611), in John Wesley, *A Christian Library. Consisting of Extracts from and Abridgements of the Choicest Pieces of Practical Divinity, which have been publish'd in the English Tongue*, 50 vols. (Bristol, 1749), 50:366.

30. "An Extract of the Life of de Renty, A Late Nobleman of France," in *The Works* 11:36–128, 38.

31. "Life of Mr. Gregory Lopez," p. 390.

32. "Life of de Renty," p. 48.

33. "Life of Mr. Gregory Lopez," pp. 385, 388.

34. "Life of de Renty," p. 133.

35. Wesley maintained rigorous control over his societies in a way that was quite foreign to the spirit of Old Dissent. Reports were made on the spiritual development of each person. Though not required to give "evidence of conversion but merely a desire for salvation, members had to prove the sincerity of their quest by their conduct" (Watts, *The Dissenters*, p. 444).

36. Thomas Jackson, ed., *Lives of the Early Methodist Preachers, Chiefly Written by Themselves*, 3 vols. (London, 1838). In the preface Jackson writes, "Mr.

Wesley requested many of the Itinerant Preachers who were employed under his sanction to give him in writing an account of their personal history, including a record of their conversion to God, of the circumstances under which they were led to minister the word of life, and of the principal events connected with their public labours. . . . To render these sketches of autobiography generally useful, they are here published in a separate form."

37. Mather, *Arminian Magazine*, p. 202.

38. Mather, *Arminian Magazine*, p. 203.

39. Rivers, "Strangers and Pilgrims," p. 200.

40. *Arminian Magazine, Consisting of Extracts and Original Treatises on Universal Redemption* (London, 1778), 1:iii, iv.

41. Thomas Scott, *The Force of Truth: An Authentick Narrative* (London, 1779), p. 28.

42. Haime, *Arminian Magazine* 3 (May 1780), 271.

43. Scott, *The Force of Truth*, p. 107.

44. "An Extract of the Life of the Late Rev. Mr. David Brainerd," in *The Works* 12:327.

45. Silas Told, *Arminian Magazine* 10 (December 1787), 628.

46. "An Account of Mr. S. Staniforth," *Arminian Magazine* 6 (February 1783), 71. It appears in three segments, January through March.

47. Haime, *Arminian Magazine* 3 (May 1780), 257; 271.

48. Haime, *Arminian Magazine* 3 (April 1780), 210.

CHAPTER 5

Manly Subjects: Boswell's Journals and *The Life of Johnson*

Epigraph: From the typed transcription of the memoranda, Boswell Office, Sterling Library, Yale University, pp. 85–86. I am grateful for permission to reprint this selection.

1. The sketch, translated from the French, is included in Frederick Pottle, *James Boswell: The Earlier Years, 1740–69* (New York: McGraw-Hill, 1966), p. 2.

2. For an excellent analysis of the popular prodigal son stories, see Jay Fliegelman, *Prodigals and Pilgrims: The American Revolution against Patriarchal Authority, 1750–1800* (Cambridge: Cambridge Univ. Press, 1982), p. 46.

3. James Boswell, *The Life of Johnson*, ed. George Birkbeck Hill, rev. L. F. Powell (Oxford: Clarendon Press, 1934–50), 1:392. Subsequent references to volume and page numbers in this edition are given parenthetically in the text. See also Elizabeth W. Bruss, *Autobiographical Acts: The Changing Situation of a Literary Genre* (Baltimore: The Johns Hopkins University Press, 1976), pp. 61–92; Robert H. Bell, "Boswell's Notes Toward a Supreme Fiction from *London Journal* to *Life of Johnson*," *Modern Language Quarterly* 38 (1977), 132–48; Fredric V. Bogel, "Crisis and Character in Autobiography: The Later Eighteenth Century," *SEL* 21 (1981), 499–512; and Felicity Nussbaum, "Father and Son in Boswell's *London Journal*," *Philological Quarterly* 57 (Summer 1978), 383–97.

4. James Boswell, *Boswell on the Grand Tour: Germany and Switzerland, 1764*, ed. Frederick A. Pottle (New York: McGraw-Hill, 1953), pp. 50–51. Subsequent references to this edition are given parenthetically in the text.

5. "On Diaries," *Hypochondriack*, no. 66 (March 1783), reprinted in *Boswell's Column: Being his Seventy Contributions to The London Magazine under the pseudonym The Hypochondriack*, introduction and notes by Margery Bailey (London: William Kimber, 1951), no. 66, p. 331. Subsequent references to page numbers are given parenthetically in the text.

6. J. W. Smeed, *The Theophrastan 'Character': The History of a Literary Genre* (Oxford: Clarendon Press, 1985), p. 54.

7. Henry Gally's "Essay on Characteristick Writings" is cited in Smeed, *The Theophrastan 'Character,'* pp. 263–64.

8. For definitions of identity, see, for example, A. J. Greimas and J. Courtés, *Semiotics and Language: An Analytical Dictionary*, trans. Larry Christ et al. (Bloomington: Indiana Univ. Press, 1982), pp. 148–49.

9. James Boswell, *The London Journal, 1762–1763*, ed. Frederick A. Pottle (New York: McGraw-Hill, 1950), p. 206. Subsequent references to page numbers in this edition are given parenthetically in the text. Lord Auchinleck apparently broke the seals on the journal packets to invade Boswell's private correspondence with John Johnston. Boswell, violently angry, drew a generalized moral from his own particular case: "It was doing what no Parent has a right to do, in the case of a Son who is a Man, and therefore an independent Correspondence" (p. 275 n. 8).

10. James Boswell, "Remarks on the Profession of a Player," *London Magazine* 39 (August–October 1770), 470. Subsequent references to page numbers are given parenthetically in the text. See also R. Freeman's comments in *Gentleman's Magazine* 8 (July 1738), 355: "A Person, said he, [Pascal], born to an elevated Rank, and consequently born to be exposed to all the Temptations incident to such Rank, ought to consider himself in the same Light as a Man would do, who, thrown upon an Isle full of People, of Wealth, and Trade, where the King had lately been lost, and where a Resemblance in Features made himself to be taken for and treated as their King; such a one, says he, would have constantly two Sets of Thoughts in his Mind; the one suited to the Part he sustained, the other to his real Character."

11. James Boswell, *Boswell: The Ominous Years, 1774–1776*, ed. Charles Ryskamp and Frederick A. Pottle (New York: McGraw-Hill, 1963), p. 212.

12. My source is the galleys of the Boswell Catalogue, consulted with kind permission at the Boswell Office, Yale University. As Frederick A. and Miriam Pottle have remarked, "This daily series shows what Boswell planned to do, while the journal for the period, thoughtfully written at intervals, records what actually happened" (pp. 303ff.). As late as 1795 he occasionally represented experience in memoranda form, not in the imperative self-examining mode of the earlier years but as an abbreviated original draft of a more finished construction of reality.

13. Roland Barthes, "There is No Robbe-Grillet School," in *Critical Essays*, translated from the French by Richard Howard (Evanston: Northwestern Univ.

Press, 1972), pp. 91–95. On the second-person address in fiction, see also Steven G. Kellman, *The Self-Begetting Novel* (New York: Columbia Univ. Press, 1980).

14. James Boswell, *Boswell in Holland, 1763–64*, ed. Frederick A. Pottle (New York: McGraw-Hill, 1952), pp. 110, 133, 189. Subsequent references to page numbers are given parenthetically in the text.

15. Shifting from future to past tense by 1766, the memoranda move from self-criticism to provide material for the day's journal and to spur Boswell's memory of the day's events when he expands the notes. See the Boswell Catalogue, p. 306.

16. James Boswell, *Boswell in Search of A Wife, 1766–1769*, ed. Frank Brady and Frederick A. Pottle (New York: McGraw Hill, 1956), p. 49. Subsequent references to page numbers are given parenthetically in the text.

17. James Boswell, *Boswell in Extremes, 1776–1778*, ed. Charles McC. Weis and Frederick A. Pottle (New York: McGraw-Hill, 1970), p. 61.

18. For details of this affair see Gordon Turnbull, "Criminal Biographer: Boswell and Margaret Caroline Rudd," *SEL* 26 (1986), 511–35; and James Boswell, *Boswell: The Ominous Years, 1774–1776*, ed. Charles Ryskamp and Frederick A. Pottle (New York: McGraw-Hill, 1963). The interview with Mrs. Rudd is cited in Frank Brady, *James Boswell: The Later Years, 1769–1795* (New York: McGraw-Hill, 1984), p. 134.

19. *Monthly Review*, n.s. 8 (January 1792), 3–4.

20. *Gentleman's Magazine*, 61 (May–June 1791), 466, 499–500.

21. John Wilson Crocker, ed., *Boswell's Life of Johnson* (London, 1831).

22. See, for example, Donald Greene ("Reflections on a Literary Anniversary," *Queen's Quarterly* 70 [1963], 198–208), who requires the *Life* to fit twentieth-century standards of biography, and Richard B. Schwartz, "Epilogue: The Boswell Problem," *Boswell's "Life of Johnson": New Questions, New Answers*, ed. John A. Vance (Athens: Univ. of Georgia Press, 1985), pp. 248–59. For a contrary view, see Frederick A. Pottle, "The Adequacy as Biography of Boswell's *Life of Johnson*" in the Vance volume, pp. 147–60.

23. For arguments concerning the art and truth of the *Life*, see especially *Boswell's "Life of Johnson": New Questions, New Answers*. See also David Passler, *Time, Form, and Style in Boswell's "Life of Johnson"* (New Haven: Yale Univ. Press, 1971); William R. Siebenschuh, *Form and Purpose in Boswell's Biographical Works* (Berkeley and Los Angeles: Univ. of California Press, 1972); Ralph W. Rader, "Literary Form in Fictional Narrative: The Example of Boswell's *Johnson*," in *Essays in Eighteenth-Century Biography*, ed. Philip B. Daghlian (Bloomington: Indiana Univ. Press, 1968), pp. 3–42; and Irma Lustig, "Fact into Art: James Boswell's Notes, Journals, and the *Life of Johnson*," in *Biography in the 18th Century*, ed. John D. Browning, Publications of the McMaster University Association for 18th-Century Studies, no. 8 (New York: Garland, 1980), pp. 112–46.

24. For a deconstructive reading, see William Dowling's *Language and Logos in Boswell's "Life of Johnson"* (Princeton: Princeton Univ. Press, 1981), which suggests that the reader of the *Life* longs for "an internal presence belonging solely to literary reality" (p. xiv). For a recent new-historical study of Boswell as accumu-

lating "credit" in writing the *Life*, see William H. Epstein, *Recognizing Biography* (Philadelphia: Univ. of Pennsylvania Press, 1987).

25. Marshall Waingrow, *The Correspondence and Other Papers of James Boswell Relating to the Making of the "Life of Johnson"* (New York: McGraw-Hill, 1969), p. 1.

26. For discussions of the dispute, see Mary Hyde, *The Impossible Friendship: Boswell and Mrs. Thrale* (Cambridge: Harvard Univ. Press, 1972), and Irma S. Lustig, "Boswell at Work: The 'Animadversions' on Mrs. Piozzi," *Modern Language Review* 67 (January 1972), 11–30.

27. On the Savage question, see especially the introduction to Clarence Tracy's *Life of Savage* (Oxford: Clarendon Press, 1971), pp. xi–xx: Clarence Tracy, *The Artificial Bastard: A Biography of Richard Savage* (Toronto: Univ. of Toronto Press, 1953); Robert Folkenflik, *Samuel Johnson, Biographer* (Ithaca: Cornell Univ. Press, 1978), pp. 195–213; and John Dussinger, "Style and Intention in Johnson's *Life of Savage*," *ELH* 37 (December 1970), 564–80.

28. Isaac D'Israeli, "On the Influence of the Female Character in Politics and Religion," *Miscellanies; or, Literary Recreations* (London, 1796), pp. 340–41.

29. D'Israeli, "On the Influence of the Female Character," pp. 342–43.

CHAPTER 6
The Gender of Character

1. James Nelson, *An Essay on the Government of Children, Under Three General Heads: viz. Health, Manners and Education*, 2d ed. (London, 1756), p. 274.

2. Recent studies of autobiography that pay particular attention to the eighteenth century include Karl Weintraub, *The Value of the Individual Self and Circumstance in Autobiography* (Chicago: Univ. of Chicago Press, 1978); William C. Spengemann, *The Forms of Autobiography; Episodes in the History of a Literary Genre* (New Haven: Yale Univ. Press, 1980); John Morris, *Versions of the Self: Studies in English Autobiography from John Bunyan to John Stuart Mill* (New York: Basic Books, 1966); Paul Delany, *British Autobiography in the Seventeenth Century* (London: Routledge and Kegan Paul, 1969); Wayne Shumaker, *English Autobiography: Its Emergence, Materials, and Form* (Berkeley and Los Angeles; Univ. of California Press, 1954); and Donald Stauffer, *The Art of Biography in Eighteenth Century England* (Princeton: Princeton Univ. Press, 1941).

3. For these correctives to recent studies, see Domna Stanton, "Autogynography: Is the Subject Different?" in *The Female Autograph*, ed. Domna Stanton, gen. ed. Jeanine Parisier Plottel, 12–13 (New York: New York Literary Forum, 1984), pp. 5–22; Sidonie Smith, *A Poetics of Women's Autobiography: Marginality and the Fictions of Self-Representation* (Bloomington: Indiana Univ. Press, 1987); and Linda H. Peterson, *Victorian Autobiography: The Tradition of Self-Interpretation* (New Haven: Yale Univ. Press, 1986). Patricia Meyer Spacks's book is *Imagining A Self: Autobiography and Novel in Eighteenth-Century England* (Cambridge: Harvard Univ. Press, 1976).

4. Spacks, *Imagining a Self*, p. 89.

5. For a discussion of dual systems theory and its problems, see *Women and Revolution: A Discussion of the Unhappy Marriage of Marxism and Feminism*, ed.

Lydia Sargent (Boston: South End Press, 1981). An analytic formulation of current problems in feminist theory appears in Gail Omvedt, "'Patriarchy': The Analysis of Women's Oppression," *Insurgent Sociologist* 13.3 (Spring 1986), 30–50.

6. In a recent study, Carolyn Heilbrun follows the gynocentric model to locate peculiarly female plots in "Women's Autobiographical Writings: New Forms," *Prose Studies* 8 (1985), 14–28. See also Estelle Jelinek, *The Tradition of Women's Autobiography* (Boston: G. K. Hall, 1986); *Women's Autobiography: Essays in Criticism*, ed. Estelle Jelinek (Bloomington: Indiana Univ. Press, 1980); *Personal Chronicles: Women's Autobiographical Writings*, ed. Dale Spender, special issue of *Women's Studies International Forum*, 10 (1987); and Carol Gilligan, *In a Different Voice: Psychological Theory and Women's Development* (Cambridge: Harvard Univ. Press, 1982).

7. Elaine Showalter, "Feminist Criticism in the Wilderness," in *The New Feminist Criticism: Essays on Women, Literature, and Theory*, ed. Elaine Showalter (New York: Pantheon, 1985), p. 262.

8. Hélène Cixous, "The Laugh of the Medusa," in *New French Feminisms*, ed. Elaine Marks and Isabelle de Courtivron (New York: Schocken, 1981), p. 255.

9. Alice Jardine, *Gynesis: Configurations of Woman and Modernity* (Ithaca: Cornell Univ. Press, 1985), p. 37.

10. Julian Henriques, Wendy Hollway, Cathy Urwin, Couze Venn, and Valerie Walkerdine, in *Changing the Subject: Psychology, Social Regulation, and Subjectivity* (London: Methuen, 1984), and Elena Lieven, in "Subjectivity, Materialism, Patriarchy," in *Women in Society*, ed. Cambridge Women's Studies Group (London: Virago, 1981), take issue with Lacanian readings of gender. Feminist psychoanalytic critiques include Juliet Mitchell, *Psychoanalysis and Feminism* (London: Allen Lane, 1974); Nancy Chodorow, *The Reproduction of Mothering: Psychoanalysis and the Sociology of Gender* (Berkeley and Los Angeles: Univ. of California Press, 1978); and Dorothy Dinnerstein, *The Mermaid and the Minotaur: Sexual Arrangements and the Human Malaise* (New York: Harper and Row, 1976).

11. See Stanton, "Autogynography: Is the Subject Different?" and Smith, *A Poetics of Women's Autobiography.*

12. Stanton, "Autogynography: Is the Subject Different?" p. 19.

13. Smith, *A Poetics of Women's Autobiography*, p. 18.

14. Michèle Barrett, "Feminism and the Definitions of Cultural Politics," in *Feminism, Culture, and Politics*, ed. Rosalind Brunt and Caroline Rowan (1982; reprint, London: Lawrence and Wishart, 1986), pp. 42, 46. For other materialist feminist discussions, see also Michèle Barrett, *Women's Oppression Today: Problems in Marxist Feminist Analysis* (London: Verso, 1980); Christine Delphy, *Close to Home: A Materialist Analysis of Women's Oppression* (London: Hutchinson, 1984); *Feminism and Materialism: Women and Modes of Production*, ed. Annette Kuhn and Ann Marie Wolpe (London: Routledge and Kegan Paul, 1978); Lise Vogel, *Marxism and the Oppression of Women: Toward a Unitary Theory* (New Brunswick, N.J.: Rutgers Univ. Press, 1983); and Judith Newton and Deborah Rosenfelt, *Feminist Criticism and Social Change* (New York: Methuen, 1985).

15. Rosalind Coward, "Are Women's Novels Feminist Novels?" *Feminist Re-*

view, 5 (1980), 63; and Rosalind Coward, *Patriarchal Precedents: Sexuality and Social Relations* (London: Routledge and Kegan Paul, 1983).

16. See *Women and Revolution*, ed. Sargent.

17. See Frederick Engels, *The Origin of the Family, Private Property, and the State* (Harmondsworth, Eng.: Penguin, 1985); and Eli Zaretsky, *Capitalism, the Family, and Personal Life*, rev. and expanded ed. (New York: Harper and Row, 1976, 1986). For a feminist revision, see Karen Sacks, "Engels Revisited: Women, the Organization of Production and Private Property," in *Women, Culture, and Society*, ed. Michele Zimbalist Rosaldo and Louise Lamphere (Stanford: Stanford Univ. Press, 1974), pp. 301–18.

18. Omvedt, "'Patriarchy': The Analysis of Women's Oppression," pp. 30–50.

19. Veronica Beechey, "On Patriarchy," *Feminist Review* 3 (1979), 66–82.

20. Discussions of late seventeenth-century memoirs by women appear in Sara Heller Mendelson, "Stuart Women's Diaries and Occasional Memoirs," *Women in English Society, 1500–1800*, (London: Methuen, 1985), pp. 181–210; Mary Beth Rose, "Gender, Genre, and History: Seventeenth-Century Women and the Art of Autobiography," in *Women in the Middle Ages and the Renaissance: Literary and Historical Perspectives* (Syracuse: Syracuse Univ. Press, 1986); Paul Delany, *British Autobiography in the Seventeenth Century* (London: Routledge and Kegan Paul, 1969), pp. 158–74; Hilda L. Smith, *Reason's Disciples: Seventeenth-Century English Feminists* (Urbana: Univ. of Illinois Press, 1982); and John Loftis, ed., *The Memoirs of Anne, Lady Halkett and Ann, Lady Fanshawe* (Oxford: Clarendon Press, 1979), pp. ix–xxi.

21. Terry A. Boswell, Edgar V. Kiser, and Kathryn A. Baker in "Recent Developments in Marxist Theories of Ideology," *Insurgent Sociologist* 13.4 (Summer 1986), 5–22, usefully observe, "An adequate conceptualization of ideology must allow the possibility of counter-hegemonic ideologies which perform the function of unmasking relations of domination/subjugation" (p. 19).

22. The ancient public square provided an arena for vindication of character. For a discussion in relation to ancient (male) biography and autobiography, see Mikhail Bakhtin, *The Dialogic Imagination: Four Essays*, ed. Michael Holquist, trans. Caryl Emerson and Michael Holquist (Austin: Univ. of Texas Press, 1981), esp. p. 132.

23. Mary Astell, *The Christian Religion as Profess'd by a Daughter of the Church of England* (1705), in *The First English Feminist: Reflections on Marriage and other Writings by Mary Astell*, ed. Bridget Hill (New York: St. Martin's Press, 1986), p. 201. See also Ruth Perry, *The Celebrated Mary Astell: An Early English Feminist* (Chicago: Univ. of Chicago Press, 1986).

24. Mary Astell, *A Serious Proposal to the Ladies*, pt. 1 (1696), in *The Christian Religion*, p. 144. Subsequent references to page numbers are given parenthetically in the text.

25. "Of Women and their Vices, with Instructions for their Behaviour in general," *Essays Relating to the Conduct of Life: Upon the Following Subjects. . . .* (London, 1717), p. 34.

26. Michel Foucault, *Language/Counter-Memory/Practice: Selected Essays and*

Interviews, ed. Donald F. Bouchard, trans. Donald F. Bouchard and Sherry Simon (Ithaca: Cornell Univ. Press, 1977), p. 148; and *An Introduction*, vol. 1 of *The History of Sexuality*, trans. Robert Hurley (New York: Random House, 1980). Foucault's account pays insufficient attention to the economic and political uses of these hystericizing medical discourses.

27. William Perfect, *Cases of Insanity, the Epilepsy, Hypochondriacal Affection, Hysteric Passion, and Nervous Disorders, Successfully Treated*, 2d ed. (Rochester, [1780], p. 73. See also John Mullan, "Hypochondria and Hysteria: Sensibility and the Physicians," *The Eighteenth Century: Theory and Interpretation* 25 (1984), 141–74. In *Dora's Case: Freud—Hysteria—Feminism*, ed. Charles Bernheimer and Claire Kahane (New York: Columbia Univ. Press, 1985), offers a recent feminist psychoanalytic approach.

28. Richard Blackmore, *A Treatise of the Spleen and Vapours: or, Hypochondriacal and Hysterical Affections* (London, 1725), p. 102.

29. Robert Whyte, *Observations on the Nature, Causes and Cure of those Disorders which have been commonly called Nervous, Hypochondriac, or Hysteric*, 2d ed. (Edinburgh, 1765), p. 117.

30. William Cullen, *First Lines of the Practice of Physic with Practical and Explanatory Notes by John Rotherman*, 2 vols. (New York, 1793), 2:249.

31. John Astruc, *A Treatise on All The Diseases Incident to Women, trans . . . 1740* (London, 1743); and Alexander Hamilton, *A Treatise on the Management of Female Complaints, and of Children in Early Infancy* (New York, 1795), p. 87. Not surprisingly, in the 1751–65 record of admissions to St. Luke's Hospital for Lunaticks, 370 men were admitted and 814 women.

32. Feyjuo y Montenegro, *An Essay on the Learning, Genius, and Abilities, of the Fair-Sex*, translated from the Spanish of *El Teatro Critico* (London, 1774), pp. 217–18. Subsequent references to page numbers are given parenthetically in the text. Earlier editions were apparently printed in 1765 and 1768. Feyjuo y Montenegro (1676–1764, also Feijóo), a Benedictine monk born in Spain, taught theology at Oveido University.

33. Lucy Aiken, *Epistles on Women, Exemplifying Their Character and condition in Various Ages and Nations* (London, 1810), pp. v–vi.

34. E. P. Thompson, "Eighteenth-Century English Society: Class Struggle Without Class?" *Social History* 3.2 (May 1978), 150–51. See also Thompson's essay, "Patrician Society, Plebeian Culture," *Journal of Social History* 7.4 (Summer 1974), 382–405.

35. Thompson, "Eighteenth-Century English Society," p. 156.

36. For an exploration of this issue, see Donna Landry, "The Resignation of Mary Collier: Some Problems in Feminist Literary History," in *The New Eighteenth Century: Theory/Politics/English Literature*, eds. Felicity Nussbaum and Laura Brown (New York: Methuen, 1987), pp. 99–120.

37. Ann Cromartie Yearsley, "Autobiographical Narrative," (1787), in *First Feminists: British Women Writers, 1578–1799*, ed. Moira Ferguson (Bloomington: Indiana Univ. Press; Old Westbury, N.Y.: Feminist Press, 1985), p. 86.

38. William Blackstone, *Commentaries on the Laws of England in Four Books* (Philadelphia: Robert Bell, 1771–72), 1:442. Subsequent references to volume

and page numbers are given parenthetically in the text. See also Janelle Green-berg, "The Legal Status of English Women in Early Eighteenth-Century Law and Equity," *Studies in Eighteenth-Century Culture* 4 (1975), 171–81.

39. Robert W. Malcolmson, *Life and Labour in England, 1700–1780* (New York: St. Martin's Press, 1981), p. 104. See also Peter Laslett, *Family Life and Illicit Love in Earlier Generations* (Cambridge: Cambridge Univ. Press, 1977); David C. Levine, *Family Formation in the Age of Nascent Capitalism* (New York: Academic Press, 1977); and John Gillis, *For Better, For Worse: British Marriages, 1600 to the Present* (New York: Oxford University Press, 1985).

40. Cited in M. Dorothy George, *London Life in the Eighteenth Century* (New York: Capricorn Books, 1965), p. 172.

41. George, *London Life*, p. 317.

42. Malcolmson, *Life and Labour in England*, p. 37.

43. Malcolmson, *Life and Labour in England*, p. 19. Of that 20 percent who were not laborers, Malcolmson judges that less than 5 percent were gentlemen and ladies.

44. Francis Place, *The Autobiography of Francis Place, 1771–1854*, ed. Mary Thale (Cambridge: Cambridge Univ. Press, 1972), p. 95.

45. Malcolmson, *Life and Labour in England*, p. 57.

46. Alexander Pope, *Epistles to Several Persons (Moral Essays)*, ed. F. W. Bateson, Twickenham Edition of the Poems of Alexander Pope (London: Meth-uen, 1951), vol. 3, pt. 2, 45–74.

47. Feyjuo y Montenegro, *An Essay on the Learning, Genius, and Abilities, of the Fair-Sex*, pp. 217–18.

48. Henry Fielding, *Miscellanies by Henry Fielding, Esq.*, ed. Henry Miller, Wesleyan Edition of the Works of Henry Fielding (Middletown, Conn.: Wes-leyan Univ. Press, 1972), 1:155. Subsequent references to volume and page numbers are given parenthetically in the text. The title of *Characterism* con-tinues: *In Two Parts. First, Of the ladies, Second, of the Gentlemen* (London, 1750), p. 13 and preface.

49. For a semiotic approach, see Joel Weinsheimer, "Theory of Character: *Emma*," *Poetics Today* 1.1–2 (1979), 185–211. See also Roland Barthes, *S/Z: An Essay*, trans. Richard Miller (New York: Hill and Wang, 1974), p. 179; and Thomas Docherty, *Reading (Absent) Character: Toward a Theory of Characteriza-tion in Fiction* (New York: Oxford Univ. Press, 1985). Docherty usefully ques-tions the essential unity of character, though he limits the implications of his study to recent writing. On eighteenth-century character, see Patrick Coleman, "Character in an Eighteenth-Century Context," *The Eighteenth Century: Theory and Interpretation* 24.1 (Winter 1983), 51–63; and Paul J. Korshin, *Typologies in England, 1650–1820* (Princeton: Princeton Univ. Press, 1982).

CHAPTER 7
"Of Woman's Seed": Women's Spiritual Autobiographies

1. Elizabeth West, *Memoirs or Spiritual Exercises of Elizabeth West: Written by her own Hand* (Glasgow, 1767).

2. Mary Mollineux, *Fruits of Retirement: or, Miscellaneous Poems, Moral and Divine. Being Some Contemplations, Letters & c. Written on Variety of Subjects and Occasions* (London, 1702). A woman friend who published Mary Mollineux's testimonies remarks on Mollineux's reticence about making her writings public, "tho' she had nothing against the Publishing thereof afterwards" (n.p.).

3. See especially David Cressy, *Literacy and the Social Order: Reading and Writing in Tudor and Stuart England* (Cambridge: Cambridge Univ. Press, 1980). On the Dissenting academies see also Michael R. Watts, *The Dissenters From the Reformation to the French Revolution* (Oxford: Clarendon Press, 1978).

4. Robert W. Malcolmson, *Life and Labour in England, 1700–1780* (New York: St. Martin's Press, 1981), p. 95.

5. James Nelson, *An Essay on the Government of Children, Under Three General Heads: viz. Health, Manners and Education*, 2d ed. (London, 1756), p. 284.

6. Margaret Spufford, "First Steps in Literacy: The Reading and Writing Experiences of the Humblest Seventeenth-Century Spiritual Autobiographers," *Social History* 4 (1979), 407–35. See also R. S. Scholfield, "The Measurement of Literacy in Pre-Industrial England," *Literacy in Traditional Societies*, ed. J. R. Goody (Cambridge: Cambridge Univ. Press, 1968), pp. 318–25.

7. Ruth K. McClure, *Coram's Children: The London Foundling Hospital in the Eighteenth Century* (New Haven: Yale Univ. Press, 1981).

8. John Wesley, *The Journal of the Rev. John Wesley, A.M.* ed. Nehemiah Curnock (1912; reprint, London: Epworth Press, 1938), 3:39.

9. See David Cressy, *Literacy and the Social Order*, chap. 6; and Luella M. Wright, *The Literary Life of the Early Friends, 1650–1725* (1923; reprint, New York: Columbia Univ. Press, 1966), p. 8. Nearly fifty sects splintered from the Church of England, according to Mabel R. Brailsford, *Quaker Women 1650–1690* (London: Duckworth and Company, 1915). For various estimates, see also Michael R. Watts, *The Dissenters from the Reformation to the French Revolution* (Oxford: Clarendon Press, 1978), p. 270; Barry Reay, *The Quakers and the English Revolution* (London: Temple Smith, 1985), p. 27; and William C. Braithwaite, *The Beginnings of Quakerism* (1912; reprinted Cambridge: Cambridge University Press, 1955), p. 22. R. H. Tawney, *Religion and the Rise of Capitalism: A Historical Study* (1926; reprinted Gloucester, Mass.: Peter Smith, 1962) argues for a close relationship between economic and religious radicalism. For particular attention to women in the sects, see Keith Thomas, "Women and the Civil War Sects," *Past and Present* 13 (1955), 42–62; and Ethyn Williams, "Women Preachers of the Civil War," *Journal of Modern History* 1 (1929), 562–70.

10. For a discussion of the translation and dissemination of the English Bible, see Stephen Greenblatt, *Renaissance Self-Fashioning: From More to Shakespeare* (Chicago: Univ. of Chicago Press, 1980), pp. 93–114.

11. Wright, *Literary Life of the Early Friends*, p. 45. For various accounts of Quaker autobiography, see William C. Braithwaite, *The Beginnings of Quakerism* (1912; reprint, Cambridge: Cambridge Univ. Press, 1955); Cynthia S. Pomerleau, "The Emergence of Women's Autobiography in England," in *Women's Autobiography: Essays in Criticism*, ed. Estelle C. Jelinek (Bloomington: Indiana Univ. Press, 1980), pp. 21–38, and, in the same volume, Carol Edkins, "Quest

for Community: Spiritual Autobiography of Eighteenth-Century Quaker and Puritan Women in America," pp. 39–52; and Doris M. Stenton, *The English Woman in History* (London: Allen and Unwin, 1957).

12. In fact, the very name of "Quaker" may have been gendered female at its early stages. In 1647 a group of religious women were associated with feminine and foreign traits: "a sect of women they are at Southwark come from beyond sea called Quakers, and these swell, shiver, and shake, and when they come to themselves,—for in all this fit Mahomet's Holy Ghost hath been conversing with them—they begin to preach what hath been delivered to them by the Spirit," Clarendon MSS. No. 2624, cited in W. D. Braithwaite, *The Beginnings of Quakerism* (Cambridge: Cambridge Univ. Press, 1955), p. 57.

13. Michael R. Watts, *The Dissenters from the Reformation to the French Revolution* (Oxford: Clarendon Press, 1978), p. 319.

14. B. Reay, "Quakerism and Society," *Radical Religion in the English Revolution*, ed. J. F. McGregor and B. Reay (Oxford: Oxford Univ. Press, 1984), p. 145. See also R. T. Vann, *The Social Development of English Quakerism, 1655–1755* (Cambridge: Harvard Univ. Press, 1969). Of the 1383 Quakers in British and Welsh prisons in 1685, at least 200 were women, according to Mabel R. Brailsford, *Quaker Women 1650–1690* (London: Duckworth and Company, 1915), pp. 87 and 91.

15. John Lilburne, 16 June 1646, "Free Man's Freedom Vindicated," pp. 11–12, cited in H. N. Brailsford, *The Levellers and the English Revolution*, ed. by Christopher Hill (Manchester: Spokesman Books, 1976), p. 119.

16. P. G. Rogers, *The Fifth Monarchy Men* (London: Oxford Univ. Press, 1966), pp. 146–47.

17. William C. Braithwaite, *The Second Period of Quakerism* (Cambridge: Cambridge Univ. Press, 1961) finds women's meetings and speaking were newly suppressed in 1701 when the Quaker minutes chide women for "taking up too much time in our mixed public meetings," p. 287. G. E. Aylmer, *The Levellers in the English Revolution* (Ithaca: Cornell Univ. Press, 1975) notes though women were prominent "in the Leveller cause (notably Elizabeth Lilburne and Mary Overton, but numerous others as well), it is curious that no mention of women's rights ever appears in their programme," p. 29.

18. Joan Vokins, *God's Mighty Power Magnified; As Manifested and Revealed in his Faithful Handmaid Joan Vokins, Who Departed this Life the 22 of the 5th Month, 1690, Having finished her Course, and Kept the Faith* (London, 1691). Subsequent references, to page numbers, are given parenthetically in the text. After her missionary travels, Vokins returned to England to defend women's meetings. Elaine Hobby's *Virtue of Necessity: English Women's Writing 1649–88* (London: Virago, 1988) traces the emergence of a tradition of women's spiritual writings. Her fine book appeared too late to incorporate fully its arguments here.

19. Wright, *Literary Life of the Early Friends*, p. 155.

20. Luella M. Wright has established these statistics in *The Literary Life of the Early Friends*, p. 156. See also, for example, *Early Quaker Writings, 1650–1700*, ed. Hugh Barbour and Arthur O. Roberts (Grand Rapids, Mich.: William B. Eerdmans, 1973). For other recent work on women's early spiritual autobiogra-

phy, see Sara Heller Mendelson's bibliographical essay, "Stuart Women's Diaries and Occasional Memoirs," *Women in English Society, 1500–1800,* ed. Mary Prior (London: Methuen, 1985), pp. 181–210; and Mary Anne Schofield, "'Womens Speaking Justified': The Feminine Quaker Voice, 1662–1797," *Tulsa Studies in Women's Literature* 6 (Spring 1987), 61–78. Schofield's approach differs substantially from mine in her attempt to locate "the distinct voice of the Quaker woman" and "a true portrait of the voice and the person behind the voice."

21. *The Power and Pleasure of the Divine Life: Exemplify'd in the Late Mrs. Housman, of Kidderminster, Worcestershire. As Extracted from her own Papers. Methodized and Published by the Rev. Mr. Richard Pearsall* (London, 1744). Subsequent references, to page numbers, are given parenthetically in the text.

22. Elizabeth Bury, *An Account of the Life and Death of Mrs. Elizabeth Bury 11 May 1720,* 2d ed. (London, 1720), introd. Subsequent page references, to page numbers, are given parenthetically in the text.

23. Elizabeth Harper, *An Extract from the Journal of Elizabeth Harper* (London, 1769), introd. Subsequent references, to page numbers, are given parenthetically in the text.

24. Keith Thomas, "Women and the Civil War Sects," *Past and Present* 13 (1958), 50. E. P. Thompson finds Puritan beliefs to be a consistently conservative force. See also Arnold Lloyd, *Quaker Social History: 1669–1738* (London: Longmans, 1950), pp. 107–20.

25. Margaret Fell, *Womens Speaking Justified, Proved and Allowed of by the Scriptures,* 2d ed. (1667), Augustan Reprint Society no. 194 (Los Angeles: William Andrews Clark Memorial Library, 1979), p. xii.

26. Swarthmoor mss. i. 196–97, cited in Mabel Brailsford, *Quaker Women,* p. 48. See also Bernard Capp, *The Fifth Monarchy Men: A Study in Seventeenth-Century Millenarianism* (London: Faber, 1972).

27. Jane Pearson (1735–1816), *Sketches of Piety, in the Life and Religious Experiences of Jane Pearson. Extracted from her own Memorandum* (London, 1817).

28. Elizabeth Andrews, *A Narrative of Mrs. Elizabeth Andrews Containing an Account of Her Conversion, Sickness and Death: Written by her surviving consort Benajah Andrews and Published at the Particular Request of a Number of her connections and Friends* (Stockbridge, Eng.: 1800), p. 11.

29. Phyllis Mack has called attention to the fluidity of identity in the early Quaker women prophets. She notes "the importance of ecstatic prophecy as a source of spiritual authority which was potentially independent of the clerical and political elites, and which was particularly suited to the capacities of women" ("Women as Prophets during the English Civil War," *Feminist Studies* 8 [1982], 22, 19–45). In a more recent essay, "The Prophet and Her Audience: Gender and Knowledge in *The World Turned Upside Down*" in *Revising the English Revolution: Reflections and Elaborations on the Work of Christopher Hill,* eds. Geoff Eley and William Hunt (New York: Verso, 1988), pp. 139–52, Mack cautions against drawing too close a correlation between radical political activity and sexual equality in given sects. It is important, however, to note the way engaging in certain practices sometimes granted women the rights of governance or preaching; and though sectarian women were not officially authorized to enter the po-

litical sphere, they nevertheless come to wield political power. This, then, enables them to challenge the traditional stereotypes of womanhood rather than simply confirming them.

30. Elizabeth Bathurst, *The Sayings of Women, which were spoken upon sundry occasions, in several places of the Scriptures* (London, 1683).

31. Bathurst, *Sayings of Women*, p. 23.

32. Jane Hoskens, *The Life of that Faithful Servant of Christ Jane Hoskens, A Minister of the Gospel Among the People Called Quakers*. Though the life was published in Philadelphia in 1837, Hoskens, born in London in 1693, died in 1770.

33. Elizabeth [Taylor] Stirredge (1634–1706), *Strength in Weakness Manifest in the Life, Various Trials, and Christian Testimony of that Faithful Servant and Handmaid of the Lord*, [1711] (Philadelphia, 1726), p. 1. Subsequent references, to page numbers, are given parentically in the text.

34. Elizabeth Ashbridge (1713–1755), *Some Account of the Early Part of the Life of Elizabeth Ashbridge, Who Departed this Life in Truth's Service, in Ireland, the 16th of the 5th Month, 1755. Written by Herself. To Which is Added a Testimony Concerning Her, From the National Meeting of Ireland* (York, 1820), p. 2. Subsequent references to page numbers are given parenthetically in the text.

35. Margaret Lucas (1701–1769), *An Account of the Convincement of Margaret Lucas [1770]* (Philadelphia, 1800). Subsequent references to page numbers are given parenthetically in the text.

36. Catherine Phillips, *Memoirs of the Life of Catherine Phillips* (Philadelphia, 1798). Subsequent references, to page numbers, are given parenthetically in the text.

37. Pearson, *Sketches of Piety*. Subsequent references, to page numbers, are given parenthetically in the text.

38. Elizabeth West, *Memoirs or Spiritual Exercises of Elizabeth West: Written by her own Hand* (Glasgow, 1767), p. 15.

39. Mary Gilbert, *An Extract of Miss Mary Gilbert's Journal with Some Account of the Lady Elizabeth Hastings, & c.* (London 1769), pp. 2, 13.

40. Gilbert, *An Extract*, p. 43.

41. Mabel R. Brailsford, *Susanna Wesley, The Mother of Methodism* (London: Charles H. Kelly, 1910). Susanna Wesley's strong pro-Jacobite sympathies contributed to a year's separation from her husband who favored William and Mary's assumption of the throne.

42. John Wesley, *The Journal of the Rev. John Wesley, A.M.*, ed. Nehemiah Curnock (1909; reprint London: Epworth Press, 1938), 3:33. Subsequent references are in the text. See also John A. Newton, *Susannah Wesley and the Puritan Tradition* (London: Epworth Press, 1968). Dale A. Johnson, *Women in English Religion, 1700–1925*, Studies in Women and Religion, no. 10 (New York: Edwin Mellen Press, 1983), notes, "Some women ministers traveled widely, at times with husbands who were also ministers, often with other women" (p. 41). See also Earl Kent Brown, *Women of Mr. Wesley's Methodism*, Studies in Women and Religion, no. 11 (New York: Edwin Mellen Press, 1983).

43. John Wesley, *The Letters of John Wesley* (London, 1931), 5:130; and a

1787 letter to Sarah Mallet cited in Thomas Morrow, *Early Methodist Women* (London: Epworth Press, 1967), p. 15.

44. Journal of Mary Bosanquet Fletcher, 12 September 1810, cited in Morrow, *Early Methodist Women*, pp. 98–99. Baptists also opposed women's speaking. See J. F. McGregor, "The Baptists: Fount of All Heresy," *Radical Religion in the English Revolution*, ed. J. F. McGregor and Barry Reay (London: Oxford Univ. Press, 1984), pp. 123–63.

CHAPTER 8
Heteroclites: The Scandalous Memoirs

1. Laetitia Pilkington, *Memoirs of Laetitia Pilkington, 1712–50.* Written by herself, first published 1748–54), ed. Iris Barry (London: George Routledge and Sons, 1928), p. 159.

2. Wayne Shumaker, *English Autobiography: Its Emergence, Materials, and Form* (Berkeley and Los Angeles: Univ. of California Press, 1954), pp. 83, 23–24. John Morris, in *Versions of the Self: Studies in English Autobiography from John Bunyan to John Stuart Mill* (New York: Basic Books, 1966), makes no mention of the scandalous memoirs. For brief treatments of the scandalous memoirists, see John O. Lyons, *The Invention of the Self: The Hinge of Consciousness in the Eighteenth Century* (Carbondale: Southern Illinois Univ. Press, 1978); Donald A. Stauffer, *The Art of Biography in Eighteenth Century England* (Princeton: Princeton Univ. Press, 1941); and, most recently, Sidonie Smith, *A Poetics of Women's Autobiography: Marginality and the Fictions of Self-Representation* (Bloomington: Indiana Univ. Press, 1987), pp. 102–22. Smith argues that Charke serves "the pleasure of the patriarchs and the ordination of masculine autobiography." John Richetti, in *Popular Fiction before Richardson: Narrative Patterns, 1700–1739* (Oxford: Clarendon Press, 1969), Patricia Meyer Spacks, in *Imagining A Self: Autobiography and Novel in Eighteenth-Century England* (Cambridge: Harvard Univ. Press, 1976), and Susan Staves, in "British Seduced Maidens," *Eighteenth-Century Studies* 14 (1980), 109–34, provide critiques of the fictional memoirs. Only Spacks treats the nonfictional texts in any detail.

3. See Mikhail Bakhtin, *The Dialogic Imagination: Four Essays*, ed. Michael Holquist, trans. Caryl Emerson and Michael Holquist (Austin: Univ. of Texas Press, 1981), p. 132.

4. A. C. Wood, "Nottingham Penances, 1590–1794," *Transactions of the Thornton Society of Nottinghamshire*, 48 (1944), 52–63.

5. Michèle Barrett, "Feminism and the Definition of Cultural Politics," in *Feminism, Culture, and Politics*, ed. Rosalind Brunt and Caroline Rowan (1982; reprint, London: Lawrence and Wishart, 1986), pp. 42, 39–40.

6. Catherine Belsey, *The Subject of Tragedy: Identity and Difference in Renaissance Drama* (London: Methuen, 1985), pp. 191, 221.

7. *London Magazine* 20 (1751), 136.

8. Bonnell Thornton, *Have-at-you-all* (London, 1752), p. 29.

9. *The Tablet, or Picture of Real Life* (London, 1752).

10. Samuel Richardson, letters to Sarah Chapone, 6 December 1750 and 11 January 1751, in *Selected Letters of Samuel Richardson*, ed. John Carroll (Oxford: Clarendon Press, 1964), p. 173.

11. Richardson, *Selected Letters of Samuel Richardson*, pp. 202–3.

12. *A Letter to the Right Honorable the Lady V—ss V—. Occasioned by the Publication of Her Memoirs in the Adventures of "Peregrine Pickle"* (London, 1751), p. 4.

13. Henry Fielding, *Amelia*, ed. Martin C. Battestin, Wesleyan Edition of the Works of Fielding (Middletown, Conn.: Wesleyan Univ. Press, 1983), 4:i.

14. *An Apology for the Conduct of a Lady of Quality, Lately traduc'd under the Name of Lady Frail* (London, 1751), pp. 5, 2.

15. Virginia Woolf, *The Common Reader*, 1st and 2d series combined (New York: Harcourt, Brace, and Co., 1948), p. 168.

16. Patricia Meyer Spacks, "Ev'ry Woman Is at Heart a Rake," *Eighteenth-Century Studies* 8 (1974), 33, 38.

17. Among those published in London during the eighteenth century were *Thérèse Philosophe* (ca. 1748) by Jean-Baptiste, Marquis d'Argens; *Les Faiblesses d'une jolie femme, ou Mémoires de madame de Vilfranc* (1785) by Pierre Jean-Baptiste Nougaret; *Félicia, ou Mes fredaines* (1775); *The Secret History of Mlle. Lubert* (1774); *La Nouvelle Madeleine, ou la Conversion* (1789); and *Justine, ou les Malheurs de la Vertu* (1791).

18. Richetti, *Popular Fiction*, p. 123.

19. R. Gill, *A New Collection of Trials for Adultery, 1780–1802* (London, 1802), 2: preface. See also *Trials for Adultery: or, the History of Divorces. . . . the Whole Forming a Complete History of the Private Life, Intrigues, and Amours of many Characters in the most elevated Sphere. . . . Taken in Short-Hand, by a civilian* (London, 1779).

20. What had previously been private was made public when Charles II transferred criminal cases to the quarter sessions and assizes making publication of the trials possible. Peter Wagner, in "Trial Reports as a Genre of Eighteenth-Century Erotica," *British Journal for Eighteenth-Century Studies* 5 (1982), 117–22, has noted a considerable decrease in trial reports between 1737 and 1770. But it seems possible that memoirs and fictions took up the space vacated by these reports.

21. Richetti, *Popular Fiction*, p. 125.

22. *An Apology for the Conduct of A Lady of Quality*, p. 6.

23. Jay Fliegelman, *Prodigals and Pilgrims: The American Revolution against Patriarchal Authority, 1750–1800* (Cambridge: Cambridge Univ. Press, 1982); and Avrom Fleishman, *Figures of Autobiography: The Language of Self-Writing in Victorian and Modern England* (Berkeley and Los Angeles: Univ. of California Press, 1983), esp. p. 90.

24. Mary Robinson, *Memoirs of the Late Mrs. Robinson. Written by Herself* (New York, 1802), 1:96.

25. She writes to "vindicate her Character from the Base Calumnies maliciously thrown upon it" in *An Apology for the Conduct of Mrs. Teresa Constantia Phillips*, 2d ed. (London, 1748), 1:12. Subsequent references to volume and page numbers are given parenthetically in the text. Con Phillips, born in Chester, was

the daughter of Captain Thomas Phillips of the Fifth Dragoon Guards. Mistress to the Earl of Chesterfield, she was linked in a bigamous liaison with a M. de Vall from 1722, and married Henry Muilman on 9 February 1723. Phillips opened a shop in Half-Moon Alley in 1738 but, plagued by debt and prison went to Jamaica in 1754. E. J. Burford's *Wits, Wenches and Wantons: London's Low Life, Covent Garden in the Eighteenth Century* (London: Robert Hale, 1986) gives a popularized account of Phillips whom he calls a "nymphomaniac."

26. R. M. Wiles, in *Serial Publication in England before 1750* (Cambridge: Cambridge Univ. Press), judges Phillips harshly for her attention to the profit motive. He terms her a "scheming minx" determined "to sell her story" (p. 143).

27. Wiles, *Serial Publication*, pp. 144–45.

28. See James L. Clifford's edition, revised by Paul-Gabriel Boucé, of Smollett's *The Adventures of Peregrine Pickle in which are included Memoirs of a Lady of Quality* (Oxford: Oxford Univ. Press, 1983), p. 458. Subsequent references to page numbers are given parenthetically in the text. The introduction includes a summary of events related to its publication and of a competing text, Dr. John Hill's *The History of a Woman of Quality: or, the Adventures of Lady Frail* (1751).

29. Pilkington, *Memoirs of Laetitia Pilkington*. Subsequent references, to page numbers, are given parenthetically in the text. Born in Dublin, the daughter of a male midwife, she early married Matthew Pilkington, an Irish minister, who was soon unfaithful. Her own subsequent infidelity with painter James Worsdale became a public scandal. Excessive debt led to her imprisonment in 1748. Colley Cibber, in his seventies at the time, was instrumental in her release and encouraged her to write the memoirs.

30. Charlotte Charke, *A Narrative of the Life of Mrs. Charlotte Charke. Written By Herself*, 2d ed. (Gainesville, Fla.: Scholar Facsimile and Reprints, 1969). Subsequent references to this edition, by page number, are given parenthetically in the text. Charke's publications include *The History of Henry Dumont and Miss Charlotte Evelyn . . . with some critical Remarks on Comic Actors*, 2d ed. (London, 1756); *The Lover's Treat: or, Unnatural Hatred* (London, 1758); *The Mercer, or Fatal Extravagance* (London, ca. 1755). Two plays, *The Carnival, or Harlequin Blunderer* (1735) and *Tit for Tat, or Comedy and Tragedy at War* (1743), were acted but never printed. *The Art of Management; or Tragedy Expelled* (London, 1735) is a satirical diatribe against Fleetwood's incompetent management of the Theatre Royal in Drury Lane. For an excerpt of Charke's life, see also *First Feminists: British Women Writers, 1578–1799*, ed. Moira Ferguson (Bloomington: Indiana Univ. Press; Old Westbury, N.Y.: Feminist Press, 1985), pp. 284–310.

31. Introduction to the *Narrative of the Life of Mrs. Charlotte Charke*, Constable's Miscellany of Original Publications (London: Hunt and Clarke, 1929), p. 222.

32. The Sally Paul case is described in *Monthly Review* 22 (1760), 522. See also Terry Castle, "Matters Not Fit to be Mentioned: Fielding's *The Female Husband*," *ELH* 49 (1982), 602–22; and Sheridan Baker's "Henry Fielding's *The Female Husband*: Fact and Fiction," *PMLA* 74 (1959), 213–24.

33. Hannah Snell, *The Female Soldier; or, the Surprising Life and Adventures of Hannah Snell . . . Who took upon herself the Name of James Gray; and, being de-*

serted by her Husband, put on Mens Apparel, and travelled to Coventry in quest of him, where she enlisted in Col. Guise's Regiment of Foot. . . . (1750), p. 59.

CHAPTER 9
Managing Women: Thrale's "Family Book" and *Thraliana*

1. Hester Thrale, *Thraliana: The Diary of Mrs. Hester Lynch Thrale (Later Mrs. Piozzi), 1776–1809*, ed. Katharine C. Balderston, 2d ed., 2 vols. (Oxford: Clarendon Press, 1951), p. 257. Subsequent references to page numbers are given parenthetically in the text.

2. Lynn Z. Bloom and Orlee Holder, "Anais Nin's *Diary* in Context," in *Women's Autobiography: Essays in Criticism*, ed. Estelle Jelinek (Bloomington: Indiana Univ. Press, 1980) cite Suzanne Juhasz and Estelle Jelinek's unpublished papers, p. 207. See also Suzanne Juhasz, "Towards a Theory of Form in Feminist Autobiography: Kate Millet's *Flying* and *Sita; Maxine Hong Kingston's The Woman Warrior,*" p. 230 in the same volume.

3. Estelle Jelinek, introduction to *Women's Autobiography*, p. 17.

4. Isaac D'Israeli, "On the Influence of the Female Character in Politics and Religion," *Miscellanies; Or, Literary Recreations* (London, 1796), p. 359.

5. For a description of these texts and the definitive biography of Thrale, see James Clifford, *Hester Lynch Piozzi*, rev. ed. (Oxford: Clarendon Press, 1968). For a view unreflective on its gender-bias, see Lawrence Stone, *The Family, Sex, and Marriage in England 1500–1800* (New York: Harper and Row, 1977), p. 463. Stone writes, "Dominant, authoritarian, demanding, possessive and wholly selfish in her pursuit of ego-gratification through her children, as a mother Mrs. Thrale/Piozzi was a total failure."

6. "The Family Book," long in the private possession of the Salusbury family and eventually in the Hyde collection, was first published in *The Thrales of Streatham Park*, ed. Mary Hyde (Cambridge: Harvard Univ. Press, 1976). Mary Hyde remarks, "A major problem I found in editing Thrale's journal was the subject of illness" (p. viii). Subsequent parenthetical text references are to page numbers in this edition. For discussions of the late eighteenth-century woman, see especially Mary Poovey, *The Proper Lady and the Woman Writer: Ideology as Style in the Works of Mary Wollstonecraft, Mary Shelley, and Jane Austen* (Chicago: Univ. of Chicago Press, 1984).

7. Londa Schiebinger, "Skeletons in the Closet: The First Illustrations of the Female Skeleton in Eighteenth-Century Anatomy," *Representations* 14 (Spring 1986), 42–80.

8. See Thomas Laqueur, "Orgasm, Generation, and the Politics of Reproductive Biology," *Representations* 14 (Spring 1986), 1–41.

9. Thomas Beddoes, *A Guide for Self Preservation, and Parental Affection; or Plain Directions for Enabling People to Keep Themselves and their Children Free from several Common Disorders*, 3d ed. (Bristol, 1794), p. 9. The pamphlet sold for threepence.

10. Thrale, "Family Book," p. 161. The first work of its type, William Buchan's *Domestic Medicine: or, the Family Physician . . . Chiefly calculated to rec-*

ommend a proper attention to Regimen and Simple Medicines, 9th ed. (London 1786), first appeared in 1769, at the relatively low cost of six shillings and reappeared in nineteen editions during Buchan's lifetime. It was also translated into several European languages, including Russian.

11. See William Blackstone, *Commentaries on the Laws of England in Four Books* (Philadelphia: Robert Bell, 1771–72), I:442, 445.

12. William Cadogan, M.D., *An Essay upon Nursing and the Management of Children, from their Birth to Three Years of Age,* 4th ed. (London, 1750), p. 3.

13. Cadogan, *An Essay upon Nursing,* p. 3.

14. William Buchan, *Advice to Mothers, on the Subject of their own Health; and on the Means of Promoting the Health, Strength, and Beauty of the Offspring* (London, 1803), p. 1.

15. Hugh Downman, M.D., *Infancy. A Poem in Three Books* (London, 1774), stanza 11, lines 20–23.

16. [John Hill 1714?–1775], *On the Management and Education of Children, A Series of Letters Written to a Neice [sic] by the Honorable Juliana-Susannah Seymour* (London, 1754), p. 49.

17. Buchan, *Advice to Mothers,* p. 195.

18. Michael Underwood, *A Treatise on the Diseases of Children, with General Directions for the Management of Infants from the Birth,* 2d ed., 2 vols. in one, (Philadelphia, 1793), p. 2. Underwood was licentiate in midwifery at the Royal College of Physicians and physician to the British Lying-In Hospital. On deformity, Underwood compares children unfavorably with cattle: "How painful and humiliating did I feel the contrast, when I compared them with the softer children of art,—with bipeds of various shapes and sizes,—with the hunch-backed, crooked-legged, lame, rickety, diminutive and deformed human beings, whom I often saw walking though the same field" (p. 201).

19. [John Hill], *On the Management of Children,* p. 22.

20. James Nelson, *An Essay on the Government of Children, Under Three General Heads: viz. Health, Manners and Education,* 2d ed. (London, 1756), p. 137. Subsequent references are given parenthetically in the text.

21. [Hill], *On the Management of Children,* p. 8. Subsequent references to page numbers are given parenthetically in the text.

22. George Armstrong, *An Account of the Diseases Most Incident to Children. To Which is added, An Essay on Nursing, with a Particular View to Infants Brought up By Hand . . . and for Infant Poor* (London, 1777). In 1769 Armstrong, physician to the Foundling Hospital at Ackworth, established a London dispensary for relief of poor children.

23. Buchan, *Domestic Medicine,* p. 5.

24. Underwood, *A Treatise on the Diseases of Children,* p. 4.

25. Thrale, *Thraliana,* p. 156. In fact, she notes, "Hester is a Word signifying *Secret* we all know," which, she concludes, is a "silly name" (*Thraliana,* 800). As should be apparent, my approach differs substantially from that of Patricia Meyer Spacks ("Scrapbook of a Self; Mrs. Piozzi's Late Journals," *Harvard Library Bulletin,* 18 [July 1970], 221–47), which seeks unity and shape in Thrale's writings and attributes her diffuse writing to a psychological cause—a lack of self-confidence—

rather than a cultural phenomenon. William McCarthy, in *Hester Thrale Piozzi: Portrait of a Literary Woman* (Chapel Hill: Univ. of North Carolina Press, 1985), argues for Mrs. Thrale's creation of a highly self-dramatized notion of self as H. L. P., a self constructed in opposition to Burke, Johnson, or Hume, and an apologetic, if abrasive, one. In studying her works in detail (especially *Thraliana, Retrospection*, and *British Synonymy*) and regarding them seriously, he relies, however, almost exclusively on Sandra Gilbert and Susan Gubar, *The Madwoman in the Attic: The Woman Writer and the Nineteenth-Century Literary Imagination* (New Haven: Yale Univ. Press, 1979), to theorize her position as a woman writer and to claim a separate female tradition. I find more convincing his attempt to demonstrate that her writing forays into male genres to subvert them.

26. Princeton Ms AM1 2475, "Letters from Dr Sam Johnson published by Hester Lynch Piozzi with Trifling Biographical Anecdotes of the Editor Committed to the Care and Consign'd to the Honour of Sir James Fellowes by his Obliged Friend H. L. Piozzi December 1815." Subsequent references, to page numbers, are given parenthetically in the text. I am grateful to Princeton University Library for permission to publish excerpts, and to Professor Margaret Doody for directing me to the manuscript.

27. Though I differ with Mária Minich Brewer ("A Loosening of Tongues: From Narrative Economy to Women Writing," *MLN* 99.5 [1984], pp. 1141–1161) in her argument that "women's writing challenges narrative closures as well as the limits of narrative" (p. 1141) if it is applied in any transhistorical way, her observation that "it is the act of bringing subjects without common measure or value into contiguity, subjects that have their assigned place elsewhere, that challenges the narrative closures in which they are ordinarily held" (p. 1150) is relevant in the particular instance of Thrale's diaries.

28. D'Israeli, "On the Influence of the Female Character," p. 361.

Index

DATE DUE

JUL 0 7 1994		
SEP 2 8 1995		
MAR 1 4 1996		
AUG 1 5 2002		
DEC 0 5 2002		
GAYLORD		PRINTED IN U.S.A.